eBay Application Development

RAY RISCHPATER

eBay Application Development
Copyright ©2004 by Ray Rischpater

ISBN (pbk): 1-59059-301-4

Printed and bound in the United States of America 10987654321

Trademarked names may appear in this book. Rather than use a trademark symbol with every occurrence of a trademarked name, we use the names only in an editorial fashion and to the benefit of the trademark owner, with no intention of infringement of the trademark.

Technical Reviewer: Lauren Darcey

Editorial Board: Steve Anglin, Dan Appleman, Gary Cornell, James Cox, Tony Davis, John Franklin, Chris Mills, Steve Rycroft, Dominic Shakeshaft, Julian Skinner, Jim Sumser, Karen Watterson, Gavin Wray, John Zukowski

Lead Editor: Jim Sumser

Assistant Publisher: Grace Wong

Project Manager: Kylie Johnston

Copy Editor: Ami Knox

Production Manager: Kari Brooks

Production Editor: Noemi Hollander

Proofreader: Thistle Hill Publishing Services, LLC

Compositor: Kinetic Publishing Services, LLC

Indexer: Kevin Broccoli

Artist: Kinetic Publishing Services, LLC

Cover Designer: Kurt Krames

Manufacturing Manager: Tom Debolski

Distributed to the book trade in the United States by Springer-Verlag New York, Inc., 175 Fifth Avenue, New York, NY 10010 and outside the United States by Springer-Verlag GmbH & Co. KG, Tiergartenstr. 17, 69112 Heidelberg, Germany.

In the United States: phone 1-800-SPRINGER, email orders@springer-ny.com, or visit http://www.springer-ny.com. Outside the United States: fax +49 6221 345229, email orders@springer.de, or visit http://www.springer.de.

For information on translations, please contact Apress directly at 2560 Ninth Street, Suite 219, Berkeley, CA 94710. Phone 510-549-5930, fax 510-549-5939, email info@apress.com, or visit http://www.apress.com.

The source code for this book is available to readers at http://www.apress.com in the Downloads section.

Contents at a Glance

Contents

Foreword

YOU HOLD IN YOUR HANDS one of the first books devoted solely to creating software applications that incorporate the eBay Marketplace. By applying the information in this book, you're joining a community of thousands of software developers who are taking the promise of distributed Web services and putting them into action to create and enhance real businesses today.

In this book, Ray Rischpater describes the methods that any software developer can use to automatically list items for sale on eBay, perform searches of eBay product listings, and more. The fact that Ray chose both Perl and C# for code examples illustrates how any language or platform can be used to create eBay applications. Whatever language or tools you choose, whichever platform you prefer, our XML-based API makes it easy to create customized eBay functionality today.

At the end of 2003, the eBay Marketplace comprised more than 94 million registered users around the world. During the last holiday shopping season, one out of every three people who were on the Internet came to eBay. Nearly 40 percent of items listed for sale on eBay.com are listed through the API. In 2004, the eBay API will service an estimated 10 billion calls from developers. Developers are using the eBay platform to build solutions that make trading easier for eBay buyers and sellers. The revolution of Web services is real, and eBay is proud to be part of that revolution.

The opportunities to build a business or accelerate an existing business with the eBay Marketplace have never been greater. We at eBay love to help developers who come up with innovative ideas to help users and improve the marketplace, and there's no better way to do that than creating a new application using the eBay API. We're looking forward to seeing what you come up with!

The eBay Developers Program Team
http://developer.ebay.com
February, 2004

About the Author

Ray Rischpater is a software engineer and writer who has focused on mobile computing since 1995. During that time, he has developed countless applications for Fortune 500 companies using handheld computers and wireless interfaces for enterprise and commercial deployment. He is the author of 8 books and 48 articles on mobile and wireless computing.

Ray Rischpater is a member of the American Radio Relay League as well as the Institute of Electrical and Electronics Engineers and is presently employed as a staff engineer at Rocket Mobile, Inc. When not writing books or software, Ray spends time with his family and provides emergency service using amateur radio in the San Lorenzo Valley in Northern California.

About the Technical Reviewer

Lauren E. Darcey is a software engineering professional specializing in large-scale software architecture. For the past two years, Laurie has led a crackerjack enterprise software development group that is developing a custom business solution for a major player in the international finance industry. She spends her copious free time traveling the world, and is an avid nature photographer. Most recently, Laurie traveled to South Africa where she dove with 4-meter-long great white sharks and got stuck between a herd of rampaging hippopotami and an irritated bull elephant. Laurie lives in sunny Santa Cruz, California, with her fiancé, Shane, and their six lagomorphic friends named Bit, Nibble, Heap, Qubit, Stack, and Null. Lauren recently started her own company, Mamlambo, Inc.

Acknowledgments

IT'S TIME TO MAKE a little-known confession: Writing the acknowledgments for a book is the most fun of all. Not because it's the last thing I have to write (meaning after this I can stop, take stock of the situation, and promise to just say no the next time I have an idea for a book!), but because it gives me a chance to recognize all of the people who made the book you now hold possible.

First and foremost, I must thank Maurice Sharp, Debbie Brackeen, and Jeff McManus at eBay for supporting me in writing this book. The opportunity to work so closely with the eBay team has been an excellent one, and I am deeply indebted to them and their team for their efforts. Without them, at best this book could only have drawn on what was externally available, and may well not have been written at all.

Next, I must thank Lauren Darcey for her timely and careful commentary as technical reviewer on every page of the manuscript. An accomplished developer in using both the latest in Microsoft technologies and other technologies including Perl, she not only provided excellent review of the technical content, but also helped round out many pieces of otherwise wretched prose, and kept an able eye out for where my UNIX background got the better of me. (Any remaining transgressions, of course, are solely my responsibility, and not that of editors, technical or otherwise!)

The staff at Apress remain my favorite people to work with, both in and out of the publishing world. Apress's founders, Gary Cornell and Dan Appleman, show an amazing degree of flexibility and grace in reviewing author proposals for books, and Gary seems always able to take a bit of time from his hectic schedule when an author like me comes calling with an idea or a question. This is my second book working with Jim Sumser at Apress, and I hope it won't be my last. Kylie Johnston proved to be an able pilot, navigating our ship . . . er, book . . . through the various shoals and storms of production, from the time the mostly complete manuscript was completed until the final layout was complete. I'd also like to thank Ami Knox, my copy editor, for helping ensure that I avoided the gravest of sins throughout the manuscript; and Noemi Hollander for her work in producing the printer-ready version of the manuscript, a sight far kinder on the eyes than the Microsoft Word files everybody else had to look at through the book's production.

I need to thank my coworkers at Rocket Mobile, Inc., who gave me moral support and encouragement throughout the process, and professed interest when I nattered on about various aspects of developing applications for eBay in front of the water cooler, at our lunch seminars, and virtually anywhere else that they had to put up with me.

My family once again earned immeasurable gratitude by supporting me throughout the project. My son, Jarod, has been a constant companion since I began writing books four years ago. He's now old enough to understand what it is that I do, and I am deeply grateful that he supports me with his encouragement and smiles and curiosity about what it is that I do with a computer. My wife, Rachel, encouraged me to start the project immediately after finishing my last book, something about which I had grave doubts, and tolerated the countless times I answered her queries of "Let's go/do/be . . . wouldn't it be fun?" with a growled, "I can't this weekend. I need to work on the book." Throughout the process, she has encouraged me with her infinite love and patience—to her I owe my world.

Introduction

How would you like to have a piece of the action involving one of today's largest online marketplaces? Perhaps you've got an idea for an innovative electronic storefront, but don't want to build the back end or try to build the marketing campaign you need to attract the millions of users that you know you'll please. Or maybe you're looking to integrate your enterprise with an existing e-tailer. Or perhaps you have another idea altogether, and just need the customers to support it. Look no further than eBay. With the eBay Software Developer's Kit (SDK) and lower-level Web-based Application Programming Interface (API), you can craft applications that tap eBay's vast product, server, and customer resources. Your application can be hosted on a Web server, your customers' desktop workstations, or on the latest mobile gadgets such as a Personal Digital Assistant or smart phone.

This book shows you how to do just that. After reading this book, you'll understand what the eBay interfaces provide through both their SDK and their API; how you can partner with eBay to design, develop, certify, and deploy your application; and most important, the technical nuts-and-bolts behind actually writing applications that use both the SDK and API.

Who Needs to Read This Book

If you're a software developer interested in leveraging one of the world's largest online marketplaces, this book is unquestionably for you. As you read the book, you'll gain a crucial understanding of the technical aspects of interfacing your applications with eBay, as well as the business background you need to succeed in making the connection between your business and eBay's customers a reality.

For software developers, the book has 11 fully written sample applications and dozens of code snippets to help explain the eBay SDK and API. To understand them, you need only have experience with developing applications in a high-level language—I explain the rest you need to know as I go along. Many of the applications are in C#, which lets you leverage the power of eBay with little need to worry about the complexities behind the scene. If you're not familiar with C#, you'll quickly learn it along the way, because it looks a lot like C++ or Java, and I don't rely on specific language features. Still others—including those that introduce the lower-level API—are written in Perl. You needn't worry about being a Perl guru to understand them, though, because I take care to explain the nuances of Perl syntax I use, and keep sophisticated use of Perl at bay. In fact, if you flip through the book now, you may find it a little difficult to tell the Perl examples from the C# examples, because throughout the book I've been careful to keep my use of both

Perl and C# to the sorts of logic and flow control you're likely to encounter in a simple C program!

If you're a product or marketing manager looking to leverage eBay's technologies for your company, many parts of this book—especially the introductory material in the first three chapters and in Chapter 7—is crucial to understanding the relationship between your firm and eBay, and the corresponding relationship between your applications and eBay's servers.

What You Will Find in This Book

This book approaches the eBay tools from two perspectives: the high-level SDK, with which you can craft rich applications quickly, and the lower-level API, which is the engine under the hood of the SDK that lets you bring connectivity with eBay to platforms that don't support the SDK itself.

In **Chapter 1, "Introducing the eBay Software Platform,"** I give you a first glimpse at both the SDK and the API. After reading this chapter, not only will you understand what you can do with these tools, but you will gain an important understanding of the business behind writing applications that integrate with eBay. Because your application must integrate with eBay's servers directly, I show you the ins and outs of the eBay developer program, including how to access their test servers—called the Sandbox—during development, as well as how to obtain eBay certification so you can ship your application with access to the production servers at eBay.

In **Chapter 2, "Understanding the Fundamentals of eBay Development,"** I present a thumbnail sketch of the concepts crucial to understanding how to use the SDK. This provides you with the background you need to understand how to use the SDK, including the fundamental mechanism—the Component Object Model (COM)—used by the SDK to represent eBay objects and interfaces. You'll see how to use COM and the SDK using both C# and Perl, paving the way to understanding the examples throughout the book.

In **Chapter 3, "Introducing the eBay SDK,"** I present a technical survey of the SDK itself. You'll see the various interfaces and objects that the SDK presents, as well as how they fit together.

In **Chapter 4, "Managing Users with the eBay SDK,"** I move from generalities to specifics. You'll learn about how to manage user information and transaction payment information via the IAccount and IUser interfaces. Of course, the chapter includes sample code that shows you how to use these interfaces as well as how to use the various classes that support them.

In **Chapter 5, "Managing Items with the eBay SDK,"** I continue showing you individual interfaces, demonstrating how to manage individual items with the IItem interface, as well as exploring other interfaces. You'll learn how these interfaces connect to let you track an item from listing through its final sale, as well as how to perform common operations such as searching for items on eBay, listing items on eBay, completing a sale, and leaving feedback.

In **Chapter 6**, **"Introducing the eBay Integration Library,"** you'll see how to improve your application's performance using the eBay-provided Integration Library, which lets your application manipulate data from eBay servers offline, periodically synchronizing data with eBay for transactions.

In **Chapter 7, "Reviewing Internet Programming,"** I return again to the fundamentals, this time discussing what you need to know to use the underlying eBay API. I give you a quick tour of sockets, HTTP, secure HTTP transactions, and XML, the tools you need to know if you're going to communicate directly with eBay through the API.

In **Chapter 8, "Using the eBay API,"** the focus shifts to the API, the low-level method of integrating your application with eBay. In this chapter, I present the programming model behind the API. I show you the fundamentals of making requests and receiving responses from eBay servers via the API. Using the information you glean from this chapter, you'll be able to bring integration with eBay to a host of new platforms that don't presently support the SDK itself.

In **Chapter 9, "Using the eBay API Within a Web Site,"** I show you how to integrate eBay within your Web site. Focusing on the task of using the eBay API, I show you how to use the eBay API with Perl to add eBay interfaces to your Web site, giving your site seamless integration between your data and eBay's. Along the way, I explore the gamut of eBay API calls.

A Word on Presentation

As with other technical books, it helps to make a distinction between what's meant for people to read and what's meant for computers to read.

Any text in this book that looks like this is either a variable or class name. Whole listings of code are set in the same style, with line numbers, like this:

```
1:          Console.Write( "Enter API Developer Id: " );
2:          devID = Console.ReadLine();
3:          Console.Write( "Enter API Application Id: " );
4:          appID = Console.ReadLine();
5:          Console.Write( "Enter API Certificate: " );
6:          crtID = Console.ReadLine();
```

It is widely held that a picture is worth a thousand words. I've tried to use illustrations here for two purposes: to show you screen shots of the various sample applications I present throughout the book, or to describe relationships between the interfaces provided by the eBay SDK and API. To do this, I frequently use the Unified Modeling Language. UML provides a powerful way to represent different aspects of systems in a compact notation that is clear and intuitive.

Getting the Latest Resources

The Internet is a fast-moving place, and eBay is ahead of the pack. To ensure you have the latest information, all of the examples in this book, along with late-breaking news and details, can be found at the Downloads section of the publisher's Web site, http://www.apress.com/.

Of course, as you get started, you should go straight to the source for the latest information and version of the eBay SDK. You can find that and more at eBay's developer Web site, http://developer.ebay.com/.

Looking Ahead

If you're looking to bring your software ideas, products, and services to a bevy of satisfied consumers, look no further than the eBay SDK. You have the skills and tools to bring your idea to market—add this book and you're ready to go. So sit down, pull out your laptop, and let's get started.

CHAPTER 1

Introducing the eBay Software Platform

To THE AVERAGE CONSUMER, eBay is one of two things: either a member of that rare breed, the wildly successful dot-com corporation, or a buyer's and seller's mecca. In truth, these are so tightly interrelated as to be the same thing: eBay is phenomenally successful simply because it unites buyers and sellers from all places and all walks of life. Key to its success, however, is its focus—a company that trades in data, rather than physical merchandise. By offering the eBay SDK and API services, eBay extends to you not just that data, but also an opportunity to share in their success by tapping both buyers and sellers, bringing you a market for your ideas, services, and products.

In this chapter, I introduce the fundamentals behind the eBay platform: how people use eBay and how they can benefit from your skills, why you might choose eBay for a partner when developing a new application, how to integrate eBay in your application, and how you develop your application with eBay as a partner. Think of this chapter as your 30,000-foot introduction to the world of eBay application development; after this chapter, you'll be ready to disembark and begin meeting the various components of the eBay SDK and API as you go about your day.

Understanding the Market for eBay Applications

The notion of eBay as an online auction house is now a central concept in the minds of hobbyists, collectors, and bargain hunters around the world. Increasingly, however, eBay has added brands and categories, turning it into the equivalent of an online mall in which you can find virtually anything. Unlike a mall, though, eBay has two advantages: They are a broker, meaning that they don't need to manage inventory, and as a broker, they simply mediate the relationship between buyer and seller, letting you (as either a buyer or seller) have control over how much you spend or make on a transaction. In fact, eBay gives you complete control over the appearance and sale of your item: You can even list items as fixed-price sales, not auctions at all! With over 12 million listings *a day* in 18,000 categories, eBay helps move tens of billions of dollars' worth of merchandise annually.

As a result, most of us have the same image of eBay users, people like these:

- Beanie Baby–smitten collectors trading their surplus wares on eBay, hoping to score the rare find of a limited-edition doll

- Fanatical *otaku*—Western slang for Japanese animation and comic collectors—snapping up the latest in fan-subtitled releases and collectibles from Japan

- The neighbor down the street cleaning his attic and selling his old vinyl records to collectors on eBay

- Bargain-conscious techies looking to pick up a cell phone, PDA, or video game to try at a good price

Unfortunately, these images are one-sided, and tend to forget millions of other users, such as these four:

- The comic book storeowner who expanded her sales to eBay, now selling more merchandise online than through her retail business

- The clothing retail chain using eBay to sell excess inventory, helping maintain their profitability while bringing bargains to consumers without devaluing sales in their brick-and-mortar stores

- The savvy housewife in a single-income family, buying up baby formula from stores about to close for pennies on the dollar and reselling it at a tidy profit to help make ends meet

- The slide-rule collector who has been able to move from collecting slide rules and drawing equipment as a hobby to a bona fide full-time business using eBay as his store to reach interested customers

Understanding How People Use eBay

To date, the overwhelming majority of users interact with eBay in the same way: via the ubiquitous online interface. Using this interface to sell an item, you must do the following:

1. Obtain an eBay ID, giving you access to eBay to sell an item. When you do this, you also need to provide information about how you will pay eBay for listing your item, thereby becoming a seller on the eBay site.

2.   Create a description of your item, including photographs if desired, the category in which it belongs on eBay, your desired starting price, an optional reserve price, and an optional "Buy It Now" price that users can use to bypass an auction and purchase your item immediately.

3.   Enter all of this data into eBay's servers using Web-based forms in HTML.

4.   During the auction, many buyers like to track the progress of their auction by monitoring the number of bids and pace of bidding, as well as how the auction compares to other auctions. At the conclusion of your auction, contact the buyer for payment and shipping using information from eBay's Web site.

5.   Package your item for shipment and send it to the buyer.

6.   Leave feedback for your buyer regarding how she handled the transaction on the eBay Web site.

7.   Pay (via your seller's account) a *final value fee*, typically a percentage of the transaction, and *your insertion fee* for listing the item to eBay.

8.   Periodically remit payment for your seller's account fees, managing your seller's account using eBay's Web site.

Much of the work in listing an item is involved in step 2, and much of the eBay SDK and API you will encounter in later chapters provide ways for you to automate this process on behalf of users. In fact, given the rather cumbersome nature of listing many items on eBay with their Web site, there is a healthy market for applications that make listing items easier.

The process for a buyer is similar:

1.   Obtain an eBay ID, giving you access to eBay to bid on an item.

2.   Find an item you'd like to purchase by searching eBay's Web site, browsing categories, or a combination of these two.

3.   Place a maximum bid on an item using eBay's Web site, and periodically revisit the auction to see if your maximum bid has been exceeded.

4.   When the auction has closed, the seller contacts the buyer via eBay's Web site or e-mail to send payment and shipping information.

5.   If you won the auction, when you receive the item, leave feedback for the seller using eBay's Web site regarding your satisfaction with the purchase process and item you've received.

As you can see, a great deal of the activity centers on eBay's Web site. While easy to use, it quickly becomes an arduous chore for those seeking to make a living on eBay.

The eBay API, SDK, and related tools such as the eBay Integration Library let you eliminate the time-consuming process of entering each item into eBay's auction service, allowing you to track auctions, list items, post feedback, and review your eBay account activity programmatically. Instead, using these Web interface tools, companies can integrate their existing inventory, shipping, and accounts-payable applications, removing the need to manage eBay sales manually. In essence, these applications enable such companies to treat eBay as an additional storefront, much like their existing brick-and-mortar or Internet storefronts.

It doesn't end there, however. Until recently, the Developers Program for eBay was prohibitively expensive for many to join. The latest options in the Developers Program, however, make it *free* to have access to the SDK, API, and the eBay Sandbox, a safe area with real data from past auctions where you can test your application. This enables everyone, from the visionary CTO looking to streamline his company's inventory management or find a new outlet for existing products and services, to the foundation of a startup—two folks in a garage with a novel way to help a segment of eBay users process their sales listings quickly and easily.

How Your Applications Can Help eBay Users

As you can see from the last section, even if you've never used eBay, there's a lot of room for automation in the work of many frequent eBay users, especially eBay sellers. Obviously, one segment is already undergoing change as developers craft eBay applications—inventory control for medium and large-scale retail firms. In many cases, these applications are one-off applications, parts of large-scale information technology overhauls for major corporations. While very profitable for IT and management consultants, it's admittedly a limited market, especially if you don't have the right connections.

That's where eBay's strength from numbers comes in: With millions of buyers and sellers, there are plenty of opportunities to come up with applications to help a sizable number of eBay users. Virtually every group of sellers can benefit from an application that helps them manage the list-sell-ship-rate-reimburse cycle, with features specific to the kinds of items sold, or the kinds of databases specific users use, and so on. Consider Sandy, the owner of the comic book store that I mentioned in a previous section. With her inventory in a standard database product, you can write an application that integrates with the database product, letting her mark specific items to be listed on eBay if they're in excess inventory for over six months. In turn, the application periodically queries her to be sure that the items suggested should be listed, lists items, generates reports for sold items as buyers pay for them, and even generates shipping labels once items are paid for.

Of course, not all eBay applications need to be desktop-centric like this. Because the eBay SDK and eBay API are Web-based and can run on many different platforms, applications can reside on Web servers as well. Using the SDK, you could construct an application to query eBay on behalf of other Web users, such as members of an organization following antiques or other collectibles on eBay. The application might optimize searches in specific ways for users, or periodically aggregate the results of searches and send them via e-mail to users' desktops or mobile phones.

Finally, there's a whole host of value-added applications that might not necessarily contribute to your retirement fund, but may well address the needs of small groups of people. You should be careful when considering some of these, however, as the API license you must sign before having your application manipulate live eBay data does place restrictions on some applications, such as mining eBay data for your own purposes.

Selecting eBay for Your Application

If you're considering writing an application or service, you may wonder why you want to integrate with eBay at all. Perhaps your application is designed to provide stand-alone auction management services for collectors, or you're writing a database application to track collections, or you're looking to enhance your corporation's inventory management system. What, you ask, does the eBay connection bring to the table for you?

The obvious answer is simple: millions of potential customers (75 million registered users as of September 2003!). If you're involved in a part of the industry where you're selling products or services, you can't beat that. Ready for your products and services, these customers are already proficient at buying and selling on eBay, so leveraging eBay's auctions and stores simply makes sense. If you're writing software to help these customers, integrating with eBay is a logical step. By taking one of the most time-consuming parts of using eBay and streamlining it in your application, you can save them time, making your application even more valuable to them.

Maybe you've already decided to leverage eBay—there's a host of applications and services that do this using *screen scraping,* the process of programmatically parsing the HTML that makes up a page on eBay and then using the resulting data to drive your application. Why wouldn't you just use screen scraping, rather than coming up to speed on a new interface and taking the time to integrate it with your application?

First, from a technical perspective, maintaining a screen-scraping application is painful at best. As eBay—and their users in custom storefronts—change their HTML and server scripts, you must be prepared to make changes to your screen-scraping code. Inevitably, this becomes a continual process, as you track changes to eBay's site and respond accordingly. More importantly, it's openly discouraged by eBay; the API and SDK are there precisely to ensure that you don't have to use screen scraping in the first place. Screen-scraping applications can place a heavy load on the servers at eBay, and don't give them the control they need over the dissemination of their data. Using eBay's development tool offerings gives you the assurance that your application will be flexible to eBay's changes, reliable in the face of those changes, and not subject to technical or business restrictions that screen-scraping applications face. Finally, as you will learn throughout this book, using the tools and services eBay offers in your application is actually *easier* than parsing out HTML and making decisions based on its content. Instead, the SDK provides a .NET and Component Object Model (COM) and .NET interface to eBay data, while the companion API provides a flexible interface to eBay's data using the eXtensible Markup Language (XML) over a secure HyperText Transfer Protocol (HTTPS) connection. By using widely adopted technologies including .NET Framework, COM, XML, and HTTPS, writing applications for eBay is far easier with their tools than without.

Integrating eBay in Your Application

So what does it take to write an eBay-connected application? Surprisingly little, actually. You begin by signing up with eBay to get an application certificate identifying your application and obtaining the appropriate tools from eBay (which I discuss in the following section, "Developing Your Application with eBay"). Your application itself needs to be implemented on a platform with basic network services, including HTTPS, or you'll need to be prepared to implement HTTPS as part of your application (say, on simple Internet appliances or some wireless handsets). If you want to use the high-level SDK, which is implemented in .NET and exposed as COM and Java packages, the dependence on .NET essentially limits the use of the SDK to Microsoft Windows–based platforms. On the other hand, the underlying API requires only support for Web services—namely, HTTPS and XML—and the XML is simple enough that if necessary you can port or craft an XML parser to your target platform for your application. Finally, for this to be of any use to your application's users, they must have accounts with eBay to actually access eBay data with your application.

Using the eBay development tools, you can perform common operations including

- Searching for items that are for auction

- Gathering information about items for auction

- Listing new items for auction or revising or ending existing items

- Listing fixed-price items for sale

- Managing item shipping costs and accessing the eBay Shipping Calculator to determine shipping costs

- Obtaining information about eBay users

- Fetching lists of transactions you had in a specified period of time

- Fetching lists of change events to your items' status

- Fetching lists of bidders and sellers for items for sale

- Obtaining feedback about buyers and sellers

- Leaving feedback to users that you had transactions with

- Managing and searching eBay categories

You should be aware, however, that there are some key things that you *can't* do with the eBay tools. In most cases, the reason for this is obvious: to ensure a level playing field between all buyers and sellers on eBay. Some of the things you can't do programmatically are

- Bid or buy an item for auction using either the SDK or the API.

- Create a new eBay user ID.

- Manage nonpayer bidder processing or fair-value fee refunds from eBay to seller accounts.

> **NOTE** *eBay is continually improving the eBay API and SDK. This list was current as this book was written, but you should check the latest SDK documentation to see what things have been added since then.*

Selecting the eBay SDK or the eBay API

There's a key difference between the eBay SDK and API you must be aware of from the beginning if you're to make the right choices about whether to use one or the other. Figure 1-1 shows the relationship between the eBay SDK, API, and the underlying features of the eBay platform.

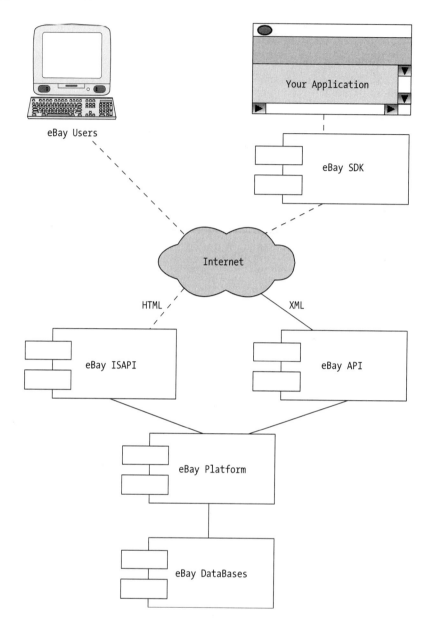

Figure 1-1. The relationship between the eBay SDK, API, and eBay platform

In a very real sense, the eBay SDK provides a high-level interface to the features of the eBay API, freeing the average application developer from needing to worry about Web-based transactions, XML, or the other complexities of Internet programming (a topic I review in Chapter 7). eBay SDK is currently implemented only in Microsoft .NET. It provides COM-compliant .NET assemblies. Consequently, you're free to write your application in any language that supports linking to .NET assemblies or COM components, including Java, C++, VB .NET, Visual Basic, VBScript or

Perl. The SDK runs on Microsoft Windows platforms starting at Microsoft Windows 2000 (Windows 98 support is under development) and going forward, making the SDK an excellent choice for applications that will reside on any modern Microsoft-based system. An important segment of the eBay SDK is the eBay Sample Selling Tool (which I discuss in detail in Chapter 6)—an open source application that is built upon the eBay SDK Integration Library. Using the Sample Selling Tool, you can list items, and manage items, sales, and feedback that are cached and synchronized in your database.

> **NOTE**   *The Sample Selling Tool is just what its name implies: a* sample.

Under the eBay SDK is the eBay API. The eBay API isn't an API in the sense you may be used to. Instead, the eBay API is an *XML application*—a series of predefined XML tags and attributes. You use these XML tags to send queries to eBay via HTTPS, and responses returned by eBay are also encoded with these XML tags. In an abstract way, this is in fact an API, although if you're not careful, you can get mired in the details of XML and HTTPS (a topic I discuss in Chapter 7 as well). Because the API has fewer requirements on a host platform—needing only XML and HTTPS atop a reasonable operating system—the API is well-suited to developing eBay applications on a host of platforms, from high-end computers running Mac OS X or Linux to diminutive handheld computers running the Palm-powered operating system or cell phones with QUALCOMM BREW or J2ME.

Conceptually, you can think of the eBay API as a segment of the API used by eBay internally, even if that's not necessarily so. Under the API—and alongside it—are the other various server-side scripts that access the eBay platform on servers at eBay directly, shuffling all of the details of user accounts, buyer and seller transactions, item listings, and the like, making the virtual market a real one for millions of people.

Developing Your Application with eBay

When you decide to integrate your application with eBay, you take on eBay as a partner. You'll be using not just their data, but also some of their intellectual property—the interfaces provided by the eBay SDK and API, as well as some of their physical property, the servers that process the API requests on your behalf whether you're using the eBay SDK or eBay API. Consequently, developing an application that interacts with eBay involves some additional steps from a traditional software development project.

At the outset, your development process, in which you construct scenarios and use cases for your application, will be much the same. You'll be hammering out exactly what it is that your application will do, and what value the eBay connection brings to your application. Even at this early stage, you should visit the eBay Developer Web site at http://developer.ebay.com/ to take a look at what the Developers Program offers and how its pricing will affect your application.

While entry to the Developers Program is free, applications using the eBay interfaces aren't. There are good reasons for this, too, especially because the pricing is very reasonable. Applications that use eBay interfaces must limit their use of API calls to a set number every day or month to ensure that they don't swamp eBay's server resources with excessive requests. Consequently, eBay provides a tiered developer program in which you can choose to be an individual developer (with relatively few API calls per day permitted), or pay increasing amounts and obtain a greater number of API calls per day and other benefits (such as direct developer technical support). Weighing the options available to you early in your development process lets you select the kinds of use cases you can implement at set economic cost to you or your application users.

Once you're ready to begin development, you must actually sign up with the eBay Developers Program to obtain access to the eBay API (although you can download the eBay SDK without signing up) and the eBay Sandbox. Signing up is essential, if only because you will use the eBay Sandbox throughout the development life cycle. It's easy to do, too—you simply fill out a Web-based form, pay an annual membership fee if you choose to purchase support for your application development, and receive a login and password to access the eBay Developer Zone, a password-protected site that includes all of the eBay SDK and eBay API documentation, as well as access to the eBay Sandbox.

The eBay Sandbox is an eBay-in-miniature, where you're able to test your application against real-world eBay servers chock full of past auction data. Using the eBay Sandbox, you can create test users, list items for sale, and set up real-world test cases for your application—all without running the risk of costly application failures with real people on eBay's production servers. It's a critical part of developing and testing your application, because the eBay Sandbox acts just as the real eBay servers do, letting your application get the workout it needs as you write, test, and debug.

Once your application is ready to be delivered to customers, you submit it to eBay for certification, typically paying a flat fee to eBay to cover the cost of testing. This certification ensures that your application plays well with eBay's servers and data, verifying that you comply with the API agreement that specifies how you may use the APIs, and that you use them efficiently, avoiding practices that incur unnecessary processor and network loads on eBay servers. Because of this, certification is mandatory; but it provides additional benefits to you, because after certification your application can access the real data on eBay's production

servers, and you can advertise the application as having met eBay certification—
something not available to developers without certification or those using
technologies other than those available from eBay.

Certification is essentially black-box testing—that is, eBay testers run your
application, examine the user interface, and explore how it interacts with the
eBay service by looking at the network traffic it generates. They don't perform
code reviews, code audits, or anything else of the sort, so you can rest assured
that the details of any proprietary algorithms stay where they belong, safe inside
your company's brain trust.

Of course, once your application is complete, you'll probably find the need
to make changes as you add features. Generally, you need only recertify your
application when your license to use either the eBay API or eBay SDK expires, or
when you make specific changes to your application that changes how it uses the
eBay API or SDK. Other changes, such as user-interface changes, changes to the
splash screen or help documentation, and the like, don't require recertification
because they don't change how your application interacts with the eBay service.

Key Points

In this chapter, you learned that

- Not just individuals use eBay, but hundreds of smaller and larger corporations do to buy and sell inventory. Using the eBay developer tool offerings,
you can create software valuable to both buyers and sellers who use eBay
to conduct their business.

- Using eBay's development tool offerings is the only eBay-sanctioned way
to programmatically access data from eBay's servers.

- The eBay SDK provides an interface to eBay data using .NET and the
Component Object Model (COM), suitable for developing applications
on the Microsoft Windows platform.

- The eBay API provides an interface to eBay data using XML over secure
HTTP, suitable for developing applications on any platform with a minimum of network services.

- You must be a member of eBay's Developers Program to develop applications that use eBay's data, the eBay SDK, and the eBay API. The Developers
Program is a tiered program, with a free level so that even individual developers can afford to develop applications.

- A key element of the eBay Developers Program you will use in developing your application is the eBay Sandbox, a set of servers stocked with data from past auctions you can use with test users and your application to ensure that it functions correctly.

- Before you ship your application, you must have it certified by eBay, to ensure that it follows eBay's Terms of Service and doesn't interact maliciously with eBay servers and data.

CHAPTER 2

Understanding the Fundamentals of eBay Development

BEFORE YOU DIVE INTO the eBay SDK, it's worth taking some time to review the fundamentals of developing applications using the eBay SDK itself. Understanding how the eBay SDK relates to your application and how people use eBay will help you create robust applications quickly.

In this chapter, I show you the fundamental concepts you need to know when using the eBay SDK. I first show you the organization behind the eBay service and the eBay SDK, so that you understand how the different pieces of the SDK fit together and how to make an SDK API call. Next, I step back from the eBay SDK and talk in general terms about the .NET assemblies and the Component Object Model (COM) interfaces you use when writing applications with the SDK and how you use these with both C# and Perl, two of today's popular programming languages. Once you understand how to use COM to access the eBay SDK, I return to the topic of the eBay SDK itself, showing you your first application at the end of this chapter in both C# and Perl.

Understanding the eBay SDK

While the eBay SDK is not complex, it has an organization and a vocabulary all its own that is essential for you to understand when using the SDK. If you're new to eBay, it's imperative that you understand these concepts before moving forward; if you're a veteran user or developer, understanding these concepts and how they're used in the context of eBay development helps you use the SDK correctly.

> **NOTE**   *Before you even set out to use the SDK, you should understand what it is and isn't. The eBay SDK gives Microsoft Windows developers a high-level interface to the eBay service. It's* not *the same as the eBay API (which I discuss in Chapters 8 and 9), which lets* any *Web-enabled platform access the eBay service.*

Installing the eBay SDK

Before you can work with the eBay SDK, you must first install it on your development workstation. This is easy: After signing up as an eBay developer (see "Developing Your Application with eBay" in Chapter 1), simply download the eBay SDK installer from `http://developer.ebay.com/DevProgram/developer/` `sdk.asp` and execute it on your workstation. It will create a folder (by default, c:\Program Files\eBay\SDK\) that contains all of the components of the eBay SDK, including the developer samples, necessary dynamic linked libraries (DLLs), resources, and documentation.

Understanding the Life Cycle of an Auction on eBay

An item's auction goes through a set of distinct phases on eBay. Understanding these phases is crucial, because your understanding not only affects how your application operates, but also helps you determine how your application adds to an eBay user's experience. In broad strokes, these stages include

1. The initial item listing

2. Viewing by potential buyers once the item is listed

3. Bidding on the item by interested buyers

4. The closing of the auction

5. Settling the auction transaction

6. After-auction activities

An auction begins when you officially list the item for sale, either through a special page on eBay (the Sell Your Item page), or via the eBay SDK or eBay API. As you list the item for sale, you describe it, post pictures of the item, and so forth. You also specify the conditions under which the auction concludes, such as the minimum price you will accept, how long the auction should take place, how a buyer must pay for an item, and where you're willing to ship the item. Listing an item incurs fees that are calculated and shown to the user as part of the process.

Once the item is listed, it goes up for auction. Each auction can be different, however. Some auctions allow a single user to purchase an item immediately, while other auctions meet the more traditional notion of an auction, complete with a competitive bidding process. Table 2-1 lists the kinds of auctions eBay presently supports.

Table 2-1. Auctions Supported by the eBay Platform

Type of Auction	Definition
Chinese auction	One item per auction. Ends *only* when the auction's time expires. Auction is won by competitive bidding, and only one winner is allowed. May be an eBay store item.
Dutch auction	Two or more items per auction. Ends *only* when the auction's time expires. May have one winning bidder for each item in the auction. May be an eBay store item.
Ad-Type auction	One real-estate item per auction. Auction is never won, being an advertisement for the real estate property.
Stores Fixed-Price auction	One or multiple items per auction. Ends when last item sold or duration expires. One winning bidder for each item. Item must be listed inside seller's eBay Stores storefront.
Buy It Now auction	One item only per auction. The first bidder has the option of exercising the Buy It Now option at the indicated price and winning the item. If she does not, auction continues as per Chinese auction and ends when auction expires.

NOTE   *As you can see from Table 2-1, eBay has the notion of eBay Stores, a separate part of their Web site that allows sellers to cobrand their sales with eBay. Using an eBay store, sellers can present a unique look and feel, obtain a dedicated URL that takes buyers directly to their items on eBay, and obtain regular reports of sales performance.*

Table 2-1 shows that there are some broad differences between kinds of auctions:

- The number of physical items listed within an auction

- Whether the auction is listed as part of an eBay storefront for a user

- Whether the auction is fixed or variable price

Once the item has been listed, it's visible on the eBay Web site in a number of places, depending on the type of item and the type of auction. Most users will see the item first under a listing Web page that shows the results of a search by item or category. Selecting an item from the listing page shows the item itself, along with its current price, how many bids have been placed for the item, the start time and end time of the auction, payment and shipping terms, and a form for you to enter a bid to purchase the item.

Once you have placed a bid on an item, it's added to your My Ebay page, a special page attached to your user account that you can view at any time to get a synopsis of the status of the items you've bought, sold, and are interested in buying.

Once the auction is over—either because the auction's time has elapsed, or because the item has been purchased via Buy It Now during a Buy It Now auction—the auction is closed. If the item has sold, the buyer and seller must settle the terms of the auction; otherwise, the seller is free to relist the item as she chooses.

To settle the auction, buyer and seller may contact each other, exchange payment and item, and optionally leave feedback for each other. The settlement can be done a variety of ways, from e-mail to using eBay's PayPal service. If buyer and seller use PayPal, eBay provides an automated Checkout service that lets buyers send payment automatically via their PayPal account; otherwise the process is more manual, typically through the use of a money order or personal check. In any case, once payment is received, the seller sends the item to the buyer. Finally, feedback (consisting of a brief textual comment and a numerical rating) is given by the buyer to the seller and by the seller to the buyer, indicating each party's degree of satisfaction with the transaction. Feedback is essentially peer-driven reputation building, and permits others to have a relative notion of the reliability of a specific buyer or seller.

> **NOTE** *Leaving feedback is an optional yet crucial part of the process, because feedback is the means by which buyers and sellers maintain ratings and provide a peer-reviewed mechanism for ensuring trust between eBay users.*

Understanding the Vocabulary of the eBay SDK

The eBay SDK has a precise vocabulary describing the kinds of entities that the eBay SDK manipulates. Understanding these terms from the get-go will help you understand how the eBay SDK interfaces map to the real-world elements behind an online auction at eBay.

Central to the notion of the eBay SDK interface is a *user*. This term encapsulates the notion of a user of the eBay auction service, and possesses attributes including the user's e-mail address, an "about me" URL to a Web page with details about the user, cumulative feedback score from previous transactions, whether or not the user owns a specific eBay store, and so forth. Each user has an *account,* which contains information about how that user pays eBay for carrying and completing auctions. Of course, you can't go accessing users' accounts willy-nilly, but you can access the account of users who're signing in with your application, so that your application can help users track the details of their eBay accounts, if they have more than one (which can happen if a user has more than one eBay store, for example).

Something for auction on eBay is called an *item.* Sellers list items for sale, and buyers bid on those items. Your application can observe an item's main properties, including the number of bids pending on an item, the current bidding price, the Buy It Now price at which the item can be bought and the auction closed, the currency associated with the price, the country from which the item is being sold, and so on. Most of an item's properties are fixed once the item is listed, or at least cannot be changed by SDK calls: It would make little sense for a user of the SDK to artificially change who is selling an item, for example! The notion of an item is a little slippery, as it may be more than one tangible thing (such as in a Dutch auction). To eBay, an item is simply something up for sale classed by a specific item ID.

All items fall into at least one *category* (and possibly two), one of the thousands of classifications that make objects easy to find. eBay employs hierarchical categories, with broad categories towards the top of the hierarchy and smaller, more specific categories below. For example, Music is a category contained by Entertainment, and Music itself contains other categories, including Cassettes, CDs, Records, and even 8-Tracks (which technically falls into the Other Formats category of Music).

Once an auction has concluded, the auction itself is known to the SDK as a *sale.* The sale contains information such as a reference to the item that has been sold, the amount the buyer as agreed to pay for the item, the user information for the buyer, and the unique transaction ID that represents the sale.

After completing a sale, both buyer and seller leave *feedback* regarding the other party. A unique item of feedback includes a textual comment describing the transaction, a numeric score, the ID of the user who left the feedback, their role in the transaction, and when the comment was recorded. Every user has an aggregate score showing their feedback standing, giving other users a notion of how trustworthy an individual user is.

Understanding How the eBay SDK Is Organized

The eBay SDK is a set of .NET assemblies that are also COM compliant. By being so, they ensure that the SDK components are available to a host of development platforms running on Microsoft Windows, including C, C++, C#, Perl, PHP, Visual Basic, and VB.NET.

Within the eBay SDK are two specific components: the API Library, which provides a wrapper around the underlying eBay API, and the Integration Library, which provides a number of added-value functions that lets you streamline access between your application and the eBay service. In the discussion that follows, I emphasize the eBay API Library because you will learn about the eBay Integration Library in Chapter 6. This division, and the other divisions within these components, are maintained via *namespaces*—hierarchical naming that begins with the prefix eBay.SDK. Each namespace is divided with periods. Here are a few valid eBay SDK component names:

- eBay.SDK.Model.Account: Represents an account

- eBay.SDK.API.APISession: Manages the underlying API calls that operate behind the eBay SDK

- eBay.SDK.Model.Item.Fees: Represents the fees a seller pays to list and sell items

> **TIP** *Even if you never intend to use the eBay Integration Library, you should still peruse Chapter 6, because the eBay Integration Library provides a lot of support in its data model for interacting with eBay. Understanding the eBay Integration Library will help you understand patterns of use your application is likely to follow as well as create a robust application design.*

As you might imagine, the libraries behind the SDK contain two kinds of components: classes, which implement the various components of the SDK; and interfaces, which describe how you can access a class programmatically.

The eBay API Library is divided up into two logical sections: the *model* and the *api*. The model section of the eBay API Library, contained in the namespace eBay.SDK.Model, consists of the classes and interfaces that represent components of the eBay data model, such as sales, items, users, accounts, and transactions. The api section of the eBay API Library, contained in the eBay.SDK.API namespace, provides interfaces for each eBay API call. You use both in the course of building your application; the eBay.SDK.Model components will help you organize your application, while the eBay.SDK.API components perform the actual work of making eBay API calls.

Using the eBay SDK COM Components in Applications

Component-oriented programming is not new. The first discussions centering on the notion of creating pluggable components for assembling software like electronics, with interchangeable components, dates back to a North Atlantic Treaty Organization (NATO) conference on the state of software engineering in 1968. At the conference, Douglas McIlroy presented a paper titled "Mass Produced Software Components," suggesting that a component-oriented approach to organizing code would facilitate large-scale software development.

The Microsoft COM approach to software components dates back to the early 1990s in the form of Microsoft's Object Linking and Embedding (OLE) technology for supporting interapplication communication. With the rise of other component-oriented approaches such as the Common Object Request Broker Architecture (CORBA) to facilitate the construction of applications using predefined, interchangeable chunks of code on a single computer or distributed across a network, Microsoft repeatedly enhanced and renamed OLE through the following five years, finally announcing COM, an all-encompassing component framework, in 1997.

To most developers, COM is an umbrella over the underlying software components. However, to platform vendors such as eBay, it's far more. COM includes the underlying protocols and code for platform vendors to add additional components, enabling a developer to make virtually anything available as a component. To make access to eBay easier for developers like you and me, eBay's engineers created a set of COM components that encapsulates the underlying eBay API (see Figure 1-1 in Chapter 1) so that you can access eBay servers without needing to use the underlying API. Consequently, in order to use the eBay SDK, you must first be comfortable using COM in building your applications.

Using the eBay SDK in C# Applications

Because the eBay SDK is a set of .NET assembly libraries, its integration with other .NET applications and languages is trivial. If you've struggled with integrating other COM components into your .NET applications, don't panic: eBay has done the work for you.

> **TIP** *Even when you go to write your own application from scratch, you may want to have a look at the C# container sample that accompanies the source code with this book. This sample shows how you add the eBay SDK assemblies to your project and include their declarations in your source code.*

To begin with, be sure you have installed the C# components of Visual Studio .NET on your development workstation. Once you do that, accessing the eBay SDK from your C# application requires only that you perform the following steps:

1. Include the directory where you installed the eBay SDK (the default is C:\Program Files\eBay\SDK\) in the References Path field of your project's Common Properties section in the project's Property Pages dialog box (see Figure 2-1).

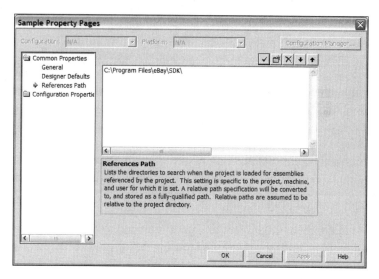

Figure 2-1. Including the eBay SDK path in your C# .NET project

2. Include the necessary eBay SDK DLLs (typically eBay.SDK.dll and eBay.SDK.Integration.dll) in your project's references by right-clicking References in the Solution Explorer, selecting Browse, and adding the eBay SDK DLLs (see Figure 2-2).

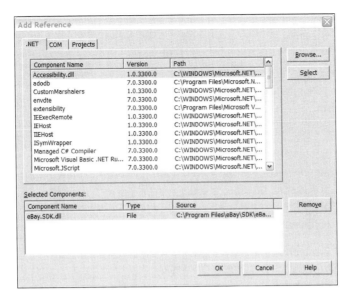

Figure 2-2. Including references to the eBay SDK DLLs in your C# .NET project

3. Include the various components in each file where they'll be accessed with the C# using directive, like you see in Listing 2-1, which includes the necessary support for the eBay.SDK.API, eBay.SDK.Model, and eBay.SDK.Model.Item components.

Listing 2-1. Including eBay SDK Components with C#'s using Directive

```
1: using eBay.SDK.API;
2: using eBay.SDK.Model;
3: using eBay.SDK.Model.Item;
```

Once you do this, you can declare instances of eBay SDK interfaces just as you would any other component.

Using the eBay SDK in Perl Applications

One of the great beauties of working in Perl these days is that it seems that with only a little typing, all things are possible. This is certainly true when it comes to using COM components such as those provided by the eBay SDK. With Perl's Win32::OLE library, available for the Microsoft Windows platform under ActiveState's ActivePerl (at http://www.activestate.com/), using eBay SDK components is almost as easy from Perl as it is from a native Microsoft language like C# or Visual Basic.

To begin with, you must first have installed ActivePerl, including the Win32::OLE library, via the installer available from http://www.activestate.com/Products/ActivePerl/. Once you do this, you must include the Win32::OLE library using Perl's use keyword with your other includes, as you see in Listing 2-2.

Listing 2-2. Including the Win32::OLE Library

```
1: use Win32::OLE;
```

After that, conjuring up an eBay SDK component is as easy as using the library's new method and naming the desired component, as you can see from Listing 2-3. This works because the components within the eBay SDK are registered with the operating system for general use, so that the Win32::OLE module can find the underlying libraries.

Listing 2-3. Creating an eBay SDK Component Using Win32::OLE

```
1: $apiSession = Win32::OLE->new("eBay.SDK.API.ApiSession");
```

The resulting variable is a Perl object that has fields mapping to the component's properties. Thus, you can configure a data model object by assigning its fields the appropriate values, and make an SDK call using the object's methods. To see this in detail, see "Validating a Test User in Perl" in the next section.

NOTE *If you're not familiar with Perl, the notion of a Perl object might be a little intimidating, especially if after reading the last paragraph you put the book down and did a bit of searching with Google for articles about Perl objects. Rest assured that you needn't concern yourself with the language semantics. At a high level, practitioners of languages such as C, C++, C#, or Java can pretend that a Perl object is something like a C++ object: a structure with associated fields and member functions. (In reality, it's actually quite a bit more powerful and sophisticated than that, but I won't be taking advantage of the features of object-oriented Perl to any great degree here.)*

Your First Application Using the eBay SDK

It's time to write your first application that uses eBay. This first application is very simple, almost deceptively so; all it does is take a test user and validate the account that is required for the test user to sell items in the eBay Sandbox. You will find that this application is handy to use, both because you need to have a way to have validated sellers to test your own application, and because it lets you get a feel for what it takes to begin testing your application in the eBay Sandbox and using the eBay SDK.

Starting with the eBay Sandbox

Before you can run your application against the eBay Sandbox for testing, you must have your developer ID, application ID, and certification ID that eBay assigned to you when you joined the eBay Developers Program. These are character strings that are best kept both electronically in a file on your development workstation and as printed backup in case you lose or change the file, because eBay must reissue these certificates in the event that you lose them. Together, these three IDs provide the keys you need to access the eBay Sandbox, where all of your application testing will take place with eBay data. The eBay Sandbox looks just like the eBay Web interface real users use (see Figure 2-3).

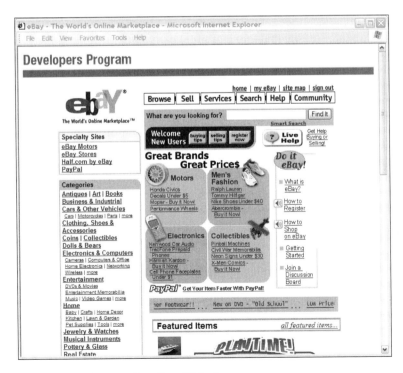

Figure 2-3. The eBay Sandbox Web site

The other thing you need when testing your application are *test users*. Test users are accounts in the eBay Sandbox that play the part of real-world users of the eBay service, listing items for sale, bidding, buying, and leaving feedback. To add test users (you'll need at least two, because you can't bid on your own items), simply click the Register Now button on the first page of the Sandbox. You'll be met with a form that is identical to the form that users fill out when joining the real eBay service.

When filling out the form, you must specify valid data, including for the e-mail address. It's imperative when specifying an e-mail address that you use a valid e-mail address that's unique to this test user, because eBay uses the e-mail address to validate the user. (This is even true for test users.) This e-mail address should go to a valid ISP, and not a free e-mail hosting service such as Yahoo! or Microsoft Hotmail. Figure 2-4 shows the new user registration form.

> **TIP** *When you're first setting out with your application development, make a table of the names and e-mail addresses of buyers and sellers, and ask your system administrator to create e-mail accounts for each. Doing so will help you stay organized and eliminate making regular requests of your system administrator for just one more e-mail address for testing.*

Once you create a test user, you need to check your test user's e-mail account for instructions on how to verify your test user. This e-mail, similar to the one you see in Figure 2-5, includes a URL to a Web page you must load to finish your registration.

The users you create in this manner can bid on items in the eBay Sandbox, but can't actually list items for auction. To sell items, users must be validated. In the production eBay environment, this means that the user has given eBay a valid credit card number. In the eBay Sandbox, however, you need only make a call to the eBay API interface `ValidateTestUserRegistrationCall`, available through the SDK with the class `eBay.SDK.API.ValidateTestUserRegistrationCall`.

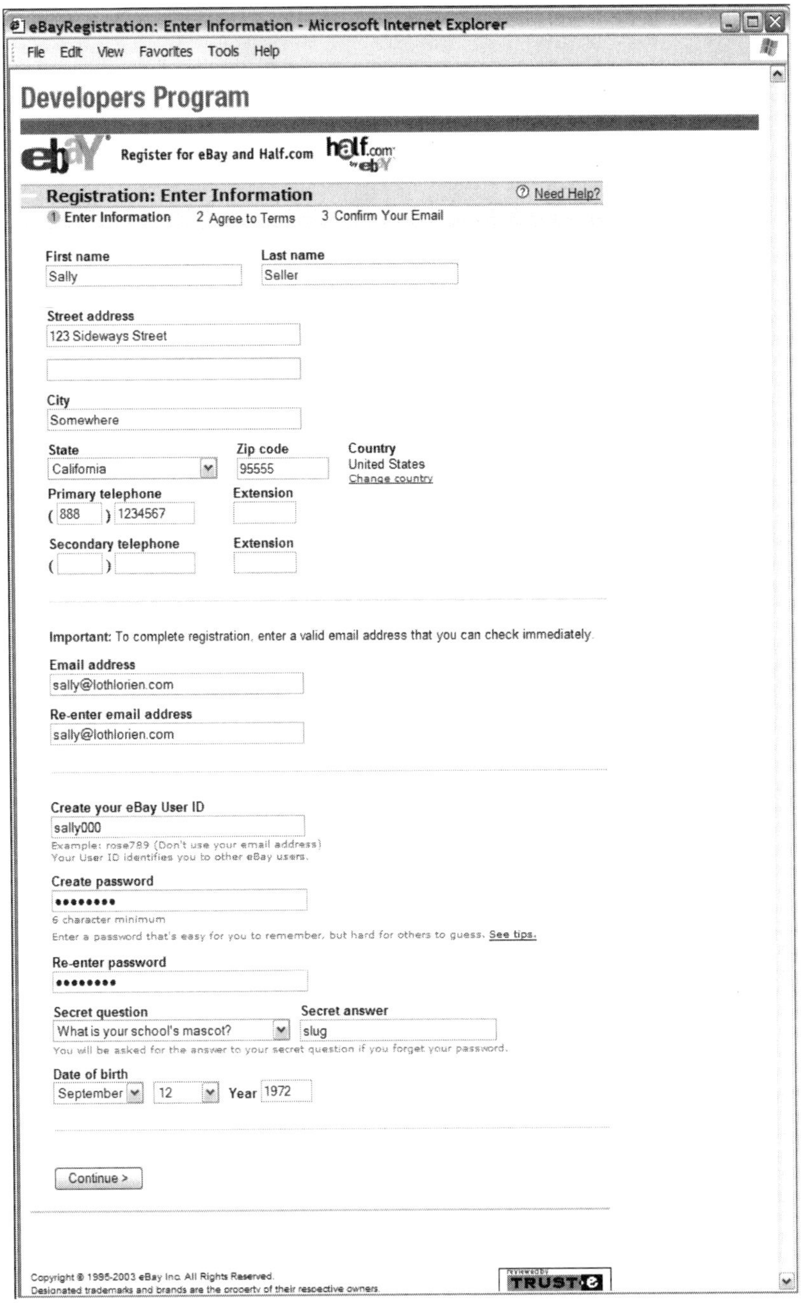

Figure 2-4. The eBay Sandbox new user registration form

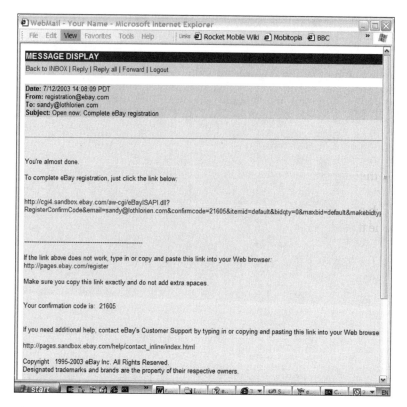

Figure 2-5. The eBay verify user e-mail message

Understanding the ValidateUser Sample Application

The flow of the ValidateUser application is quite simple, but illustrates the necessary sequence of events when using the eBay SDK. To use the eBay SDK, your application must

1. Create an `eBay.SDK.API.ApiSession` object. This session object encapsulates the HTTPS and XML code responsible for exchanging messages with eBay servers via the eBay API.

2. Set the session object's `Url` property to the URL for the eBay server. When testing your application, you use the URL for the eBay Sandbox, `https://api.sandbox.ebay.com/ws/api.dll`.

3. Set the session's `Developer` property to the developer key you received when joining the eBay developer program.

4. Set the session's `Application` property to the application key you received when joining the eBay developer program.

5. Set the session's `Certificate` property to the certificate key you received when joining the eBay developer program.

6. Create any necessary eBay SDK model components and set their properties or access their methods.

7. Create any necessary eBay SDK API components.

8. For each eBay API component you created, set its `ApiCallSession` property to the session object you created in step 1.

9. For each eBay API component you created, invoke its method and examine the results.

The ValidateUser application follows this flow, first creating and initializing an `eBay.SDK.API.ApiSession` object, and then using it with an `eBay.SDK.API.ValidateTestUserRegistrationCall` call to validate the test user you specify.

Figure 2-6 shows the application in action, using eBay keys fetched from a configuration file, ebayrc, in the same directory as the application. (If you don't place your eBay keys in the ebayrc file, the application will prompt you for each of the keys in turn.)

Figure 2-6. The eBay ValidateUser application

> **NOTE** *Unix aficionados will recognize the ebayrc file as a bastardized version of their favorite configuration mechanism, the* dotfile *(so called because it usually begins with a single period to hide it from normal directory listings). By using such a simple configuration mechanism, you avoid the need to retype keys for each user you must validate, while still keeping the sample application in both C# and Perl simple. You might want to store the keys as entries in the Microsoft Windows registry; by all means, go ahead! You can obtain the source code for this—and all other examples—at the Apress Web site at* http://www.apress.com/, *and change it to your heart's content.*

Validating a Test User in C#

The ValidateUser application has three broad sections in a single class, ValidateUser. The first section at the beginning sets up the necessary ApiSession object. The second section obtains the eBay keys and the desired test user name and password. The final section creates and uses an instance of eBay.SDK.API.ValidateTestUserRegistrationCall to validate the user you specify in the second step. Listing 2-4 shows ValidateUser.cs.

Listing 2-4. The ValidateUser Application in C#

```
 1: // Dependencies
 2: using System;
 3: using System.IO;
 4: using eBay.SDK.API;
 5:
 6:
 7: namespace ValidateUser
 8: {
 9:   class ValidateUser
10:   {
11:     private static string devID;
12:     private static string appID;
13:     private static string crtID;
14:
15:     static void Main(string[] args)
16:     {
17:       IApiSession apiSession;
18:       ValidateTestUserRegistrationCall api;
19:
20:       // Create ApiSession object.
21:       Console.Write( "Creating eBay.SDK.API.ApiSession " );
22:       Console.WriteLine( "object..." );
23:       apiSession = new ApiSession ();
24:       apiSession.LogCallXml = true;
25:       apiSession.Url = "https://api.sandbox.ebay.com/ws/api.dll";
26:
27:       // Get the eBay keys.
28:       getKeys ();
29:       apiSession.Developer = devID;
30:       apiSession.Application = appID;
31:       apiSession.Certificate = crtID;
32:
```

```
33:        // Find out which account we should validate.
34:        Console.Write( "Enter eBay User ID of " );
35:        Console.Write( "the seller account: ");
36:        apiSession.RequestUserId = Console.ReadLine();
37:
38:        Console.Write( "Enter password to the " );
39:        Console.Write( "seller account: " );
40:        apiSession.RequestPassword = Console.ReadLine();
41:
42:        // Create the API request.
43:        Console.Write( "Creating " );
44:        Console.Write( "eBay.SDK.API." );
45:        Console.Write( "ValidateTestUserRegistrationCall " );
46:        Console.WriteLine( "object..." );
47:        api = new ValidateTestUserRegistrationCall();
48:        api.ErrorLevel =
49:            ErrorLevelEnum.BothShortAndLongErrorStrings;
50:        api.ApiCallSession = apiSession;
51:
52:        // Issue the call.
53:        Console.Write( "Issuing ValidateTestUserRegistration() " );
54:        Console.WriteLine( "call..." );
55:        try
56:        {
57:          api.ValidateTestUserRegistration();
58:          Console.Write( "Congratulations! " );
59:          Console.Write( "The user has been validated " );
60:          Console.WriteLine( "successfully!" );
61:        }
62:      catch( Exception e )
63:        {
64:          Console.Write( "**Error**: " );
65:          Console.Write( e.Message );
66:        }
67:        // Linger until the user dismisses the app.
68:        Console.ReadLine ();
69:      }
70:
71:      //
72:      // Fetches the eBay developer keys from either
73:      // a dotfile or from the input line if the dotfile
74:      // isn't available.
75:      //
```

```
76:     static void getKeys( )
77:     {
78:        FileStream stream;
79:        StreamReader streamreader;
80:        String keystring;
81:        String [] keys;
82:        Char [] eol = {'\n'};
83:        try
84:        {
85:          stream =
86:            new FileStream( "ebayrc", System.IO.FileMode.Open );
87:          streamreader = new StreamReader( stream );
88:          keystring = streamreader.ReadToEnd();
89:          keys = keystring.Split( eol );
90:          devID = keys[0].Trim();
91:          appID = keys[1].Trim();
92:          crtID = keys[2].Trim();
93:        }
94:      catch
95:        {
96:          Console.Write( "Enter API Developer Id: " );
97:          devID = Console.ReadLine();
98:          Console.Write( "Enter API Application Id: " );
99:          appID = Console.ReadLine();
100:          Console.Write( "Enter API Certificate: " );
101:          crtID = Console.ReadLine();
102:        }
103:      }
104:    }
105: }
```

Lines 1–4 indicate the namespaces used by the ValidateUser application. The application uses classes from .NET's System namespace (most significantly, the Console class for I/O), the System.IO namespace (the FileStream and FileReader classes), and the eBay.SDK.API namespace, for access to eBay SDK components.

On line 7, the entire application is encapsulated in its own namespace, the ValidateUser namespace. While this is overkill for such a simple example, it's good practice, and the Visual C# .NET application wizard provides the namespace anyway. The application itself consists of a single class, ValidateUser, which has two methods: Main (lines 15–69), the entry point for the application, and getKeys (lines 76–103), which obtains your eBay keys from either the ebayrc file or from the console.

On lines 17–18, the Main method declares two local variables: apiSession, which contains an instance of IApiSession the application uses to communicate with the eBay service; and api, which contains the actual eBay SDK component that validates the user, a ValidateTestUserRegistrationCall instance. Line 23 creates the apiSession object, while the following two lines initialize its LogCallXml and Url properties. The LogCallXml property, as you will see in the next chapter, lets you perform some handy debugging by dumping the underlying XML behind a session transaction to a file so you can see what the eBay SDK is making of an application request. The Url property, on the other hand, must point to the URL of the eBay service the application will use. The URL you see here on line 25 is the URL for the Sandbox.

Lines 28–31 use the class function getKeys to determine the keys necessary to access the Sandbox, and set the apiSession's Developer, Application, and Certificate properties appropriately. (I discuss the getKeys function later in this section.)

The next chunk of code (lines 33–40) is the application's user interface: two humble console input lines, prompting you for the test user to activate. The apiSession needs both the test user's account name (line 36) and password (line 40) in order to issue a successful request.

Line 47 creates an instance of the ValidateTestUserRegistrationCall, the eBay SDK class that encapsulates the eBay API logic to validate a test user, and stores it in the variable api. Line 48 sets its ErrorLevel property to report verbose errors; the enumeration ErrorLevelEnum has two values, OnlyShortErrorStrings and BothShortAndLongErrorStrings. The eBay SDK reports errors to you as C# exceptions, and you can use the Exception class's Message property to obtain the text of an error reported by the SDK.

Lines 55–66 use the api object to actually make the eBay API call ValidateTestUserRegistration. You wrap the actual API invocation on line 57 with a C# try/catch block to differentiate between success and failure. On success, the eBay SDK executes the necessary HTTPS transaction to validate your test user on line 57 and then prints the success message on lines 58–60; if anything goes awry, the eBay SDK generates an exception, and the catch block on lines 62–66 prints the contents of the exception's Message property so you know what went wrong.

The utility method getKeys, spanning lines 76–103, attempts to read the three eBay keys from the file named ebayrc in the current directory. It does this by assuming that the file exists and opening it as a .NET System.IO.FileStream on lines 85–86. If this succeeds, the function uses the System.IO.StreamReader instance created on line 87 to read the entire file into a string, keystring, on line 88. The function expects the keys to appear in the file separated by line breaks, like so:

```
1: developer-key
2: application-key
3: certificate-key
```

so the function splits the string keystring by end-of-line characters on line 89. Finally, lines 90–92 set the class variables devID, appID, and crtID to the first three lines of the file, respectively, trimming any white space.

In the event that any of this fails—typically because there's no ebayrc file in the first place—none of this will work. As a result, the file management logic is wrapped in an error-catching try block, and on any failure, the code on lines 96–101 gets executed instead, prompting you for the three eBay keys from the console.

Validating a Test User in Perl

Like the C# version of ValidateUser, the Perl version of ValidateUser has three broad sections: a brief section at the beginning that creates the ApiSession object, the necessary file system or user input to obtain the eBay keys and the desired test user name and password, and the actual creation and use of the eBay.SDK.API.ValidateTestUserRegistrationCall object to validate the test user. Listing 2-5 shows the ValidateUser application listing in Perl.

Listing 2-5. The ValidateUser Application in Perl

```
 1: use Win32::OLE;
 2: sub getKeys;
 3:
 4: # Create ApiSession Object.
 5: print "Creating eBay.SDK.API.ApiSession object...\n";
 6: $apiSession = Win32::OLE->new("eBay.SDK.API.ApiSession");
 7: $apiSession->{'LogCallXml'} = True;
 8: $apiSession->{'Url'} =
 9:     "https://api.sandbox.ebay.com/ws/api.dll";
10:
11: # Get the eBay keys.
12: ( $apiSession->{'Developer'},
13:   $apiSession->{'Application'},
14:   $apiSession->{'Certificate'} ) = getKeys();
15:
16: # Find out which account we should validate.
17: print "Enter eBay User ID of the seller account: ";
18: chomp($input = <>);
19: $apiSession->{'RequestUserId'} = $input;
20:
21: print "Enter password to the seller account: ";
22: chomp($input = <>);
23: $apiSession->{'RequestPassword'} = $input;
24:
```

```perl
25: # Create the API request.
26: print "Creating ";
27: print "eBay.SDK.API.ValidateTestUserRegistrationCall ";
28: print "object...\n";
29: $api = Win32::OLE->new(
30:   "eBay.SDK.API.ValidateTestUserRegistrationCall");
31: $api->{'ApiCall'}->{'ErrorLevel'} = 1;
32:
33: # Perl doesn't seem to know how to query multiple interfaces
34: # so we have to use the ApiCall property of the api.
35: # $api->{'ApiCallSession'} = $apiSession;
36: $api->{'ApiCall'}->{'ApiCallSession'} = $apiSession;
37:
38: # Issue the call.
39: print "Issuing ValidateTestUserRegistration() call...\n";
40: $api->ValidateTestUserRegistration();
41: $result = Win32::OLE->LastError();
42:
43: # Show the results.
44: if($result)
45: {
46:   print "**Error**: $result!\n";
47: }
48: else
49: {
50:   print "Congratulations! ";
51:   print "The user has been validated successfully!\n";
52: }
53: print "\n";
54:
55: # Fetches the eBay developer keys from either
56: # a dotfile or from the input line if the dotfile
57: # isn't availalble.
58: sub getKeys
59: {
60:   # Try to open the file.
61:   open( IDS, "ebayrc" ) or $ttyInput = 1;
62:
63:   # If the open failed prompt the user for each key.
64:   if ( $ttyInput )
65:   {
66:     print "Enter API Developer Id: ";
67:     chomp($input = <>);
68:     $devid = $input;
69:
```

```
70:      print "Enter API Application Id: ";
71:      chomp($input = <>);
72:      $appid = $input;
73:
74:      print "Enter API Certificate: ";
75:      chomp($input = <>);
76:      $crtid = $input;
77:    }
78:  else
79:  {
80:    # Read them from the file.
81:    # The file should have the keys in the order
82:    # developer id
83:    # application id
84:    # certificate id
85:    $line = 0;
86:    while ( <IDS> )
87:    {
88:      chomp( $_ );
89:      $devid = $_ if $line == 0;
90:      $appid = $_ if $line == 1;
91:      $crtid = $_ if $line == 2;
92:      $line++;
93:    }
94:  }
95:  # return a list with the keys
96:  return ( $devid, $appid, $crtid );
97: }
```

Lines 1–2 are the bookkeeping the script needs to continue, first ensuring that the Win32::OLE library will be loaded, and then providing a forward declaration for the getKeys function, which simply loads the eBay keys from either the ebayrc file or the command line if the file doesn't exist in the current directory.

Lines 4–9 create the eBay.SDK.API.ApiSession object the application needs to communicate with the eBay service. On line 4, the variable $apiSession is given the new object created by the Win32::OLE->new function. The application sets the resulting ApiSession object's LogCallXml and Url fields on lines 7–8. (Newcomers to Perl should note that the syntax you see on line 7—and elsewhere when you set an object's property—in which the object's property name is in bracketed single quotes is how you access an object's field.) The LogCallXml property, which I discuss in the next chapter, lets you create a log file for debugging that you can examine if you need to see the resulting XML exchanged between your application and the eBay service. The Url field must contain the URL of the server at eBay your application should interact with.

> **CAUTION**   *The code I show in this section does very little by way of either error handling or debugging, because I want to show you how to use the eBay SDK in its simplest terms. As you will see in the following chapter, you never want to begin using the results of creating new eBay SDK components willy-nilly without ensuring that they exist! If allocation of an eBay SDK component fails without error checking, your application will come to a screeching (and embarrassing) halt when it tries to use the component later on.*

Lines 10–14 use the getKeys() utility function (which is defined at the end of this program) to determine the developer, application, and certificate eBay keys from either the input line or the ebayrc file. If you're not used to Perl, the syntax of this statement may be a bit confusing. In Perl, you can perform multiple variable assignments by placing the variable names in a list on the right-hand side of the expression, and the values in the left-hand side, like this:

```
1: ( $e, $pi, $minus_one ) = ( 2.71828, 3.14159, -1.0 );
```

Because getKeys returns a list of the three keys, this statement simply assigns each key to the appropriate property of the $apiSession object.

Lines 16–23 comprise the user interface for the application. Lines 17–19 prompt for and accept your input of the seller account name, while lines 21–23 do the same for the seller account's password. Perl denotes a file handle as a variable (typically uppercase) between angle brackets; the expression

```
1: $variable = <>;
```

simply assigns the value of the line you enter to the variable $variable. The chomp function removes the trailing carriage return and linefeed from its argument and replaces its argument with the truncated string, so that on line 19 the RequestUserId property of $apiSession is set to the text you enter without the trailing carriage return and linefeed. Similarly, on line 23 the RequestPassword property of $apiSession is set to the password you enter.

Lines 24-30 create another SDK object the application needs to actually validate the test user, the eBay.SDK eBay.SDK.API.ValidateTestUserRegistrationCall object the application needs to actually validate the test user. Line 31 sets the desired error reporting level for the API call to show both short and long error strings so that in the event of the eBay SDK reporting an error you have some idea what went wrong. (This value is the same as the eBay SDK .NET's notion of the ErrorLevelEnum.)

Lines 33–36 are an outright hack; the Perl object hierarchy using Win32::OLE doesn't like the notion of setting the ApiCallSession property directly, so instead you set it indirectly, using a documented trick provided by the eBay SDK. In a perfect world, you could perform the assignment shown in the comment on line 35, but things being what they are, the code on line 36 does the trick. Regardless, the purpose of this assignment is to tell the newly created $api what session it should use when carrying out its eBay API request.

Lines 38–40 make the eBay ValidateTestUserRegistration API call using the $api object over the $apiSession. This is the syntax for invoking any eBay API call: Create an appropriate eBay SDK API object, initialize it with the API's arguments and the previously allocated ApiCallSession to use, and then invoke the object's API method by the same name as the eBay SDK API method.

> **NOTE** *To avoid confusion, all the names of the classes in the* eBay.SDK.API *namespace that correspond to eBay API calls end with the word* Call.

Lines 41–53 constitute the application's error handling; they simply test the result of calling Win32::OLE->LastError() to determine the last error encountered by the Win32::OLE library. If the library reports an error, the resulting string (usually generated by the eBay SDK) will contain information about the error. Otherwise, a simple message indicating success is printed on lines 49–53.

The remainder of the listing on lines 55–97 are a friendly hunk of Perl that simply tries to load your eBay keys from the file ebayrc, or, if the file doesn't exist, prompts you to enter them on the keyboard instead. Given the rather cryptic nature of the keys, it doesn't make sense to make you enter them by hand each time you run the application, so instead you can place them in the text file. Line 58 defines the function using the Perl keyword sub and the function name getKeys; the function block itself is on lines 59–97.

This function takes no arguments, and returns a list of three arguments: the eBay developer key, the eBay application key, and the eBay certificate key. The function begins on line 61 by trying to open the file named ebayrc and assigning the open file descriptor to the Perl file descriptor IDS. If the attempt to open the file fails, the local variable $ttyInput is set to 1, indicating that the function should prompt the user for the keys. Line 64 tests this flag, either prompting the user for each key (lines 65–77) using the print-chomp <>-*assignment* logic you saw previously on lines 17–23, or read each line from the configuration file on lines 79–93.

The logic on lines 79–93 is simple, even if the syntax is new to you. For each line in the file read from the descriptor IDS, Perl stores the line in the temporary variable $_. After reading the line, the script strips off the termination character (line 88), and then based on which line it's currently reading (lines 89–91) interprets the line as either the developer key, the application key, or the certificate key. Finally, the routine increments the line counter on line 92. The loop, which began on line 86, ends when the file contains no more lines to read. Consistent with the remainder of this example, there's little or no error checking.

Once the function has collected the three keys from either the console input or the file, it returns them as a list on line 96.

Key Points

In this chapter, you learned the following important points about the eBay SDK:

- The life cycle of an auction on eBay consists of the initial item listing, item viewing by potential buyers, bidding by potential buyers, the close of the auction, the settling of the auction transaction, and after-auction activities including the acceptance of payment, shipment of the item, and settling of auction fees with eBay.

- The eBay platform supports several kinds of auctions, including the traditional notion of an auction with a single item (the Chinese auction), an auction with multiple items won by multiple bidders (the Dutch auction), and Ad-Type and Stores Fixed-Price auctions.

- The eBay SDK consists of two discrete kinds of classes and interfaces: those pertaining to the eBay data model, in the eBay.SDK.Model namespace; and those pertaining to the eBay API, in the eBay.SDK.API namespace.

- The eBay SDK provides a Microsoft .NET assembly for you to use when using Microsoft .NET languages including C# and VB .NET.

- The eBay SDK provides Microsoft COM components for you to use with other languages that support Microsoft COM, such as Perl or PHP. For example, when using Perl, you can create an object from the eBay SDK using the Win32::OLE library and its new function.

- Before you can test your application, you must obtain developer, application, and certificate keys from the eBay developer Web site.

- Before you can test your application, you must create test users within the eBay Sandbox, a configuration of eBay servers that simulates real users and auctions.

- Each test user in the eBay Sandbox must have its own unique e-mail address.

- For a test user in the eBay Sandbox to be able to list items for auction, it must first be validated using the eBay API's ValidateTestUserRegistration function, also available via the eBay SDK eBay.SDK.API.ValidateTestUserRegistrationCall class.

CHAPTER 3

Introducing the eBay SDK

IN THE LAST CHAPTER, I took you on a whirlwind tour of the eBay SDK. You saw how the eBay SDK was divided into two sections: the data model representing abstractions of key data types used in eBay's business logic, and the API section encapsulating eBay API calls. You saw how your application accesses the Sandbox, and even explored your first eBay application using the Sandbox.

In this chapter, you build on that knowledge, getting the formal background on how the parts of the eBay SDK fit together, and which parts you need to use to craft specific bits of functionality for your application. I begin by giving you a detailed walkthrough of the eBay data model, building on the eBay-specific terminology you learned in the last chapter. You then see the API section of the eBay SDK in the same detail, and find out what happens under the hood when you use a member of the eBay SDK's API namespace. Finally, I conclude the chapter with another sample application that lets you explore eBay's tens of thousands of categories, a valuable tool you can use when crafting your own applications that lets users list items for sale on eBay.

Examining the eBay SDK Data Model

A key component of the eBay SDK is its *data model*—the interfaces and classes that encapsulate objects pertaining to everyday concepts in the world of eBay business. The data model includes fundamental objects representing accounts, feedback, items, sales, and users, along with a slew of other kinds of data your application can manipulate when working with the eBay service.

These objects are first-class citizens in the API, with their own methods and properties, just like the elements of the eBay.SDK.API namespace such as the eBay.SDK.API.ValidateTestUserRegistrationCall object you encountered in Chapter 2. By using these objects, you can avoid creating data structures or classes that encapsulate the same data as these do when using the eBay SDK. All of these objects include useful utility methods that stem from the Object class in the .NET Framework, including the following:

- The Equals method lets you test two objects for equivalency.

- The GetHashCode method lets you get a unique hash code for an object.

- The GetType method returns the item's type as a type object.

- The Finalize method performs necessary cleanup when the application is done using the object.

- The ToString method returns a String instance that describes the contents of the object.

These .NET-specific methods are not accessible from SDK COM components and Java packages.

Let's take a closer look at each of the namespaces that contain data model objects to see how they're organized.

Inside the eBay.SDK.Model Namespace

The eBay.SDK.Model namespace is a grab bag for data models that don't necessarily fit into one of the other namespaces. This namespace contains classes that represent eBay bids, postal addresses, and so on. Members of this namespace include the following:

- The AccessRule class, available via the IAccessRule interface, represents a single access rule to a specific API.

- The Address class, available via IAddress, encapsulates contact details such as one associated with a user.

- The APIException class, accessed via the IAPIException interface, which inherits from the .NET Exception class, represents a software exception. You will frequently use its Message property to get a text message describing the extension.

- The Bid class, accessed via the IBid interface, represents a buyer's bid to purchase an item.

- The BidCollection class, accessed via the IBidCollection interface, represents a collection of bids using Bid objects. To see how collections work, see the section "Managing Collections of Data Model Objects" later in this chapter.

- The Category class represents a category on the eBay service, accessed via the ICategory interface. You will encounter categories in detail in the section "Viewing eBay Categories: A Sample Application" at the end of this chapter.

- The CategoryCollection class, manipulated using the ICategoryCollection interface, represents a set of categories.

- The CountryHelper class provides a set of helper methods you use when converting between country names and two-character country codes such as *de* (Germany).

- The CustomCategory class, accessed via the ICustomCategory interface, represents a user-defined category.

- The CustomCategoryCollection class, accessed via the ICustomCategoryCollection interface, represents a collection of CustomCategory instances.

- The ListingDesigner class, accessed via the IListingDesigner interface, represents a custom listing format on the eBay service's Web site.

- The LogoInfo class, accessed via the ILogoInfo interface, encapsulates the return value from the eBay.SDK.API.GetLogoURLCall.GetLogoURL method, which returns a String containing the URL to the eBay logo that you can display in your application.

- The SellerEvent class, accessed via the ISellerEvent interface, encapsulates a record of the sales activities of an item up for auction.

- The StringCollection class, accessed via the IStringCollection interface, provides a collection of String instances.

- The TimeLeft class, accessed via the ITimeLeft interface, represents an arbitrary time interval in days, hours, minutes, and seconds, used for things like noting how long until an auction closes.

- The UUid class, accessed via the IUuid interface, represents a unique ID used by the eBay interfaces when performing item additions to avoid repeatedly adding the same item.

You will encounter examples with these objects throughout this and the next three chapters.

Inside the eBay.SDK.Model.Account Namespace

The eBay.SDK.Model.Account namespace contains classes that represent managing an eBay seller account. The core element of this namespace, the eBay.SDK.Model.Account.Account class, represents a seller account and provides a property, Activities, that contains a record of each account transaction that occurs for that account. The eBay.SDK.Model.Account namespace has the following additional classes:

- The AccountActivity class encapsulates a specific account transaction, representing it with properties including Balance, containing the balance as of a specific transaction; Credit and Debit, which indicate whether the transaction incurred a credit or a debit; and Id, which contains the unique ID of the specific AccountActivity within the eBay service. You use the AccountActivity class via the IAccountActivity interface.

- The AccountActivityCollection class lets you manage collections of AccountActivity objects. You use the AccountActivityCollection class via the IAccountActivityCollection class.

- The AccountInvoiceView class represents an account invoice with the properties EmailAddress, containing the e-mail to which invoices are sent; InvoiceBalance, the balance of the account when the invoice was generated; and InvoiceDate, the date at which the invoice was generated in Greenwich mean time (GMT). You use this class via the IAccountInvoiceView class.

- The AccountPaymentMethodImpl class represents how an account holder pays an account via its Type property; this property indicates the type of the payment using AccountPaymentEnum, which indicates how the account is paid. This class also includes properties such as CreditCard, which contain the actual account number of the payment method. You use this class via the IAccountPaymentMethod interface.

- The AccountPeriodView class represents a view into account activity over a specific billing period. Properties such as State (described by the AccountStateEnum), CurrentBalance, LastInvoiceAmount, PaymentMethod, and LastAmountPaid make this object resemble an account summary you'd receive from your favorite credit card company. You use this class via the IAccountPeriodView interface.

- The AdditionalAccount class contains the balance and ID of an account related to a principal Account instance for a user. You use this class via the IAdditionalAccount interface. The AdditionalAccount nodes represent historical data related to accounts that the user held with a country of residency other than the current one. eBay users can have one active account.

- The AdditionalAccountCollection represents a collection of AdditionalAccount objects. You use this class via the IAdditionalAccountCollection interface.

- The CreditCardImpl class represents the properties of a credit card used for payment, including its account number and expiration date. You use this class via the ICreditCard class.

- The DateRangeImpl class implants a range between two dates (date and time), denoted by its BeginDate and EndDate properties. You use this class via the IDateRange class.

- The DirectDebitImpl class represents a direct deposit payment method.

- The EBayDirectPay class represents a payment made to eBay via a direct payment such as a check or money order. You use this class via the IEBayDirectPay interface.

- The InvoiceViewSettings class represents the settings that you can apply to an AccountInvoiceView class via its InvoiceMonth and InvoiceYear properties. You use this class via the IInvoiceViewSettings interface.

- The PeriodViewSettings class represents the settings that you can apply to an AccountPeriodView class via its DateRange and ViewRecord properties. You use this class via the IPeriodViewSettings class and the helper enumeration PeriodViewRangeEnum, which lets you define the range for a period view's settings.

NOTE *When working with dates provided by eBay, bear in mind that all dates returned by eBay are in Greenwich mean time. You'll need to convert those to the time zone where your application is running!*

You will see more about using these in Chapter 4.

> **CAUTION** *Don't confuse the eBay notion of an account with the notion of a user account. While eBay users have accounts in the Web sense, in the parlance of the eBay SDK, an* account *is the entity that tracks transactions, like your checking account, and you manipulate it using the classes in the* eBay.SDK.Model.Account *namespace. All of the stuff pertaining to a user is referred to by the name* user, *and you can find its functionality in the* eBay.SDK.Model.User *namespace.*

Inside the eBay.SDK.Model.Attributes.Motors and eBay.SDK.Model.Attributes Namespaces

A relatively new addition to the eBay service is the eBay Motors service, where you can list and sell your car, motorcycle, or boat to interested buyers, or find the dream vehicle you've been looking for. Its use and cost structure is similar to that of eBay, but given the very nature of the merchandise, it's a separate service, and the SDK has additional support for it.

The eBay.SDK.Model.Attributes.Motors namespace contains the bulk of this support, which has the following classes and interfaces:

- The Car class, accessed via the ICar interface, represents a car for sale, inheriting from eBay.SDK.Model.Attributes.Motors.Vehicle.

- The CarOptions class, accessed via the ICarOptions interface, represents the options a specific car may have, such as a cassette player, CD player, and whether or not the car is a convertible.

- The CarPowerOptions class, accessed via the ICarPowerOptions interface, describes the common powered control options a vehicle may have via its properties including AirConditioning, CruiseControl, and PowerSeats.

- The CarSafetyFeatures class, accessed via the ICarSafetyFeatures interface, describes safety features for a vehicle including whether or not it has antilock brakes, a driver-side airbag, or a passenger-side airbag, indicated by an enumeration.

- The Motorcycle class, accessed via the IMotorcycle interface, represents a motorcycle for sale. The Motorcycle class is a subclass of the Vehicle class.

- The Vehicle class, accessed via the IVehicle interface, represents features to all vehicles, including cars, motorcycles, and boats.

The eBay.SDK.Model.Attributes namespace contains the Attributes class, responsible for maintaining a motor item and the notion of whether it's a car or a motorcycle.

Inside the eBay.SDK.Model.Feedback Namespace

The eBay.SDK.Model.Feedback namespace contains the classes and interfaces that represent the feedback that buyers and sellers leave for each other. The notion of feedback is an important one in the eBay service, because it provides all users with peer-based accountability and a measurement of buyer and seller reliability. This namespace contains the following classes:

- The Feedback class and its IFeedback interface encapsulate a single feedback item for a user.

- The FeedbackCollection class and its IFeedbackCollection interface represent a collection of Feedback objects.

You will see more about using these in Chapter 4.

Inside the eBay.SDK.Model.Item Namespace

The eBay.SDK.Model.Item namespace, like its siblings the eBay.SDK.Model.Account and eBay.SDK.Model.User namespaces, contain fundamental elements you'll use when interacting with the eBay SDK for listing and searching for items. This namespace contains the following classes:

- The Fees class and its IFees interface represent the fees a user is charged when listing an item on eBay for sale, or the fees associated with a completed auction.

- The GiftSettings class and its IGiftSettings interface represent the buyer's choices for how a purchase is presented to the recipient when purchasing an item through an eBay store.

- The Item class and its IItem interface are at the heart of eBay's representation of items that are traded in eBay auctions. These classes encapsulate the description, bid status, and other information about an item for auction through its properties.

- The ItemCollection class and its IItemCollection represent a collection of Item instances.

- The ItemFound class and its IItemFound interface represent an item found by searching the eBay service for items.

- The ItemFoundCollection class and its IItemFoundCollection interface represent a collection of ItemFound objects.

- The ItemStatus class and its IItemStatus interface provide specific information about an item for auction, such as whether it's an adult-oriented item, whether the reserve is met, and so forth.

- The ListingFeatures class and its IListingFeatures interface provide details about the appearance of an item's listing, such as typesetting options on the item's Web page on the eBay service. You can serialize a ListingFeatures object using the ListingFeaturesSerializer class and its IListingFeaturesSerializer interface.

- The PaymentTerms class and its IPaymentTerms interface represent how a buyer may pay for an item listed for auction. You can serialize a PaymentTerms object using the PaymentTermsSerializer class and its IPaymentTermsSerializer interface.

- The ShippingRegions class and its IShippingRegions interface represent which regions (continents) a user will ship a specific item to. It's organized as a set of Boolean properties naming specific regions. You can serialize a ShippingRegions object using the ShippingRegionsSerializer and its IShippingRegionsSerializer interface.

- The ShippingSettings class and its IShippingSettings interface represent how the seller will ship an item and to where the item can be shipped (using a ShippingRegions object), along with whether the buyer or the seller will pay shipping charges.

You will see how many classes and interfaces in this namespace are used in Chapter 5.

Inside the eBay.SDK.Model.Sale Namespace

The eBay.SDK.Model.Sale namespace contains the classes and interfaces that represent an actual item sale (and not the listing, which is managed through the classes in the eBay.SDK.Model.Item namespace). This namespace contains the following:

- The CheckoutData class and its ICheckoutData interface provide a container for the details of the checkout session that occurs as buyer and seller settle an auction by items and sales.

- The CheckoutDetailsData class and its ICheckoutDetailsData interface provide a container for fine-grained details about a checkout transaction, such as additional shipping costs or the seller's return policy and special instructions.

- The CheckoutStatusData class and its ICheckoutStatusData interface provide a container for the current state of the checkout process.

- The Sale class and its ISale interface provide the representation of an actual item sale on the eBay service. These classes contain properties that let you determine the nature of a sale, including the amount paid, current price, and number of items purchased.

- The SaleCollection class and its ISaleCollection interface provide a container for collections of Sale objects.

You will see how to use the members of this namespace in Chapter 5.

Inside the eBay.SDK.Model.User Namespace

The eBay.SDK.Model.User namespace contains everything needed to represent a user of the eBay service. Both buyers and sellers are users, although only those users that sell items have accounts (which track the money they owe eBay for the use of its auction services). Of course, the User class and its IUser interface are at the heart of this namespace, but it also contains a few other classes:

- The SchedulingLimit class and its ISchedulingLimit interface represent the maximum number of Item listings a user may schedule, and how long in advance an item can be scheduled.

- The User class and its IUser interface represent everything that makes up an eBay user, including her e-mail address, cumulative feedback score, registration time and date, unique ID, and so forth. Many of its properties are instances of other classes.

- The UserCollection class and its IUserCollection interface, as you can guess by now, lets you manage a collection of User objects.

Managing Collections of Data Model Objects

The .NET Framework provides a type-safe mechanism by which to manage collections of like-typed objects via classes in the System.Collections namespace and the mother of all collections, the ICollection interface, which defines enumerators, size, and synchronization methods for all collections. The SDK architects at eBay wisely chose to use this model for managing collections of objects via classes such as UserCollection, SaleCollection, CategoryCollection, and so on.

The interface to a collection is quite simple: Each collection can provide you with a count of the number of items in the collection and an *enumerator,* an object that you can use to fetch sequentially each item in the collection. (In some component models, the enumerator is known by the term *cursor.*) The collections in the eBay SDK share the following methods in their interfaces:

- The Add method lets you add an object to the collection.

- The AddRange method lets you add (concatenate) one collection to the end of the other.

- The Clear method lets you remove all items from the collection.

- The Contains method lets you determine if a collection contains a specific element.

- The CopyTo method lets you copy the contents of the collection to an array.

- The GetEnumerator method lets you get an enumerator so that you can iterate over all objects in the collection.

- The IndexOf method lets you obtain the index of a specific entry in the collection.

- The Insert method lets you insert (add) an item between two items in the collection.

- The ItemAt method lets you obtain an item at a specific index of the collection.

- The ItemCount method lets you determine the number of items in the collection, just like the Count property.

- The Remove method lets you remove an item from the collection.

- The RemoveAt method lets you remove an item at a specified index position within the collection.

While you can certainly use the ItemCount method and a traditional for or while loop to iterate across all elements in a collection, it's often easier to do so using an *enumerator,* which lets you visit each item in the collection. In C#, you can access the items directly using a foreach loop through code such as that shown in Listing 3-1.

Listing 3-1. Using an Enumerator in C#

```
1: ICategoryCollection categories;
2: ...
3: foreach( eBay.SDK.Model.ICategory category in categories )
4: {
5:   Console.WriteLine( category.CategoryName );
6: }
```

Here, the C# compiler uses the base class interface for collections to fetch each Category object within the categories collection in line 3, and the loop prints the name of that category using Console.WriteLine on line 5. Listing 3-2 shows the corresponding Perl code.

Listing 3-2. Using an Enumerator in Perl

```
1: $categoryEnumerator = $categories->GetEnumerator();
2:
3: while( $categoryEnumerator->MoveNext () )
4: {
5:   $category = $categoryEnumerator->Current();
6:   print $category->{ 'CategoryName' }, "\n";
7: }
```

This code does exactly the same thing, but you need to use the while loop on line 3 and directly access the collection's enumerator via the method on line 1. On initialization, the enumerator's notion of which element to return when calling its Current method is an imaginary element *before* the first element, so the first time you call MoveNext, the Current method will return the first element, and so on. The loop terminates when MoveNext returns false, indicating that it has visited every item in the collection.

I show you how to use collections, specifically CategoryCollection, in the sample application in the section "Viewing eBay Categories: A Sample Application" at the end of this chapter.

Examining the eBay SDK API Interfaces

While you can create some pretty nifty applications using just the classes and interfaces from the data models you saw in the last section, the real value of the eBay SDK is in the `eBay.SDK.API` namespace, where there's an interface defined for each eBay API call.

In turn, each interface has a corresponding API call class that implements the eBay API call. Typically, the implementation of this class contains code to create the appropriate XML class, and then other classes such as the `eBay.API.ApiSession` class and the `eBay.API.APICall` class contain the logic necessary to make the network transaction to issue the request, receive the response, and parse the resulting XML. For each eBay API call, the class is named *apiName*Call, such as `eBay.SDK.API.ValidateTestUserRegistrationCall`, with its interface `eBay.SDK.API.ValidateTestUserRegistration`.

The superclass of all `eBay.SDK.API` classes, `eBay.API.APICall`, contains several properties that all classes of the `eBay.API` namespace inherit. To use any eBay API call, you must set these properties as follows:

- The `ErrorLevel` property must contain an integer indicating the level of verbosity for resulting error messages. These integers are defined by the `ErrorLevelEnum` enumeration. If no value is set, the default value specified by the API session in the `IApiSession` object is used.

- The `DetailLevel` property specifies which fields are returned by the eBay API call. It's not used by all functions, but lets you pick which properties should be returned by an API call.

- The `SiteId` property specifies the eBay site to which the API call pertains, such as sites in the United States or Germany, or another site. Like `ErrorLevel`, the default value specified in the API session is used if you do not set this property.

- The `Timeout` property specifies how long the API request may go unanswered before it is cancelled and an exception generated. Like `ErrorLevel`, the default value specified in the API session is used if you do not set this property.

- The `ApiCallSession` property must contain a valid `APISession` instance that has been initialized with the URL of the eBay service and your developer, application, and certification keys.

- The `Verb` property specifies the verb (e.g., `AddItem`, `GetSellerList`) of the eBay API call that you are going to make.

- The `Response` property will be set after each successful API call for you to examine the original XML message returned from the eBay API server.

- `OnPostRequestXml` is the event that you can handle to get notified when the underlying constructed XML is posted to eBay. The `OnReceiveResponseXml` event is the one to notify you when an response XML is received from eBay.

Each of the API calls in the namespace has a method that's the same name as the API itself. This method—eBay calls it the *master method*—makes the actual API call to eBay and returns an appropriate object or object collection with the response, or raises an exception in the event of an error. For example, calling `ValidateTestUserRegistration.ValidateTestUserRegistration` issues the underlying eBay API call `ValidateTestUserRegistration` to the eBay service.

To supply arguments to an `eBay.SDK.API` call, you set the arguments via the API call's properties. For example, `AddItemCall`, which adds a new item to eBay to create a new auction for an item, has the property `ItemToAdd`, which you must set to the item you wish to add to the eBay service.

Unlike the various data models, there's no subdivision of the `eBay.SDK.API` namespace. There are 27 API calls in the SDK; Table 3-1 summarizes the ones you're likely to use most often.

Table 3-1. The eBay.API.SDK Calls

Call	Interface	Purpose
AddItemCall	IAddItem	Adds an Item for auction to the eBay service
AddToItemDescriptionCall	IAddToItemDescription	Adds information about a listed Item
GetAccountCall	IGetAccount	Returns the account of an eBay user
GetAPIAccessRulesCall	IGetAPIAccessRules	Returns the rules by which your application can use the eBay API, including details such as the number of API requests you may make over a unit of time
GetBidderListCall	IGetBidderList	Returns information about the bidders for an item in an auction
GetCategoriesCall	IGetCategories	Returns a collection of categories given a parent category
GetEbayOfficialTimeCall	IGetEbayOfficialTime	Returns the official time at eBay, which presides over all auctions
GetFeedbackCall	IGetFeedback	Returns feedback regarding a user

Table 3-1. The eBay.API.SDK Calls

Call	Interface	Purpose
GetHighBiddersCall	IGetHighBidders	Returns the list of all high bidders for a Dutch auction
GetItemCall	IGetItemCall	Returns the specified item
GetItemTransactionsCall	IGetItemTransaction	Returns the transactions for a specific item
GetLogoURLCall	IGetLogoURL	Returns the URL of the eBay application logo
GetSearchResultsCall	IGetSearchResults	Returns the results of searching for an item by various criteria
GetSellerEventsCall	IGetSellerEvents	Returns price updates and sale information from eBay
GetSellerListCall	IGetSellerList	Returns the list of items for sale on eBay, bounded by the API's search criteria
GetSellerTransactionsCall	IGetSellerTransactions	Returns the list of transactions for a seller
GetStoreDetailsCall	IGetStoreDetails	Returns the details pertaining to a specific eBay store
GetUserCall	IGetUser	Returns information about a specific eBay user
GetWatchListCall	IGetWatchList	Returns the items on an eBay user's watch list
LeaveFeedbackCall	ILeaveFeedback	Leaves feedback for an eBay user
RelistItemCall	IRelistItem	Relists an existing item on eBay
ReviseItemCall	IReviseItem	Revises information about an item on eBay
ValidateTestUser RegistrationCall	IValidateTest UserRegistration	Validates a test user, just as if the user were a real seller and had entered a credit card number
VerifyAddItemCall	IVerifyAddItem	Verifies that an item was successfully added to the eBay service

> **WARNING** *To prevent your application from overloading eBay's application servers, there are a number of restrictions on how you can use these APIs, such as repeatedly using* GetCategoriesCall *to fetch individual categories, or using* GetItemCall *to get an item's highest bidder. To get a better understanding of these restrictions, consult Chapter 9 in this book, or see the documentation at the eBay Web site.*

Debugging eBay Applications

With the advent of today's modern interactive programming environments, debugging isn't nearly the unadulterated pit of despair and misery it used to be. Languages like C, C++, C#, and Perl all have interactive debuggers; depending on your preferences and budget, they can be simple command-line affairs like the famous GNU GDB application, or the amazingly powerful Microsoft Visual Studio debugger.

Debugging integration touch points—such as the ones between your application and the eBay SDK—can often be a challenge, because you don't have access to what goes on under the hood of something like the eBay SDK. As a result, if you make an incorrect assumption about how the environment operates, you can introduce a defect, and spend valuable time working out just what caused the defect in the first place. To make your life easier, here are a couple of things you can do to monitor the behavior of your eBay application when things go wrong.

Logging eBay SDK XML for the eBay API

The eBay.SDK.API.ApiSession class has the ability to log the XML requests and responses generated when executing eBay API calls. While these logs are of the most use when you're trying to debug eBay API applications (such as those I discuss in Chapters 8 and 9) and want to see how the eBay SDK uses the same eBay API calls, it can also shed light on other failures, such as when your application simply doesn't get a response from the eBay server, or when you're getting a drastically different response than you expect.

Listing 3-3 has one such eBay SDK XML log, here intentionally pruned to save space in the book.

Listing 3-3. An eBay SDK XML Log

```
1: [7/22/2003 00:37:38 AM]
2: [Request][https://api.sandbox.ebay.com/ws/api.dll]
3: <?xml version="1.0" encoding="utf-8"?>
4: <request>
```

```
 5:    <RequestUserId>******</RequestUserId>
 6:    <RequestPassword>******</RequestPassword>
 7:    <DetailLevel>1</DetailLevel>
 8:    <ErrorLevel>1</ErrorLevel>
 9:    <SiteId>0</SiteId>
10:    <Verb>GetCategories</Verb>
11:    <CategoryParent>0</CategoryParent>
12: </request>
13:
14: [7/22/2003 00:37:39 AM]
15: [Response]
16: <?xml version="1.0" encoding="utf-8"?>
17: <eBay>
18:    <EBayTime>2003-07-22 00:37:39</EBayTime>
19:    <Categories>
20:      <Category>
21:        <CategoryId>0</CategoryId>
22:        <CategoryLevel>1</CategoryLevel>
23:        <CategoryName><![CDATA[]]></CategoryName>
24:        <CategoryParentId>0</CategoryParentId>
25:        <IsExpired>0</IsExpired>
26:        <IsVirtual>0</IsVirtual>
27:        <LeafCategory>0</LeafCategory>
28:      </Category>
29:      <CategoryCount>1</CategoryCount>
30:      <UpdateGMTTime>2003-07-22 00:37:39</UpdateGMTTime>
31:      <Version>26</Version>
32:    </Categories>
33: </eBay>
```

As you can see, the log file simply keeps track of every request (marked by the keyword [Request] followed by the server URL) and response. For security, the log obscures the eBay user account name and password in the request (lines 5–6). You can see how each eBay.SDK.API call property maps to a specific XML entity, so checking the log is a good way to find out if you're forgetting an obvious property.

Getting the ApiSession object to generate a log file is easy:

1. First, set its LogCallXml property to true.

2. Next, set its Log property to a newly created eBay.SDK.LogFile instance.

3. Open the newly created log file using its Open method. If the specified file doesn't exist, it will be created.

Listing 3-4 recaps these steps in a snippet of C#, while Listing 3-5 does the same in Perl.

Listing 3-4. Enabling the eBay SDK Log in C#

```
1: IApiSession apiSession;
2:
3: apiSession = new ApiSession();
4: apiSession.LogCallXml = true;
5: apiSession.Log = new eBay.SDK.LogFile( );
6: apiSession.Log.Open( "c:\\tmp\\ebaylog.txt" );
7: apiSession.Url = "https://api.sandbox.ebay.com/ws/api.dll";
```

Listing 3-5. Enabling the eBay SDK Log in Perl

```
1: $apiSession = Win32::OLE->new("eBay.SDK.API.ApiSession");
2:
3: $apiSession->{'LogCallXml'} = True;
4: $apiSession->{'Log'} =
5:    Win32::OLE->new("eBay.SDK.LogFile");
6: $apiSession->{'Log'} ->Open("c:\\tmp\\ebaylog.txt");
7: $apiSession->{'Url'} =
8:       "https://api.sandbox.ebay.com/ws/api.dll";
```

Both of these snippets are pretty self-explanatory. After creating the ApiSession object (line 3 of Listing 3-4, line 1 of Listing 3-5), the code sets the LogCallXml property (line 4 of Listing 3-4, line 3 of Listing 3-5). Next, it sets the Log property to a newly created log file, and sets the name of the log file (lines 5–6 of Listing 3-4, lines 4–6 of Listing 3-5). Finally, the code sets the session's URL to use the eBay Sandbox.

Monitoring Network Activity

Another tool you can use (admittedly crude by today's standards of single-stepping through source code, breakpoints, watchpoints, and viewing or changing variables on the fly) is monitoring your application's use of the network when executing your application. This is akin to the activities of our forefathers (or, alas, some of *us!*) that used a computer's CPU load or the status of front-panel lights to get a feel for what our application was doing as it executed.

The easiest tool to use is the Microsoft Windows Task Manager; the Networking tab shows a graph of network activity. For it to be very meaning-ful, of course, you should shut down other applications that may use your computer's network adapters, including e-mail clients, Web browsers, and even instant messaging utilities. By single-stepping through your code, you can see if long pauses are actually due to eBay SDK network requests, and correlate the behavior with the network activity you see in the network activity graph.

Using Network Use to Indicate Application Defects

An anecdote here may well prove the point. When debugging the sample application that appears in the next section, I mistakenly asked eBay to send me *all* categories, rather than just the categories that were subcategories of a specific parent. I was doing this on the weekend from home over a dial-up line. After watching it start and apparently never return a couple of times, I decided that our connection was just being flaky, and launched the application and went to town to buy groceries. To my chagrin, it was *still* downloading something (I couldn't tell what, this being the domain of the eBay SDK) when I returned. I wasn't even sure it was downloading, until I brought up the Microsoft Windows Task Manager and clicked the Networking tab, and was met with a graph frighteningly like the one you see in Figure 3-1. As soon as I saw the graph, I realized my mistake: I was downloading all categories! A minute's worth of code changes later, and my mistake was fixed, my application ran considerably more smoothly, and the Windows Task Manager was showing me the graph in Figure 3-2.

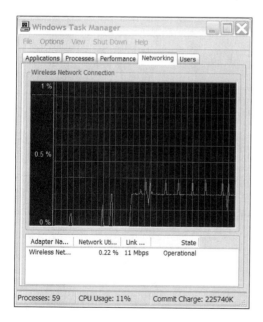

Figure 3-1. Network activity vs. time with defective application

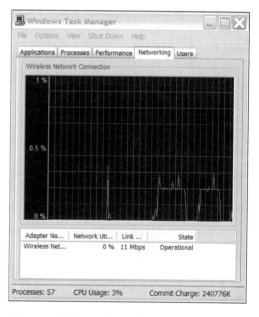

Figure 3-2. Network activity vs. time with corrected application

For more challenging bugs, or when you're using the eBay API directly, bypassing the eBay SDK, you may need to call out the heavy artillery: a network monitor. Tools like UNIX's tcpdump and the Microsoft Windows–friendly WinDump (available from `http://windump.polito.it/`) let you monitor the exact contents of a TCP/IP connection, and are invaluable tools when debugging *any* networking application.

Viewing eBay Categories: A Sample Application

This chapter's sample application is Categories, an application that lets you browse eBay's categories using a hierarchical list. Figure 3-3 shows a screen shot of Categories in action.

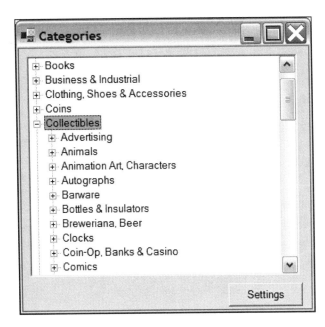

Figure 3-3. The Categories application

This application is easy to use; after launching, it downloads the top-level categories and lets you investigate subcategories by clicking the cross next to a given category. (Leaves are denoted as list items without a cross, just like in a standard hierarchical view.) Clicking the Settings button lets you enter your eBay developer, application, and certificate keys, along with a test user's account name and password. This data persists between sessions (and between the various sample applications in this book).

In doing so, the application demonstrates how to use the `eBay.SDK.API.GetCategoriesCall`, along with the `eBay.SDK.Model.ICategory` and

eBay.SDK.ModelICategoryCollection interfaces. In the discussion that follows,
I present the C# implementation of Categories. Instead of a Perl implementation
that performs these operations, in Chapter 6 you learn how to write the same
application in Perl that uses the eBay Integration Library to minimize the load
on eBay servers that your application creates.

The application's functionality can be divided up into three broad sections:

- The sample application framework, responsible for establishing the
  ApiSession and establishing its keys, target URL, and debugging log. The
  sample application also contains a secondary dialog box for entering the
  application keys, test user account name, and test user password. For
  a walkthrough of the sample application framework, see the Appendix.

- The gathering of the root categories, performed in a separate thread
  once the application starts to populate the top level of the list category. This is assisted by the function GetCategories, which uses the
  eBay.SDK.API.GetCategoriesCall method to obtain the a list of categories.

- The gathering of the categories below a specific list entry.

> **WARNING**   *In the interests of simplicity, this sample code is written to show
> you how to use these APIs, but does not show you the best way to use them.
> Repeatedly invoking* GetCategoriesCall.GetCategories *in your application is
> expensive, and presents a load to the eBay service. If your application has an
> upper ceiling of eBay API calls it can make, you may find that in the field your
> application can reach this upper limit using an algorithm such as the one
> presented here. Production applications should cache the results of common
> operations such as* GetCategoriesCall.GetCategories, *and use the cached
> results instead of repeating the same call over and over again. A good way to
> do this is to harness the power of the eBay Integration Library, which I discuss
> in Chapter 6.*

Starting the Categories Application

The Categories application is a single monolithic class, the CategorySample class
within the com.lothlorien.ebaysdkbook namespace. Listing 3-6 shows the skeleton of the application, including its members and methods, but not the actual
method implementations.

Listing 3-6. The Skeleton of the Categories Application

```
1: using System;
2: using System.Threading;
3: using System.IO;
```

```
 4: using System.Windows.Forms;
 5: using eBay.SDK;
 6: using eBay.SDK.API;
 7: using eBay.SDK.Model;
 8:
 9: namespace com.lothlorien.ebaysdkbook
10: {
11:     public class CategorySample : System.Windows.Forms.Form
12:     {
13:         // eBay Session
14:         IApiSession apiSession;
15:         // UI components
16:         private System.Windows.Forms.Button config;
17:         private System.Windows.Forms.Label status;
18:         private ConfigDialog configDialog;
19:         private System.ComponentModel.Container components = null;
20:
21:         // This application's fields
22:         private System.Windows.Forms.TreeView tree;
23:
24:         private delegate void
25:             DelegateAddRootNodes( CategoryCollection categories );
26:         private DelegateAddRootNodes AddRootNodesFunc;
27:
28:         public CategorySample()
29:         {
30:           // Inits components.
31:           // Creates a new thread to load root nodes.
32:           // Start the new thread.
33:         }
34:
35:         private void LoadRootNodes()
36:         {
37:           // Entry point for the thread to load the
38:           // root nodes and invoke the main thread
39:           // to redraw.
40:         }
41:
42:         private CategoryCollection RootNodes()
43:         {
44:           // Load the root nodes from eBay.
45:
46:         }
47:
```

```
48:       private void AddRootNodes( CategoryCollection categories )
49:       {
50:         // Add the root nodes _and_ their children
51:         // to the tree.
52:       }
53:
54:       private CategoryCollection GetCategories( int parent,
55:                                                 int level )
56:       {
57:         // Issue the API call.
58:       }
59:
60:       private void tree_BeforeExpand( object sender,
61:                                       TreeViewCancelEventArgs e)
62:       {
63:         // Populate a branch when clicked.
64:       }
65:
66:       private void InitializeEBayComponent( )
67:       {
68:         // Create the API session.
69:         // Set its log file.
70:         // Set the API session's access credentials.
71:       }
72:
73:       protected override void Dispose( bool disposing )
74:       {
75:         // Dispose the components and close the logfile.
76:       }
77:
78:       #region Windows Form Designer generated code
79:       private void InitializeComponent()
80:       {
81:         // Support the IDE.
82:       }
83:       #endregion
84:
85:       [STAThread]
86:       static void Main()
87:       {
88:         // Call application's Run.
89:       }
90:
```

```
 91:      private void config_Click(object sender, System.EventArgs e)
 92:      {
 93:         // Show the configuration dialog box.
 94:      }
 95:
 96:      private void LoadKeys()
 97:      {
 98:         // Load the configuration keys and test user.
 99:      }
100:   }
101: }
```

The application begins with the usual using directives provided by the Microsoft Visual Studio .NET environment, along with those the application needs for the eBay SDK (lines 5–7).

The application has a handful of member variables, including the apiSession the application uses (line 14), the configuration button labeled "Settings" (line 16), and a simple text-based status bar (line 17), as well as the configuration form on line 18 (which I discuss in detail in the Appendix, as it has only C#-relevant code). Visual Studio .NET uses the final UI variable, components, for its nefarious purposes (line 19). This application uses a single TreeView, declared on line 22. Finally, the application declares a delegate to support invoking a TreeView UI method from the thread that initializes the root categories on lines 24–26.

The TreeView, as you may recall, is a control that lets you store a list of TreeNode objects, which each in turn may contain additional node lists. As the user clicks nodes, the TreeView sends events that manage the opening and closing of each list item to reveal the sublists below the selected node. The Category application uses this feature to download subcategories of a given selected category.

The constructor, CategorySample, initializes the Visual Studio .NET–generated code and then executes code that loads the various keys and test user information from a configuration file. Next, it creates and starts a new thread responsible for downloading the root categories from eBay while the application UI starts up. This gives you the opportunity to immediately see the application, even though it must perform a network transaction with eBay before it can do anything useful.

This work to load the root nodes of the tree is performed by the thread in the LoadRootNodes method, which first queries eBay for the root nodes, and then adds them to the TreeView tree. This is helped along by the helper function GetCategories, which actually performs the eBay SDK API request to obtain a collection of categories given a specific parent category. Once this occurs, the thread exits.

With the tree initialized, you can click a specific category to view the subcategories in that category, which generates the .NET Framework BeforeExpand event. The application registers to receive this event in its constructor, so that when you click an item, it is invoked. It uses the GetCategories helper to obtain the categories under the category you choose, and adds them to the tree.

The remainder of the methods are application helper methods. The InitializeComponent method (lines 78–83) is created by the Visual Studio .NET application builder when you create the initial form. In a similar vein, the InitializeEbayComponent (lines 66–71) initializes the apiSession after loading the user keys with LoadKeys (on lines 96–99) and starts logging eBay messages. The Dispose method (lines 73–76) closes the eBay log file and disposes the components. The Main method is the application's entry point; it simply invokes the Application class's Run method to start the application. Finally, the config_Click method simply invokes the configuration form, which you can see in detail in theAppendix.

Obtaining Top-Level Tree Entries

The application begins by initializing its components, the eBay components, and fetching the root-level categories for the tree view. Listing 3-7 shows the relevant methods of the application (here removed from the namespace and class declarations for brevity).

Listing 3-7. Obtaining Top-Level Tree Entries at Application Start

```
1: public CategorySample()
2: {
3:    Thread loadRootNodesThread;
4:
5:    // Init our components, including the eBay one.
6:    InitializeComponent();
7:    InitializeEBayComponent();
8:    // Set up the tree's event handlers.
9:    this.tree.BeforeExpand +=
10:      new TreeViewCancelEventHandler( this.tree_BeforeExpand );
11:
12:    AddRootNodesFunc =
13:        new DelegateAddRootNodes( AddRootNodes );
14:    loadRootNodesThread =
15:        new Thread( new ThreadStart( LoadRootNodes ) );
16:    loadRootNodesThread.Name = "eBay Categories Thread";
17:    loadRootNodesThread.Start();
18:
19: }
20:
```

```
21: private void LoadRootNodes()
22: {
23:   CategoryCollection categories;
24:   categories = RootNodes();
25:   this.Invoke( AddRootNodesFunc,
26:          new object[] { categories } );
27: }
28:
29: private CategoryCollection RootNodes()
30: {
31:   Cursor.Current = Cursors.WaitCursor;
32:
33:   return GetCategories( 0, 2 );
34: }
35:
36: private void AddRootNodes( CategoryCollection categories )
37: {
38:   TreeNode node;
39:   if ( categories != null )
40:   {
41:     tree.BeginUpdate();
42:     foreach( Category category in categories )
43:     {
44:       if ( category.CategoryName != "" &&
45:          category.CategoryId == category.CategoryParentId )
46:       {
47:         // This is a top-level node.
48:         node = new TreeNode( category.CategoryName );
49:         node.Tag = category.CategoryId;
50:         tree.Nodes.Add( node );
51:         foreach( Category subcategory in categories )
52:         {
53:           if ( subcategory.CategoryName != "" &&
54:         subcategory.CategoryId != subcategory.CategoryParentId &&
55:         subcategory.CategoryParentId == category.CategoryId )
56:           {
57:             // This node is a child of the current parent node.
58:             TreeNode child =
59:               new TreeNode( subcategory.CategoryName );
60:             child.Tag = subcategory.CategoryId;
61:             node.Nodes.Add( child );
62:           }
63:         }
```

```
64:        }
65:     }
66:     tree.EndUpdate();
67:     status.Text = "";
68:     status.Refresh();
69:     Cursor.Current = Cursors.Default;
70:   }
71: }
```

This work begins in the constructor, CategorySample (lines 1–19), where you declare the thread that will load the root nodes loadRootNodesThread on line 3. Next, on lines 5–7, the constructor initializes first the Windows GUI components and then the eBay components using the helper functions InitializeComponent and InitializeEBayComponent. After that, the application adds the event handler for the tree control's BeforeExpand method on lines 9–10, and creates a delegate for the AddRootNodes function that the loadRootNodesThread will use to invoke the AddRootNodes function and update the tree control on lines 12–13. Finally, the method creates the loadRootNodesThread (lines 14–15), specifying the entry point as the LoadRootNodes function, and then starts the thread on line 17 after setting the thread's name to something meaningful for the display of running tasks in the Microsoft Windows Task Manager. Once the thread starts, the constructor exits, and the system invokes the Main method, starting the application and its event handler.

Meanwhile, while the application is accepting threads, the LoadRootNodes function (lines 21–27) is running in its own thread. This function first calls the RootNodes function, which returns a CategoryCollection of the root categories, and then uses the Form method Invoke to signal to the application that it should execute the AddRootNodes function on the main application thread.

> **NOTE** *You can only update controls from the main thread of an application. Consequently, if you look to multiple threads to maintain the interactivity of your application, you must create a delegate for any user interface update methods and use* Invoke *to ensure that they run on the main thread. If you forget to do this, your control update methods will generate an exception.*

The RootNodes method, on lines 29–33, uses the GetCategories helper to obtain the categories one and two levels deep below the category 0, the root category after first setting the cursor to Cursor.WaitCursor to inform the user that a blocking operation is taking place. You need to get both the root-level categories *and* their children so that the tree view will know which nodes have children, correctly differentiating parent nodes with a cross from leaf nodes, which have no cross and cannot be expanded.

The AddRootNodes method (lines 36–71), called on the main thread, actually does the work of manipulating the child nodes of the tree and inserting each category. The code's a little tricky, so let's take it a line at a time to understand what it does.

The code begins by declaring an empty TreeNode node to contain a newly created node from a category name on line 38. Then, if the incoming category list, categories, is not empty, it locks tree using its BeginUpdate method on line 41, to ensure that it will not process user events while the update occurs.

Lines 42–65 are the meat of this function, examining in turn each of the categories the application received from eBay. Each entry in the categories collection is one of two kinds of entries:

1. If the entry has a name and its unique ID in its CategoryId property is the same as the ID in its CategoryParentId, it's a root node and should be shown at the top of the list. If it's a root node, it should be inserted in the Nodes property of the tree.

2. Otherwise, it's a child category of a root node, and should be inserted in a specific Nodes property of a node contained in the tree's Nodes property.

The comparison on lines 44–45 determines whether or not the specific category category is a root node. If it is (that is, if it has a nonempty name and its ID is its parent's ID), a new TreeNode with its text set to the category's CategoryName property is created on line 48. Next, on line 49, the node's Tag property (a category reserved by the TreeNode class for use by the application) receives the CategoryId of the category for that node, so that when you click the entry corresponding to that TreeNode, the application can fetch its subcategories.

The inner loop, on lines 51–64, tests each category in the categories loop to determine which of the returned categories are children of the category just added to the tree. You need to do this here, because there's no other good way to denote which tree nodes have children in the user interface without actually loading those children into the appropriate tree node. It's easy to detect a subcategory of a category—its CategoryParentId property is equal to its parent's CategoryId property. Lines 53–55 test this for a category selected by the foreach loop on line 51, also including two additional tests. The first, on line 53, is simple defensive programming, ensuring that no category without a name appears on the user interface. The second, on line 54, ensures that no top-level category is accidentally treated as a subcategory. (Failing to include the test on line 54 would make each category a subcategory of itself.) If a subcategory passes these tests, a new TreeNode, child, is created, and the Tag property assigned appropriately on line 60 before adding the new child to the node.

The remainder of the function, lines 66–69, undid the user interface setup that took place earlier. Line 66 unlocks the tree, so that it will again accept user input. Lines 67–68 clear the status line, which originally read "Downloading..." to give you some indication of what the application was doing. Finally, line 69 returns the cursor to its default, resetting it from the hourglass first set on line 31 of RootNodes.

Obtaining Categories

Obtaining a category list is easy—far simpler than the gymnastics you performed with the tree control in the last section. Listing 3-8 shows how the application gets categories using the GetCategories method.

Listing 3-8. The GetCategories Method

```
 1: private CategoryCollection GetCategories( int parent,
 2:                                           int level )
 3: {
 4:    CategoryCollection categories = null;
 5:    GetCategoriesCall getCategoriesCall;
 6:
 7:    // Set up the API we'll use.
 8:    getCategoriesCall =
 9:       new GetCategoriesCall( apiSession );
10:    getCategoriesCall.ErrorLevel =
11:       ErrorLevelEnum.BothShortAndLongErrorStrings;
12:    getCategoriesCall.CategoryParent = parent;
13:    getCategoriesCall.DetailLevel = 1;
14:    getCategoriesCall.LevelLimit = level;
15:    try
16:    {
17:      categories = getCategoriesCall.GetCategories();
18:    }
19:    catch( Exception e )
20:    {
21:      MessageBox.Show( this,
22:              "Exception - GetCategories call failed: " +
23:              e.Message, "Error" );
24:    }
25:    return categories;
26: }
```

This method is straightforward; the only real logic in the routine is the error handling required to keep the application running in the event that making the GetCategories API call goes awry. The routine takes two arguments: parent, which determines the parent category of interest; and level, which specifies how deeply the eBay service should traverse the category hierarchy in generating the response. Lines 4–5 create first the return value categories and then the getCategoriesCall variable that will contain a freshly created eBay.SDK.API.GetCategoriesCall object, created on lines 8–9.

The remainder of the initialization, on lines 10–14, sets the key properties for the API invocation:

- Lines 10–11 set the desired level of verbosity for error strings. When in doubt, I always choose the most verbose error strings, especially early in application development.

- Line 12 specifies the parent of the categories to be returned using the request's CategoryParent method. In return, the API will return the named category and its children, and its children's children, up to the level limit indicated by the request's LevelLimit parameter.

- Line 13 specifies the DetailLevel property, which defines the default level of detail, indicating that in the response all fields should be populated.

- Line 14 specifies the LevelLimit property, indicating how many levels below the given category should be retrieved and returned in the collection.

The try/catch block on lines 15–24 first attempts to invoke the master method for the GetCategoriesCall, GetCategories. This can fail for a myriad of reasons: an incorrect key, user account login or password, network congestion, and so forth. Consequently, it's imperative that you wrap each call to an eBay API with try/catch (or test the results of the OLE last error if you're using a language like Perl) to ensure that the request was a success, and that you control your application's behavior in case of an error.

> **WARNING** *Failing to correctly handle API failures may cause your application to fail eBay certification.*

This event handler is simple, but accomplishes the job. In the event of any error (indicated by an Exception or its subclass, eBay.SDK.SDKException), the application displays a message box showing the text from the exception (lines 21–23).

Obtaining Tree Branch Entries

The only other action the application must perform is managing the selection of a tree item, which may require that the item expand and download new categories. When a tree item is selected, if it can expand, the control issues a BeforeExpand event, which the application registered to receive during its constructor. When the application receives this event, it invokes tree_BeforeExpand, shown in Listing 3-9.

Listing 3-9. Expanding a Tree Item

```
1: private void tree_BeforeExpand( object sender,
2:                     TreeViewCancelEventArgs e)
3: {
4:    CategoryCollection subcategories;
5:    int baseLevel = -1;
6:
7:    Cursor.Current = Cursors.WaitCursor;
8:    status.Text = "Downloading...";
9:    status.Refresh();
10:   subcategories = GetCategories( (int)e.Node.Tag, 3 );
11:
12:   tree.BeginUpdate();
13:   foreach( Category subcategory in subcategories )
14:   {
15:     // Find the appropriate node to contain this subcategory.
16:     if ( baseLevel == -1 )
17:          baseLevel = subcategory.CategoryLevel;
18:     if ( subcategory.CategoryLevel == baseLevel + 2 )
19:     {
20:       foreach( TreeNode child in e.Node.Nodes )
21:       {
22:         if ( (int)child.Tag == subcategory.CategoryParentId )
23:         {
24:           TreeNode newChild =
25:              new TreeNode( subcategory.CategoryName );
26:           newChild.Tag = subcategory.CategoryId;
27:           child.Nodes.Add( newChild );
28:         }
29:       }
30:     }
31:   }
32:   tree.EndUpdate();
```

```
33:    status.Text = "";
34:    status.Refresh();
35:    Cursor.Current = Cursors.Default;
36: }
```

This code is very similar to the AddRootNodes routine you just saw. It begins by declaring a CategoryCollection, subcategories on line 4, which will contain those categories that descend from the item you selected. Next, it creates an integer, baseLevel, used to determine which subcategories fall below the selected category. This is necessary because although the tree provides a hierarchical data structure that mirrors the eBay category hierarchy, the eBay CategoryCollection model represents this information using a flat collection of Category items, each with a CategoryLevel.

Lines 7–9 prep the user interface for another network transaction, first selecting Cursor.WaitCursor and then updating the text on the status line. Line 10 requests the category selected, its children, grandchildren, and great-grandchildren. While the selected category and its children are already known (the selected category was fetched previously, and its children were fetched at the same time to determine whether this item was a leaf or a parent), there's no good way to use this information without additional data structures, so the routine just requests it again anyway.

Once the request completes, I lock the tree on line 12. Line 13 iterates through the resulting subcategories. Lines 16–17 use a bit of skullduggery to avoid the category node that was selected, and lines 18–30 add the grand-children to the appropriate node using the same logic you first saw in AddRootNodes, ensuring that each node is correctly treated as a parent node or a leaf node.

Key Points

In this chapter, you learned the following key points regarding the eBay SDK:

- The lion's share of the eBay SDK are elements of the data model, which let you easily interact with the software analogues of real-world concepts such as users, their accounts, and the items they buy and sell.

- The eBay.SDK.API namespace contains classes and interfaces for each of the eBay APIs that the eBay SDK supports.

- The eBay SDK provides collections that inherit from the .NET collection interfaces to let you manage groups of identically typed components without resorting to using arrays. Moreover, collections *can* be used as arrays when needed.

- When using an eBay.SDK.API interface to execute an eBay API request, you must set its ApiSession property to an allocated and initialized eBay.API.ApiSession object, which contains the eBay developer, application, and certification key for your application, along with a user account ID and password.

- When you use an eBay.SDK.API interface to execute an eBay API request, the arguments for the request are stored as properties set by the interface, and the API itself is invoked using the interface's master method. In turn, this method returns the results to you, typically as an object defined in one of the namespaces contained by the eBay.SDK.Model namespace.

- You can use the eBay SDK log of your application's use of eBay SDK APIs to debug your application by setting the ApiSession's LogCallXml property to true and setting its Log property to an initialized instance of eBay.SDK.LogFile.

- The eBay category system is hierarchical. You can traverse this hierarchy by using the GetCategoriesCall and supplying both the parent ID of the topmost-level category to get, along with a depth indicating how many levels of subcategories to return.

CHAPTER 4

Managing Users with the eBay SDK

USERS AND ITEMS ARE at the heart of the eBay service. Without users, there would be no one to buy or sell items; without items, there'd be little for users to do. In this chapter and the next, I explore the various aspects of these crucial members of the data model behind the eBay SDK, including the classes that represent them and the APIs that use these classes.

In this chapter, I plumb the depths of the eBay.SDK.Account and eBay.SDK.User namespaces. After reading this chapter, you will have a deep knowledge of the classes in these namespaces and how they relate. In addition, you will see how to use them in the context of two sample applications, UserInfo and AccountStatus, which demonstrate how to use members of the eBay.SDK.Account and eBay.SDK.User namespaces, respectively.

Understanding the Relationship Between Users and Their Accounts

As I noted in the previous chapter, it's important that you don't confuse the notion of an eBay *user* with an eBay *account*. Figure 4-1 shows a use case diagram that clarifies both of these concepts.

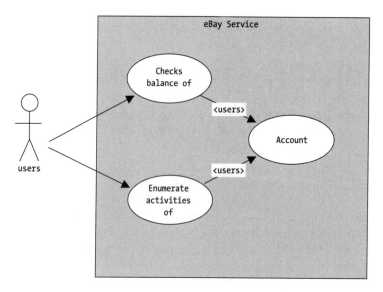

Figure 4-1. A use case diagram indicating the relationship between users and their accounts

In short, an eBay user has an account that tracks the costs of listing and selling items on eBay. Typically, a user is a single physical entity (an individual or a corporation) that sells items. In turn, this user has at least one account that indicates his or her business dealings with eBay to cover the costs of item promotion, eBay Store promotion, and item listing and sales fees.

One area where your applications can benefit eBay users is *account management:* helping eBay users determine the costs they incur using eBay and their overall profit. Such applications can be simple, providing an analogue of printed transaction records for individuals listing items on eBay; or complex applications providing cost-benefit tracking for small businesses using eBay as a channel for their products, showing their revenue and margins over time. For those looking at the opportunity of integrating eBay with existing corporate information systems, middleware or modules that integrate your firm's accounts payable software packages with eBay's account management can streamline the process of making payments for your company.

There's less of an opportunity for applications that directly manipulate user information, however. Despite the central role of users within the eBay service, there simply aren't many interfaces that let you browse or modify user attributes; moreover, there's little business reason to do so.

Looking Under the Hood at the eBay.SDK.Model.User Namespace

The members of the eBay.SDK.Model.User namespace provide you with an easy way to manage the notion of an eBay user. The chief class in the namespace is the User class, supported by the UserCollection and the SchedulingLimit classes. This class has properties that represent attributes of eBay users, including their eBay login name, e-mail address, when they registered with eBay, and so forth.

Most of the properties of the classes in this namespace are fundamental data types such as Boolean values, integers, or strings of characters. Some, however (and this is the case for many data model objects in the eBay SDK), use *helper classes* that encapsulate more complex data types, such as the SchedulingLimit class, an aggregate of a number and two times. You will find these conveniences throughout the SDK: As eBay engineers identify composite data types, they encapsulate them in classes with a specific interface, making it easy for you to manipulate complex data quickly within your application. These helper classes typically have only the most rudimentary of methods, including

- The Equals method, which you use to compare two instances of the class.

- The GetHashCode method, which you use to obtain a hash for a specific instance.

- The GetType method, which you use for introspection to determine the object's type.

- The ToString method, which you use to obtain a string representation of the object.

Representing Users with the User Class and Its Collection, the UserCollection Class

Many eBay SDK API methods require a user as an argument or return information about an eBay user as a result. To facilitate passing information about users, the eBay SDK provides the User and UserCollection classes to manage individual user data and a collection of users, respectively. The majority of your interaction with these classes is through their properties, so let's take a look at them first. Table 4-1 shows the various properties of the User class.

Table 4-1. The Properties of the User Class

Property	Purpose
About Me	TRUE if the user has a page about himself or herself.
AllowPaymentEdit	TRUE if the user allows buyers to edit payment options.
AppData	Your application can use this property to store any object relating to the User instance. This object is not sent to or received from the eBay application service.
CheckoutEnabled	TRUE if the user has enabled checkout in his or her preferences.
CIPBankAccountStored	For the German service, TRUE if a user has stored bank account information with eBay to use the CIP in checkout function.
Email	The e-mail address of the user.
FeedbackPrivate	TRUE if user has elected to keep feedback private.
FeedbackScore	The cumulative feedback score for the user. If the user has chosen to keep his or her feedback private (FeedbackPrivate), and the call is not being made by a user who is requesting his or her own FeedbackScore, this value will be 0.
IdVerified	TRUE if the user's identity has been verified through eBay's ID Verify program.
IsLAAuthorized	TRUE if the user is authorized to list Live Auction items.
PaymentAddress	Container for seller payment address information.
RegDate	The date and time that the user registered with eBay.
RegistrationAddress	Container for seller registration address information.
SchedulingLimit	Container for scheduling limits for the user.
SellerLevel	The user's PowerSeller level. Valid levels indicating PowerSellers are 11, 22, or 33. Other values are valid but do not indicate PowerSellers.
SiteId	The eBay site where the user is registered.
Star	The code for the star icon that is a visual indicator of the user's feedback score.
Status	The user's registration status.
StoreOwner	TRUE if the user is an owner of an eBay store.
UserId	The unique identifier for the user.
UserIdLastChanged	The last date and time that the user changed his or her UserId.

The User class implements the following methods:

- The Clone method, which you use to deeply clone a User object

- The Equals method, which you use to compare two instances of the class

- The GetHashCode method, which you use to obtain a hash for a specific instance

- The GetType method, which you use for introspection to determine the object's type

- The ToString method, which you use to obtain a string representation of the object

In many cases, such as when getting a list of bidders for a specific item, you're interested in a list of User objects. The eBay SDK provides this list using a UserCollection object, which you can iterate over using a foreach operator in C#, or simply use its Count property and ItemAt method to obtain each item in a for loop. Traversing UserCollection collections is identical in process to traversing other collections such as CategoryCollection (see Chapter 3) or ItemCollection (see Chapter 5).

> **NOTE** *When obtaining information in a User object, some fields may or may not be set depending on the DetailLevel of the request you're making. For specific details regarding the effect of a particular DetailLevel value and the returned properties in a User object, consult the eBay SDK documentation.*

Managing Item Scheduling Privileges with the SchedulingLimit Class

One User property, the SchedulingLimit property, indicates how many items a user can schedule at once, along with the minimum and maximum number of minutes an item can be scheduled in advance. Rather than representing these values as an array, the SDK represents the values as properties of the SchedulingLimit class. It has three properties, as you can see from Table 4-2.

Table 4-2. The Properties of the SchedulingLimit Class

Property	Purpose
MaxScheduledItems	The maximum number of items that the user can schedule
MaxScheduleTime	The maximum number of minutes that a listing may be scheduled in advance
MinScheduleTime	The minimum number of minutes that a listing may be scheduled in advance

Specifying Values with eBay.SDK.Model.User Enumerations

The eBay.SDK.Model.User namespace has two enumerations to aid in interpreting User properties: UserStarEnum and UserStatusEnum. The former provides a symbolic interpretation of the User class's Star property, while the latter provides the same for the User class's Status property.

The UserStarEnum enumeration and its container, the User Star property, are best understood in the context of a user's feedback score, which I discuss in detail in the next chapter. Put simply, each transaction allows a buyer and seller to exchange *feedback,* a mandatory comment with an associated numeric score. Higher scores assigned in a feedback exchange indicate greater satisfaction with a transaction. The user's Star property is a sum of all feedback values, giving each user a relative peer-based ranking of their reliability. On the eBay Web site, the property is displayed as a star, like the one you see in Figure 4-2. Different color stars, along with those adorned with other symbols such as lines indicating a shooting star, provide visual indication of a user's feedback score. The eBay application service provides images for each shooting star, as described in the eBay SDK documentation under the UserStarEnum documentation entry. Table 4-3 shows the values for the UserStarEnum property.

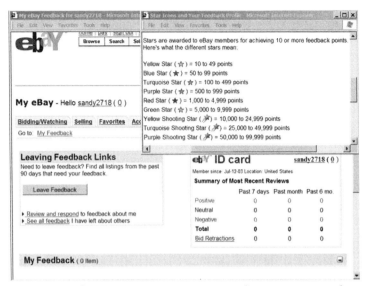

Figure 4-2. The user rating (Star property) for eBay user sandy2718 shown on the eBay Web site

Table 4-3. The Meaning of Values of the UserStarEnum Enumeration

Enumeration Value	Feedback Score Range
None	0–9
YellowStar	10–99
BlueStar	50–99
TurquoiseStar	100–499
PurpleStar	500–999
RedStar	1,000–4,999
GreenStar	5,000–9,999
YellowShootingStar	10,000–24,999
TurquoiseShootingStar	25,000–49,999
PurpleShootingStar	50,000–99,999
RedShootingStar	100,000 and above

More prosaic is the UserStatusEnum enumeration, which denotes a user's status within the eBay service. The enumeration values and their meanings are shown in Table 4-4.

Table 4-4. The Meaning of Values of the UserStatusEnum Enumeration

Enumeration Value	Meaning
AccountOnHold	The user's account is on hold, such as for nonpayment of amounts due eBay. User cannot sell or buy items.
Confirmed	The user has completed online registration and has properly responded to confirmation e-mail. Most users should fall in this category.
Deleted	Records for the specified user have been deleted.
FromHalfPending CreditCardVerification	The user has completed the registration for Half.com and opted to automatically also be registered with eBay, but the verification of credit card information is still pending.
FromHalfUnconfirmed	The user has completed the registration for Half.com and opted to automatically also be registered with eBay, but the registration confirmation is still pending.
Ghost	The user is a registered user of AuctionWeb (pre-eBay) who never reregistered on eBay.
InMaintenance	The user's record is in the process of being changed by eBay. Query user information again to get new status.
Merged	The user record has been merged with another account record for the same user.
PendingCreditCard Verification	The user has completed registration and confirmation, but is pending a verification of credit card information.
PendingTermination	The user has been scheduled for account closure. A user in this state shouldn't be considered an active user.
RegistrationCodeSent	The user has completed online registration and has been sent the confirmation e-mail, but has not yet responded to the confirmation e-mail.
Suspended	The user has been suspended from selling and buying.
Unconfirmed	The user's registration has not yet been confirmed.
Unknown	The user properties have never been set. This typically represents a problem with the user's account.

NOTE *The various eBay SDK enumerations, including* UserStarEnum *and* UserStatusEnum, *are* not defined *for languages other than those that can directly import content from the .NET Framework, such as C# and Visual Basic .NET, because in C#, enumerations are actual types, not aliased to a primitive type like you'd expect if you were coming from a language like C. Unfortunately, those of us who prefer Perl or other languages without full .NET support and use the eBay SDK via its COM interface must either implement these enumerations for their applications or take the more perilous route of referring to the constants defined by these enumerations directly.*

Looking Under the Hood at the eBay.SDK.Model.Account Namespace

The contents of the eBay.SDK.Model.Account namespace is critically important to many eBay applications, because it contains the classes, interfaces, and enumerations that pertain to managing an eBay user's online account with eBay. Within this namespace are the Account class, which provides a snapshot of account activity at an instant in time, along with the AccountInvoiceView and AccountPeriodView classes, which provide a summary of account activities (each represented by AccountActivity objects) over time.

Like the User class, all of the classes in this namespace implement the Clone, Equals, GetHashCode, GetType, and ToString methods defined by the interface to the Object parent class. As I discuss each of the classes in this namespace, I point out where a specific class deviates from this behavior.

Examining Accounts with the Account Class and Its Collection, the AccountCollection Class

The Account class is the chief class in the eBay.SDK.Model.Account namespace. This class provides a container for the various elements of an eBay user's account. Table 4-5 lists the various properties of the Account class.

Table 4-5. The Properties of the Account Class

Property	Purpose
Activities	Indicates the container node for AccountActivityCollection with AccountActivity objects denoting each account transaction.
Currency	Defines the ID of the currency used by this account.
Id	Defines the ID of this account as a string. All accounts begin with the letter E and are followed by a string that uniquely identifies the account.

Table 4-5. The Properties of the Account Class (continued)

Property	Purpose
InvoiceView	Provides the account's transaction history as an AccountInvoiceView object. This property may be null.
PeriodView	Provides the account's transaction history over a specific period as an AccountInvoiceView object. This property may be null.

The Account class is a frequent return value when working with eBay API methods, and depending on the API call, the InvoiceView and PeriodView properties may or may not be set.

The Currency property is interesting, if only because its return value isn't a country identifier (as a string or enumeration), but rather a number indicating a value in the eBay SDK enumeration eBay.SDK.Model.Account.CurrencyEnum.

Examining Account Activity with the AccountActivity Class and Its Collection, the AccountActivityCollection Class

At its core, the purpose of an Account object is to give you insight into the transactions that affect the account's balance. The eBay SDK gives you this information via the Account class property Activities, which can contain anAccountActivity Collection. This collection, in turn, contains zero or more AccountActivity instances, each with the properties you see in Table 4-6.

Table 4-6. The Properties of the AccountActivity Class

Property	Purpose
Activity	Indicates the type of activity, detailing the entry type.
Balance	Indicates the account balance as of this entry. Can be zero.
Credit	Indicates the amount this activity credits to the account. Can be zero.
Date	Specifies date the activity was posted to the account, in Greenwich mean time.
Debit	Indicates the amount this activity debits from the account. Can be zero.
Id	Specifies the unique reference number of this activity in the account.
ItemId	If the transaction is associated with an eBay item, indicates the ID of the item. Zero if no item is associated with this entry.
Memo	Indicates a string comment regarding the activity. May be an empty string.

Most `AccountActivity` objects directly correspond to either selling or buying an item on eBay, indicating the fees eBay charges to your account as a result of posting a listing or closing an auction. Consequently, to help reconcile accounts, the `AccountActivity` class has the `ItemId` field, so that you can match a specific `AccountActivity` record with the corresponding eBay `Item` (as opposed to a sale) that generated the credit or debit in question.

Viewing Account Activity with the AccountInvoiceView and AccountPeriodView Classes

Although a raw listing of account transactions in the form of an `AccountActivity-Collection` is all well and good, most of the time you want to see your account's activity in the form of a collection either as an *invoice*—what you need to pay at the end of an accounting period—or an account balance over a particular time period. The `AccountInvoiceView` and `AccountPeriodView`, usually accessed as the `InvoiceView` and `PeriodView` properties of an `Account` object, let you do just that. Table 4-7 lists the properties of the `AccountInvoiceView` class.

Table 4-7. The Properties of the AccountInvoiceView Class

Property	Purpose
EmailAddress	The e-mail address to which eBay invoices are sent
InvoiceBalance	The amount on the invoice
InvoiceDate	The date the invoice was issued, in Greenwich mean time

As you can see from Table 4-7, the `AccountInvoiceView` is remarkably brief. Think of it as the bottom line on your phone bill: All it says is what you need to pay, and by when you need to pay it.

By comparison, the `AccountPeriodView` class provides a summary of account activity. If the `AccountInvoiceView` is the bottom line on your bill, the `AccountPeriodView` is all of the other lines that come before it, except for the actual list of transactions. Table 4-8 shows the properties of the `AccountPeriodView` class.

Table 4-8. The Properties of the AccountPeriodView Class

Property	Purpose
AdditionalAccounts	Contains a collection of additional accounts associated with the account.
AmountPastDue	Indicates the amount the account is past due, or zero if the account payments are up to date.
BillingCycle	Indicates the billing cycle in which eBay sends an invoice to the user. The value is a member of the BillingCycleEnum enumeration, either OnLastDayOfTheMonth or On15thDayOfTheMonth.
CurrentBalance	Specifies the user's current balance. A signed floating-point number.
LastAmountPaid	Specifies the amount of the last payment posted.
LastInvoiceAmount	Indicates the amount of the last invoice.
LastInvoiceDate	Specifies the date when eBay sent the last invoice to the user, in Greenwich mean time. Empty if this account has not been activated yet.
LastPaymentDate	Indicates the date when the user made the last payment to eBay in Greenwich mean time. Empty if the account has not been invoiced yet.
PastDue	If true, the account is past due.
PaymentMethod	Defines how the user pays eBay.
State	Specifies the state of the account. One of Active, Pending, or Inactive, as indicated by the AccountStateEnum.

An AccountPeriodView object can encompass multiple accounts owned by the same user. These accounts, handled by AdditionalAccount objects, reflect separate accounts attached to a same user, in much the same way you can have multiple phone numbers on a single phone bill. In the case of eBay, these multiple accounts can reflect different storefronts, for example. I discuss the AdditionalAccount class and its collection class later in this chapter, in the section "Examining Ancillary Accounts with the AdditionalAccount Class and Its Collection, the AdditionalAccountCollection Class."

The PaymentMethod property of the AccountPeriodView specifies how you pay eBay for its services. This property contains an object representing the payment method, an instance of the class AccountPaymentMethodImpl. As you will see in the next section, this object contains additional information specifying how you pay eBay via properties that denote a credit card, direct debit from an account, or other payment methods.

As you work with invoice and period views, you need to be able to specify information about the period of time you wish to see the data. The eBay SDK lets you specify this using three helper classes: the InvoiceViewSettings class, the PeriodViewSettings class, and the DateRangeImpl class. The InvoiceViewSettings class is the simplest to use; it has two properties, InvoiceMonth and InvoiceYear, which let you specify the month and year for a desired invoice. Similarly, the PeriodViewSettings contains a DateRange property, which will contain a DateRangeImpl object; and a ViewPeriod property, which contains a value selected from the PeriodViewRangeEnum enumeration, with values such as SinceLastInvoice, ForTheLastDay, and ForTheLastWeek. The DateRangeImpl class, not surprisingly, has two properties: BeginDate and EndDate. These dates point to the beginning and ending date of a date range, specified in Greenwich mean time.

Representing Payment Methods with the AccountPaymentMethodImpl Class

As part of the AccountPeriodView class, its PaymentMethod property indicates how you make your payments to eBay. Table 4-9 shows the properties of this class.

Table 4-9. The Properties of the AccountPaymentMethodImpl Class

Property	Purpose
CreditCard	Credit card information if Type property equals AccountPaymentEnum.CreditCard
DirectDebit	Information for direct debit from an account if Type property equals AccountPaymentEnum.DirectDebit
DirectDebit_Pending SignatureMandate	Information for direct debit from an account if the debit has yet to be authorized and Type property equals AccountPaymentEnum.DirectDebit_PendingSignatureMandate
eBayDirectPay	Information for direct payments to eBay if Type field equals AccountPaymentEnum.eBayDirectPay
Type	The payment option the user selected when registering with eBay

If you're used to programming in C# or Java where type reflection is the norm, the notion of testing the Type field to determine the appropriate field to examine for more information will seem positively antiquated. It has an advantage, though, in that it works well with languages like Perl where introspection of Component Object Model (COM) objects isn't easily done. Each of the other properties of an

AccountPeriodView object will be null, except the specific property indicated by the Type field.

The eBay SDK provides classes to encapsulate information about each of the payment types: the CreditCardImpl class, the DirectDebitImpl class, and the EBayDirectPay class. Their properties are specific to the payment method, and include information about the payment method such as the account number. You can see the properties for these classes in the eBay SDK documentation under the section "eBay.SDK.Model.Account."

Examining Ancillary Accounts with the AdditionalAccount Class and Its Collection, the AdditionalAccountCollection Class

Some accounts, especially those for large businesses, may be umbrella accounts that encompass multiple accounts to track account activities by categories in different accounts, such as for individual eBay stores or business units within a specific company. To describe this within the eBay data model architecture, the eBay SDK provides the AdditionalAccount class and its collection, the AdditionalAccountCollection class. Table 4-10 shows the properties of the AdditionalAccount class.

Table 4-10. The Properties of the AdditionalAccount Class

Property	Purpose
Balance	The balance for the additional account.
Currency	The currency in which the balance is reported. Indicated using the eBay.SDK.Model.Account.CurrencyEnum enumeration.
Id	The eBay ID for the account, as a string. The string contains a leading E followed by the account number and an indication of the account's currency.

The AdditionalAccount object is analogous to an Account object, but contains only those properties that differentiate it from its containing account.

Using eBay API Methods with User and Account Data Model Objects

All of these data model objects are nice, but without the corresponding eBay SDK API calls, they don't let you actually do much. Using a handful of methods in the eBay.SDK.API namespace, you can get information about a specific user or get information about a user's account.

As you saw in the previous chapters when using an API method, you must always set the API object's ApiSession property to the ApiSession you create and initialize with your application keys and a valid eBay user login and password.

The results of any of these API calls can be changed by the API's DetailLevel property. In general (although it's not always the case), successively higher values of DetailLevel indicate that additional information should be returned.

Obtaining a User's Information with the GetUserCall

The GetUserCall class lets you get a User object corresponding to a specific user. For obvious reasons, your application can't traverse the eBay database of users willy-nilly; privacy is paramount. Consequently, a user's e-mail address and street address is only returned under specific circumstances.

Before invoking the GetUserCall.GetUser method, you must set its properties to indicate the arguments of the API call. There are three properties you must set:

- The UserId property contains the eBay user ID of the user to return.

- The DetailLevel property indicates the level of detail you desire in the result.

- The ItemId property can contain the item ID of an item whose action has closed. If the account making the request is the seller of the item and the appropriate detail level is set, eBay will return the e-mail and postal address of the user.

The GetUser method returns a new IUser object, with properties filled based on the value of DetailLevel. Table 4-11 shows which properties are returned for a specific value of DetailLevel.

Table 4-11. DetailLevel and the Resulting User Object

Property	0	2	4	8
AboutMe	✔	✔	✔	✔
CheckoutEnabled	✔	✔	✔	✔
Email	✔	✔	✔	✔
EOPCheckLimit	✔	✔	✔	✔
EOPCreditCardLimit	✔	✔	✔	✔
FeedbackScore	✔	✔	✔	✔
IDVerified	✔	✔	✔	✔
IsGCAuthorized	✔	✔	✔	✔
IsLAAuthorized	✔	✔	✔	✔
RegDate	✔	✔	✔	✔
RegistrationAddress			✔	
SchedulingLimit		✔		
SellerLevel	✔	✔	✔	✔
SiteId	✔	✔	✔	✔
Star	✔	✔	✔	✔
Status	✔	✔	✔	✔
StoreOwner	✔	✔	✔	✔
Sunglasses	✔	✔	✔	✔
UserId	✔	✔	✔	✔
UserIdLastChanged	✔	✔	✔	✔

Obtaining a User's Account with GetAccountCall

The GetAccountCall class is similar to GetUserCall, except that instead of returning a User object, it returns an IAccount object. Unlike the GetUserCall class, however, the GetAccountCall class's input arguments are far more complex. The GetAccountCall's GetAccount method is a veritable Swiss Army knife, returning a number of different kinds of information depending on the values of its input properties. There are five input properties you can set:

- The Currency property specifies the currency in which to return the report. If this property is null, the account will be returned in the currency of the user's country.

- The InvoiceViewOption specifies the options for the AccountInvoiceView if ViewType is AccountViewEnum.ViewByInvoice and should contain an InvoiceViewSettings object.

- The PageNumber property specifies which page of account information should be returned. The eBay SDK divides account information into multiple pages to limit the use of network bandwidth. (The default is 1, which returns the first page of information.)

- The PeriodViewOption specifies the options for the AccountPeriodView if ViewType is AccountViewEnum.ViewByPeriod and should contain a PeriodViewSettings option.

- The ViewType property indicates whether an AccountPeriodView should be returned if ViewType is AccountViewEnum.ViewByPeriod or an AccountInvoiceView if ViewType is AccountViewEnum.ViewByInvoice.

CAUTION   *The* AccountViewEnum *contains a third element,* None. *It's an error to set the* ViewType *field to* AccountViewEnum.None; *the eBay service will return an error.*

Note that the DetailLevel option is conspicuously absent: As of this writing, it has no impact on the return value from the GetAccountCall.GetAccount method. Moreover, note that you cannot get the account information for an arbitrary user. Instead, the account information is returned for the user whose eBay user name you set in the ApiSession object associated with the transaction.

To use GetAccountCall.GetAccount, you select what kind of account information to obtain by setting the ViewType to one of the values defined by AccountViewEnum, either ViewByPeriod or ViewByInvoice. Depending on what value you select, you must also pass options in either InvoiceViewOption or PeriodViewOption. After you invoke the GetAccount method, the resulting information will be in the returned Account object's InvoiceView or PeriodView, respectively.

In addition to obtaining the resulting Account object after invoking GetAccount, the GetAccountCall TotalPages property is set with the total number of pages available for the specific account.

Harnessing IUser: The UserInfo Sample Application

The UserInfo sample application uses the IUser interface, the User class, and the GetUserCall class to obtain information about a registered user of the eBay service. Figure 4-3 shows a screen shot of the UserInfo application.

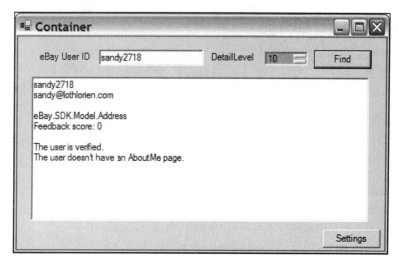

Figure 4-3. The UserInfo application (C# version)

To use the application, simply enter the desired eBay user ID in the text box on the left, and select the desired DetailLevel for the API request on the right from the list box. Once you do so, click the Find button. The application will create a GetUserCall object, issuing the GetUser request for the desired user ID with the indicated DetailLevel. The results of the request are displayed in the read-only text box at the bottom of the application. You can set your eBay developer keys and the test user and password by clicking Settings and filling out the Settings dialog box that appears.

In experimenting with the application, two things will immediately become clear: Because the application does not set the ItemId property, you'll never see an account holder's address. Once you learn how to list items (in the next chapter), you can modify UserInfo to set the ItemId property to a sold item and see a user's postal address. Similarly, the only time you see a user's e-mail address is when the eBay user ID you enter is the same as the eBay user ID you enter for the API session in the Settings dialog box. This feature of the eBay SDK and the underlying API help preserve the user's privacy, and make it more difficult for casual users of the eBay interfaces to harvest e-mail and postal mail addresses for the purposes of sending unsolicited e-mail or postal mail.

Implementing UserInfo in C#

The UserInfo application uses the user interface framework for eBay sample applications I describe in the Appendix. The implementation itself consists of a Panel that contains two child Panel objects, one with controls to let you enter the eBay user ID, and the other a Listbox to let you select the API DetailLevel for the request to determine what information will be included in the results.

The bulk of the application is trivial user interface code; you can see this in the sample code that accompanies this book. The eBay-specific work is done by the event handler for the Find button, aptly named find_Click. You can see this method in Listing 4-1.

Listing 4-1. The find_Click Method of UserInfo

```
 1: private void find_Click(object sender, System.EventArgs e)
 2: {
 3:   IGetUserCall api = new GetUserCall();
 4:   IUser theUser = null;
 5:   string resultString = null;
 6:
 7:   // We're busy.
 8:   this.Busy = true;
 9:   this.StatusText = "Downloading...";
10:
11:   // Set the API for this call.
12:   api.ErrorLevel =
13:     ErrorLevelEnum.BothShortAndLongErrorStrings;
14:   api.ApiCallSession = this.ApiSession;
15:
16:   api.UserId = this.userid.Text;
17:   api.DetailLevel = System.Convert.ToInt32(
18:     this.detaillevel.SelectedItem );
19:
20:   try
21:   {
22:     theUser = api.GetUser();
23:   }
24:   catch( Exception ex )
25:   {
26:     resultString =  "**Error**\n" + ex.Message;
27:   }
28:
```

```
29:    if ( theUser != null )
30:    {
31:      resultString = theUser.UserId + "\n" +
32:        theUser.Email + "\n" +
33:        theUser.PaymentAddress + "\n" +
34:        theUser.RegistrationAddress + "\n" +
35:        "Feedback score: " + theUser.FeedbackScore.ToString() +
36:        "\n\nThe user is " +
37:          ( theUser.IdVerified ? "" : "not" ) +
38:          "verified.\n" +
39:        "The user " +
40:          ( theUser.AboutMe ? "has" : "doesn't have" ) +
41:          "an AboutMe page.\n";
42:    }
43:
44:    this.result.SuspendLayout();
45:    result.Text = resultString ;
46:    this.result.Enabled = true;
47:    this.result.ResumeLayout();
48:
49:    // We're no longer busy.
50:    this.StatusText = "";
51:    this.Busy = false;
52: }
```

True to form, the bulk of this method is user interface code, too. It begins by
using the user interface to tell the user that the application is busy accessing the
eBay service on lines 8–9. Lines 12–14 do the usual preliminary setup of the newly
created eBay SDK API instance, in this case an instance of the GetUserCall class.
The first statement, spanning lines 12–13, chooses verbose error strings, because
the application displays the eBay-delivered error strings in the event of an error.
Line 14 initializes the api's ApiCallSession property to the ApiSession established
by the framework when the application first launched.

Lines 16–18 initialize the GetUserCall specific properties, UserId and DetailLevel.
The UserId property is set to the property you enter in the text box, while the
DetailLevel property is set to the integer value of the string you select from the cor-
responding list box.

The eBay SDK API call itself is wrapped in a try/catch block on lines 20–27.
As you can see from line 22, the GetUser call returns a newly created User object,
or null if the call fails. In the event of any error, the result string resultString is
set to the message generated by the exception.

On success, the routine creates a human-readable string summarizing the
contents of the User object on lines 29–42. You have to do this, because the default
User.ToString() method simply returns "eBay.SDK.Model.User", which isn't terribly
informative.

Once the result string is created, the routine uses it as the text of the result text box for you to see on lines 44–47. Finally, the routine restores the user interface to an active state on lines 49–51.

Implementing UserInfo in Perl

The UserInfo application in Perl uses Perl/Tk to provide a GUI similar to the C# application you saw in the last section. You can see the Perl version of the UserInfo application in Figure 4-4.

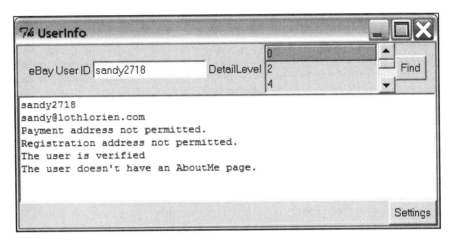

Figure 4-4. The UserInfo application written in Perl

The application opens with the usual Perl/Tk component setup drudgery, which I'll skip for brevity here. All of the eBay interaction occurs when you click the Find button; it in turn calls the find_Click subroutine, which you can see in Listing 4-2.

Listing 4-2. The UserInfo find_Click Subroutine in Perl

```
1: sub find_Click
2: {
3:    $application->Busy( 1 );
4:
5:    my $api = Win32::OLE->new( "eBay.SDK.API.GetUserCall" );
6:    $api->{ApiCall}->{ApiCallSession} =
7:    $application->{APISESSION};
8:    $api->{ApiCall}->{ErrorLevel} = 1;
```

```
 9:
10:     $api->{UserId} = $userid;
11:     my ( $detaillevelidx ) = $detaillevel->curselection();
12:     $api->{DetailLevel} = $detaillevelidx * 2;
13:
14:     my $theUser = $api->GetUser();
15:     my $result = Win32::OLE->LastError();
16:
17:     # Show the results.
18:     if( $theUser )
19:     {
20:        $result = $theUser->{UserId} . "\n" .
21:           $theUser->{Email} . "\n";
22:        $result .= $theUser->{PaymentAddress} . "\n"
23:           if $theUser->{PaymentAddress};
24:        $result .= "Payment address not permitted.\n"
25:           if !$theUser->{PaymentAddress};
26:        $result .= $theUser->{RegistrationAddress} . "\n"
27:           if $theUser->{RegistrationAddress};
28:        $result .= "Registration address not permitted.\n"
29:           if !$theUser->{RegistrationAddress};
30:        $result .= "The user is ";
31:        $result .= "not "  if !$theUser->{IdVerified};
32:        $result .= "verified\n";
33:        $result .= "The user";
34:        $result .= " has " if ( $theUser->{AboutMe} );
35:        $result .= " doesn't have " if ( !$theUser->{AboutMe} );
36:        $result .=  "an AboutMe page.\n";
37:     }
38:
39:     $resultText->delete( "1.0", "end" );
40:     $resultText->insert( "end", $result );
41:     $application->Busy( 0 );
42: }
```

If you compare Listing 4-2 with its predecessor, Listing 4-1, you immediately see one of the beauties of the eBay SDK: You can accomplish the same tasks with the same eBay SDK components in different languages, and the only real difference you encounter is the syntax of the source language.

The first line, line 3, sets the user interface framework to a busy state so that it will ignore user input. Next, on lines 5–12, the routine initializes the $api variable with an eBay.SDK.API.GetUserCall COM object, which it will use to perform the GetUser method. Most of the initialization is fairly straightforward, although the shameless code on lines 11–12 to set $api->{DetailLevel} deserves explanation. Rather than getting the selected index of the $detaillevel list box and using it to get the associated value, and then converting the value to an integer, it short-circuits all of that and uses the knowledge that the value at a specific index is just twice the value of the index anyway.

Lines 14–15 issue the GetUser call to the eBay service, capturing any error in the event that the call fails. Lines 17–37 convert the resulting User object, $theUser, to a human-readable string. Finally, lines 39–41 update the result text box with the data fetched from eBay and return the user interface to its normal state.

Harnessing IAccount: The AccountStatus Sample Application

As you can see from Figure 4-5, the user interface to the AccountStatus sample application is very similar to that of the UserInfo application. I've added controls to let you select whether you want to see a period or invoice view, and the page of the report to view, along with two more controls to let you enter date ranges when obtaining a period view. Once you enter these items, you click the Find button, and the results of the query are shown in the read-only text box below the input controls.

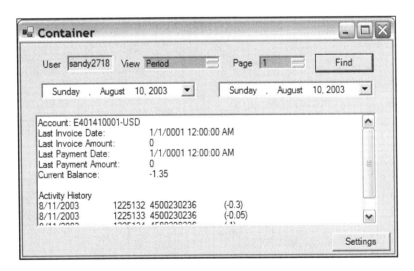

Figure 4-5. The AccountStatus application (C# version)

The application's interface reflects two important points regarding the GetAccountCall: You can only obtain the eBay account for the user logged in using the current API session, and changing the DetailLevel of the GetAccountCall has no effect on the results from the GetAccount method invocation.

Another thing you can see from Figure 4-5 is that for users who haven't had an invoice generated, the last invoice and payment dates will be invalid. This is an easy way to tell a newly created user from his or her account without needing to obtain a User object for the user.

Implementing AccountStatus in C#

Like UserInfo, the eBay-specific operations in AccountStatus are contained within the Find button's event handler. Listing 4-3 shows the implementation of the find_Click method.

Listing 4-3. The find_Click Method of the AccountStatus Application

```
 1: private void find_Click(object sender, System.EventArgs e)
 2: {
 3:   IGetAccountCall api = new GetAccountCall();
 4:   IAccount theAccount = null;
 5:   string resultString = null;
 6:   // We're busy.
 7:   this.Busy = true;
 8:   this.StatusText = "Downloading...";
 9:   // Set the API for this call.
10:   api.ErrorLevel =
11:     ErrorLevelEnum.BothShortAndLongErrorStrings;
12:   api.ApiCallSession = this.ApiSession;
13:   api.PageNumber = System.Convert.ToInt32(
14:     this.pagenumber.SelectedItem );
15:   api.ViewType =
16:     (AccountViewEnum)this.viewtype.SelectedIndex;
17:
18:   switch( api.ViewType )
19:   {
20:     case AccountViewEnum.ViewByPeriod:
21:       api.PeriodViewOption = new PeriodViewSettings();
22:       api.PeriodViewOption.DateRange = new DateRangeImpl();
23:       api.PeriodViewOption.DateRange.BeginDate =
24:         this.startdate.Value;
25:       api.PeriodViewOption.DateRange.EndDate =
26:         this.enddate.Value;
27:       break;
```

```
28:
29:    case AccountViewEnum.ViewByInvoice:
30:      api.InvoiceViewOption = new InvoiceViewSettings();
31:      api.InvoiceViewOption.InvoiceMonth =
32:        (InvoiceMonthEnum)this.Month;
33:      api.InvoiceViewOption.InvoiceYear = this.Year;
34:      break;
35:  }
36:  try
37:  {
38:    theAccount = api.GetAccount();
39:  }
40:  catch( Exception ex )
41:  {
42:    resultString =  "**Error**\n" + ex.Message;
43:  }
44:    // Create a nice string with the results.
45:  if ( theAccount != null )
46:  {
47:    resultString = "Account: " + theAccount.Id + "\n";
48:    // Summary of invoice view
49:    if ( theAccount.InvoiceView != null )
50:    {
51:      resultString += "Amount Due:\t" +
52:        theAccount.InvoiceView.InvoiceBalance + "\n";
53:      resultString += "Invoice Date:\t" +
54:        theAccount.InvoiceView.InvoiceDate.ToShortDateString() +
55:        "\n";
56:    }
57:    // Summary of period view
58:    if ( theAccount.PeriodView != null )
59:    {
60:      resultString += "Last Invoice Date:\t\t" +
61:        theAccount.PeriodView.LastInvoiceDate.ToString() + "\n";
62:      resultString += "Last Invoice Amount:\t" +
63:        theAccount.PeriodView.LastInvoiceAmount.ToString() + "\n";
64:      resultString += "Last Payment Date:\t\t" +
65:        theAccount.PeriodView.LastPaymentDate + "\n";
66:      resultString += "Last Payment Amount:\t" +
67:        theAccount.PeriodView.LastAmountPaid + "\n";
68:      resultString != "Current Balance:\t\t" +
69:        theAccount.PeriodView.CurrentBalance + "\n";
70:    }
```

```
71:    // Enumerate each of the account activities.
72:    resultString += "\nActivity History\n";
73:    foreach ( AccountActivity activity in theAccount.Activities )
74:    {
75:      resultString += activity.Date.ToShortDateString() + "\t";
76:      resultString += activity.Id.ToString() + "\t" +
77:        activity.ItemId + " " + activity.Memo + "\t";
78:      resultString += activity.Credit != 0 ?
79:        activity.Credit.ToString() : "";
80:      resultString += activity.Debit != 0 ? "(" +
81:        activity.Debit.ToString() + ")" : "";
82:      resultString += "\n";
83:    }
84:  }
85:
86:  // Update the pagenumber menu with the list pages.
87:  this.pagenumber.Items.Clear();
88:  for ( int i = 0; i <= api.TotalPages; i++ )
89:  {
90:    this.pagenumber.Items.Add( (i+1).ToString() );
91:  }
92:  this.pagenumber.SelectedIndex = 0;
93:  // Update the UI.
94:  this.result.SuspendLayout();
95:  result.Text = resultString ;
96:  this.result.Enabled = true;
97:  this.result.ResumeLayout();
98:  // We're no longer busy.
99:  this.StatusText = "";
100:  this.Busy = false;
101: }
```

If you followed the implementation of UserInfo in the previous section, this routine won't hold any surprises. It operates in exactly the same manner, and is longer only because an Account object has more to show you than a User object does. Lines 6–8 mark the user interface as busy, while lines 98–100 reverse the process, clearing the status text region and setting the cursor back to the standard pointer.

Lines 9–12 set the GetAccountCall api.ErrorLevel and api.APICallSession, and should be familiar to you by now. Lines 13–16 set the other two critical properties of the api object: PageNumber, to indicate the desired page number of the account information to fetch; and ViewType, to indicate the type of account view you select with the corresponding Listbox. As you see on line 16, you can cheat when it comes to the ViewType; by ordering the choices in the list box in the same order as the enumeration values in `AccountViewEnum`, you make it easy to set the `api.ViewType` property from the index of the `Listbox`.

The switch spanning lines 18–35 checks the `ViewType` and creates the appropriate view options based on the `ViewType`. Because the eBay SDK uses the .NET Framework, it's easy to create an eBay `DateRangeImpl` and populate it with the values from the two date entry controls, all of which use the .NET Framework `DateTime` class to encapsulate a date and time value (lines 21–26). Obtaining the month and year for the invoice view settings is a little more problematic; as you can see from lines 30–33, in the end you could get around this by creating `Month` and `Year` properties for the application that get their values from the left-hand date control. It's admittedly a hack, but a reasonable one; the alternative would be to subclass the date control and give it the appropriate methods, or to put some rather ugly .NET-specific code on these lines.

With the `api` properties in hand, line 38 executes its master method, the `GetAccount` method, returning an `Account` object or `null`. Of course, this operation is wrapped in a `try/catch` block, and if an error occurs, the exception's `Message` property will be shown to the user. If, on the other hand, all goes well and the code obtains a valid `Account` object (line 45), the results are converted to a string (lines 47–84). The manipulations to create the string representation hold few surprises, although the `foreach` loop on lines 73–83 is interesting because it demonstrates how to traverse an `AccountActivity` collection.

Once the result string has been created, the routine updates the `Listbox` for selecting the page of an account report on lines 86–92. There're any number of ways you can do this, but this example shows the clearest, which is to iterate across all of the valid page numbers, adding an item in the `Listbox` for each page number, and then selecting the first item again.

Finally, the routine updates the user interface with the result string (lines 93–97), and exits after setting the user interface to accept user events again.

Implementing AccountStatus in Perl

AccountStatus in Perl, like UserInfo in Perl before it, harnesses the Perl/Tk framework to provide a user interface similar to that of AccountStatus written in C#. As you can see from Figure 4-6, the interface is a little rougher. In part, this is due to the nature of the Perl/Tk components, but to be fair to Perl/Tk, I wasn't trying to show you a perfect clone of the original AccountStatus application written in C#, but something that was functionally equivalent and still usable. As an aside, the two-month user interfaces are provided by Slaven Rezic's Tk::Date module, available from http://www.cpan.org and other fine purveyors of Perl modules everywhere. (I've included a copy of it with the source code that accompanies this book.)

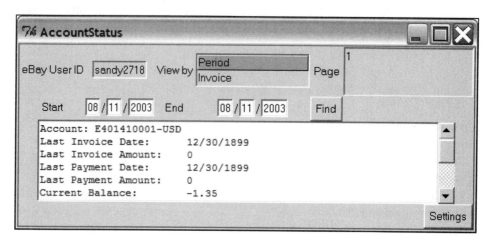

Figure 4-6. The AccountStatus application written in Perl

Listing 4-4 shows the contents of the find_Click subroutine of the AccountStatus application in Perl. As you read it, rest assured that I didn't just port the C# code with some secret C#-to-Perl converter; this is code I wrote by hand. It's really that easy to go between languages using the eBay SDK!

Listing 4-4. The find_Click Subroutine of the AccountStatus Application in Perl

```
 1: sub find_Click
 2: {
 3:    $application->Busy( 1 );
 4:
 5:    my $api = Win32::OLE->new( "eBay.SDK.API.GetAccountCall" );
 6:    $api->{ApiCall}->{ApiCallSession} =
 7:    $application->{APISESSION};
 8:    $api->{ApiCall}->{ErrorLevel} = 1;
 9:
10:    ($api->{PageNumber}) = $pagenumber->curselection();
11:    $api->{PageNumber} = 1 if !$api->{PageNumber};
12:    ($api->{ViewType}) = $viewtype->curselection();
13:    $api->{ViewType} = 0 if !$api->{ViewType};
14:
15:    if ( $api->{ViewType} == 0 )
16:    {
17:      my $popt = Win32::OLE->new(
18:        "eBay.SDK.Model.Account.PeriodViewSettings" );
19:      my $dr = Win32::OLE->new( "eBay.SDK.API.DateRangeImpl" );
20:      $dr->{BeginDate} = $startdate->get( "%Y-%m-%d" );
21:      $dr->{EndDate} = $enddate->get( "%Y-%m-%d" );
```

```
22:     $popt->{DateRange} = $dr;
23:     $api->{PeriodViewOption} = $popt;
24:   }
25:
26:   if ( $api->{ViewType} == 1 )
27:   {
28:     my $ivopt =  Win32::OLE->new(
29:       "eBay.SDK.Model.Account.InvoiceViewSettings" );
30:     $ivopt->{InvoiceMonth} = $startdate->get( "%m" );
31:     $ivopt->{InvoiceYear} = $startdate->get( "%y" );
32:     $api->{InvoiceViewOption} = $ivopt;
33:   }
34:
35:   my $theAccount = $api->GetAccount();
36:   my $result = Win32::OLE->LastError();
37:
38:   # Show the results.
39:   if( $theAccount )
40:   {
41:     $result = "Account: " . $theAccount->{Id} . "\n";
42:     if ( $theAccount->{InvoiceView} )
43:     {
44:       $result .= "Amount Due:\t" .
45:       $theAccount->{InvoiceView}->{InvoiceBalance} . "\n";
46:       $result .= "Invoice Date:\t" .
47:       $theAccount->{InvoiceView}->{InvoiceDate}->Date("MM/dd/yyyy")."\n";
48:     }
49:     if ( $theAccount->{PeriodView} )
50:     {
51:       $result .= "Last Invoice Date:\t";
52:       my $lid = $theAccount->{PeriodView}->{LastInvoiceDate};
53:       $result .= $lid->Date("MM/dd/yyyy");
54:       $result .= "\nLast Invoice Amount:\t" .
55:       $theAccount->{PeriodView}->{LastInvoiceAmount} . "\n";
56:       $result .= "Last Payment Date:\t";
57:       my $lpd =  $theAccount->{PeriodView}->{LastPaymentDate};
58:       $result .= $lpd->Date("MM/dd/yyyy");
59:       $result .= "\nLast Payment Amount:\t" .
60:       $theAccount->{PeriodView}->{LastAmountPaid} . "\n";
61:       $result .= "Current Balance:\t" .
62:       $theAccount->{PeriodView}->{CurrentBalance} . "\n";
63:     }
64:
65:     # Enumerate each of the account activities.
```

```
66:        $result .= "\nActivity History\n";
67:        my $i;
68:        for ( $i = 0;
69:              $i < $theAccount->{Activities}->ItemCount();
70:              $i++ )
71:        {
72:          my $activity = $theAccount->{Activities}->ItemAt($i);
73:          $result .= $activity->{Date}->Date("MM/dd/yyyy") . "\t";
74:          $result .= $activity->{Id} . "\t";
75:          $result .= $activity->{Credit} . "\t"
76:            if $activity->{Credit};
77:          $result .= "(" . $activity->{Debit} . ")" . "\t"
78:            if $activity->{Debit};
79:          $result .= "\n";
80:        }
81:
82:        # Update the pagenumber menu with the list pages.
83:        $pagenumber->delete( 0, "end" );
84:        for ( $i = 1; $i <= $api->{TotalPages}; $i++ )
85:        {
86:          $pagenumber->insert( "end", "$i" );
87:        }
88:
89:        $resultText->delete( "1.0", "end" );
90:        $resultText->insert( "end", $result );
91:    }
92:    $application->Busy( 0 );
93: }
```

This routine begins, like the routines before it, by blocking incoming user interface events and changing the cursor to a busy cursor by invoking the framework's Busy method on line 3. After that, it creates and initializes a new eBay.SDK.API.GetAccountCall COM object, setting its ApiCallSession and ErrorLevel slots with appropriate values.

Next, on lines 10–13, you set $api->{PageNumber} and $api->{ViewType} to the values indicated by the two list box controls. Lines 11 and 13 perform some simple error checking, providing some reasonable defaults in case you don't select items from each list box. Critics will point out that the AccountStatus sample in C# doesn't do this, and to be fair, it probably should.

Lines 15–24 create and initialize a fresh PeriodViewSettings object. This is the sort of code that casts the .NET Framework in a positive light; it's just a little more tedious than it ought to be to do this kind of thing in Perl. Nonetheless, it's not difficult, as you can see. The code begins by creating the PeriodViewSettings object and its DateRangeImpl object on lines 17–19. You could store them in temporary variables to keep the code tidy and avoid horribly long lines of code that don't read well on paper as shown in this example, but you certainly don't have to. Once you create them, use the Tk::Date module's get method to obtain the values of each of the date entry controls. This method takes a single argument, the format of the date as a string using the same keywords as the POSIX function strftime. If you omit the argument, you get the entered time in seconds since the beginning of the Unix epoch, which isn't helpful when working with eBay.

Lines 27–33 do the same thing for an InvoiceView object. As you can see from the if statements on lines 15 and 27, you need only a PeriodView or an InvoiceView, but not both.

Lines 35–36 make the GetAccount call, obtaining an error message should an error occur. The resulting $theAccount variable is used to craft a result string for human consumption on lines 39–87. There are two things worth noting here.

First, if you're not used to using the Win32::OLE module, you're probably not clear on the code on lines 47, 52, and 57. The Account OLE class, when wrapped by Perl, stores dates as Win32::OLE::Variant objects, which can encapsulate some mixed types. Thus, to get access to the date itself, you need to use its Date function and provide a format string. The full details of the format string are included in the Plain Old Documentation (POD) for Win32::OLE, but they're intuitive, as you can see from the examples here, which generate dates in *mm/dd/yyyy* format with leading zeros for single-digit dates.

Second, the loop on lines 67–80 demonstrates how to iterate the elements of an eBay collection, in this case, an ActivityCollection. The code is simple, of course—find out how many items are in the collection by calling its ItemCount method, and then use its ItemAt method with an index to fetch a specific item.

Once the $result string has been built up with pieces of $theAccount, it's copied into the $resultText object (a read-only text string of type Tk::ROText), and the user interface is returned to its normal state.

Key Points

In this chapter, you learned the following key points about how to manage users with the eBay SDK:

- You can obtain a user's information with eBay.SDK.API.GetUserCall. The result you receive is a IUser object with the desired results.

- You can obtain a user's account information with the eBay.SDK.API.GetAccountCall object. The result you receive is an IAccount object with the desired results, along with updates to the eBay.SDK.API.GetAccountCall object.

- The eBay.SDK.Model.User namespace contains the User class and helper enumerations to represent the notion of an eBay user.

- The eBay.SDK.Model.Account namespace contains the Account class and a host of helper classes and enumerations to describe how eBay users pay for their use of eBay services.

CHAPTER 5

Managing Items with the eBay SDK

ALTHOUGH USERS ARE ONE cornerstone of the foundation of the eBay SDK data model, items are another. Just as the User class and its helper classes let you manipulate users with the eBay interface calls in the eBay SDK, the Item class and its helper classes let you represent items and their sales on eBay.

In this chapter, you learn all about how to work with items using the eBay SDK. I open with an introduction to the components in the eBay.SDK.Model.Item namespace, followed by an in-depth look at eBay's SimpleList application. After that, I examine the eBay.SDK.Model.Feedback namespace and its contents.

Looking Under the Hood at the eBay.SDK.Model.Item Namespace

At the heart of the eBay.SDK.Model.Item namespace is the Item class, but it's not alone. This namespace contains a plethora of classes for describing items, most of which provide data encapsulation for specific attributes of items, such as what state an item is in with respect to an auction.

The principal use of the components in this namespace is to enable your applications to list items using the methods in the ebay.SDK.API namespace. Table 5-1 lists the API classes that use members of the eBay.SDK.Model.Item namespace.

Table 5-1. eBay.SDK.API Classes Using eBay.SDK.Model.Item Namespace Components

API	Purpose
AddItemCall	Lists a new item on eBay. Takes the item description from an Item object.
AddToItem DescriptionCall	Adds additional information to an existing item's description.
EndItemCall	Ends an auction before its duration has elapsed.
GetItemCall	Retrieves the description of a single item, returning an IItem object.

Table 5-1. eBay.SDK.API Classes Using eBay.SDK.Model.Item Namespace Components (continued)

API	Purpose
RelistItemCall	Relists an existing item that didn't sell in a new auction.
ReviseItemCall	Modifies the definition of an existing item using data from an IItem object.
VerifyAddItemCall	Validates without listing an item described by an IItem object, returning an estimation of listing fees for the described item.

Representing eBay Items with the Item and ItemFound Classes and Their Collections

At first blush, the Item class is positively overwhelming—its list of properties is simply huge. To adequately describe an item and its relationship to other eBay components in its entirety takes a plethora of properties; Table 5-2 shows the properties of the Item class accessible through the IItem interface.

Table 5-2. Important Properties of the Item Class

Property	Purpose
AppData	A generic Object field that can hold an application-specific object. Not shared with eBay.
ApplicationData	A 32-character string that the application may use to describe the item. This field is shared with and stored by eBay.
Attributes	Contains the attributes for the item. Originally used by eBay Motors, now a property of all items.
BidCount	The number of bids that have been placed on the item.
BidIncrement	The amount that each bid must be above the previous bid to qualify as a bid.
BuyItNowPrice	The amount an eBay user must pay to purchase the item and end the auction immediately.
Category2Id	The ID of the secondary category in which the item will be listed, if the user chooses to list the item in more than one category.
CategoryId	The ID of the category in which the item has been listed.
Checkout	The item's checkout details and status.

Table 5-2. Important Properties of the Item Class (continued)

Property	Purpose
ConvertedPrice	The item's price after undergoing conversion to the SiteCurrency for the eBay API transaction.
Counter	An element of the HitCounterEnum enumeration indicating how the seller wants to count page hits to the item's listing.
Country	The two-character country code of the country where the seller and his or her item are located.
Currency	The country code of the currency used to list the item.
CurrencyId	The symbol for the currency used to list the item, such as $ or €.
CurrentPrice	The current price (highest bid) for the item. If no bids have been placed, the current price is the minimum bid.
Description	The text of the description of the item.
Duration	The number of days the item will be up for auction. Used when listing an item, and values may be restricted based on the business rules for specific auctions.
EndTime	The eBay time at which the auction ends.
EstimatedFees	An estimation of the fees that eBay will charge for the item.
EstimatedFeesCurrency	Currency ID for the site where the selling user registered.
GalleryUrl	The URL for the gallery picture for the item.
GiftOptions	Gift options for the item.
HighBidder	The current high bidding user for the item.
ItemId	The unique eBay item ID for the item.
ItemRevised	If true, the item has been revised since its initial listing.
LeadCount	For advertisement items (such as real estate auctions), indicates how many leads to potential buyers are associated with this item.
ListingDesigner	eBay Listing Designer–specific information.
ListingFeatures	Listing features for the item, such as whether the title should be bold.
Location	The geographic location of the item.
MinimumToBid	The minimum acceptable bid for the item.
ModifiedProperties	List of the properties that have been modified for the item.

Table 5-2. Important Properties of the Item Class (continued)

Property	Purpose
PaymentTerms	Container for a description of the payment terms accepted by the seller.
PhotoCount	The number of pictures associated with the item using eBay's picture services.
PhotoUrl	A semicolon-delimited list of URLs to pictures of the item.
PrivateAuction	If true, indicates that the item is listed in a private auction.
Quanitity	The number of items being sold in the auction for this IItem.
QuantitySold	The number of items already sold in the auction for this IItem.
Region	The geographic region where this item is being sold.
RegionId	The numeric ID corresponding to the Region property.
RelistId	The numeric ID of the new listing when an item is being relisted.
ReservePrice	The reserve price for the auction if one has been set.
Seller	The user selling the item as an eBay User.
ShippingOptions	A container for options about how the item may be shipped.
StartPrice	The starting price for the item.
StartTime	The date and time that the item was first made available for auction.
Status	The item status, available only when using GetItemCall.
StoreCategory	Custom categories for dividing items within an eBay store.
StorefrontItem	If true, the item is in an eBay storefront.
StoreLocation	For an eBay stores item listing, the URL to the seller's eBay stores page.
TimeLeft	The time remaining for the auction.
Title	The title of the item.
TitleBarImage	If true, an image appears with the title bar for the item in the listing page.
Type	The type of listing used to sell the item on eBay.
Uuid	A globally unique identifier for the item. Assigned by eBay via an eBay SDK API call or via the creation of a new Uuid object.
Zip	The zip code of the seller.

It's important to remember when reviewing these properties that an eBay item can be one or more things. It's best to think of an *item* as a blob that's listed for auction; this blob can contain more than one item, such as is the case for Dutch auctions (see Table 2-1 of Chapter 2). Thus, you might create an item for an auction of rare pencils, and have six pencils listed in the auction, each of which can go to a different high bidder. From the perspective of the eBay SDK, this is *one* item (with a quantity of six), not six individual items, because its sale is managed through one auction.

Don't be confused by the `ApplicationData` and `AppData` properties either. The former is a container that is stored on the eBay service, which you can use as a persistent store to cross-reference the item with your application, for example, by using it to store an item's unique identifier in a non-eBay source database. The latter, however, is *not* shared with eBay, and persists for only as long as the `Item` object exists. You can use it to store an object such as a user interface control or another widget that pertains to your application's operation.

Some properties, such as `Attributes` and `LeadCount`, are applicable to only certain kinds of auctions at certain sites of eBay. These properties may not be available when obtaining an `Item` for just any auction, so you should always test for their existence first, unless your application's business logic ensures that the items it manages are for those auctions. This reflects a key design philosophy of eBay's engineers: a simple, relatively flat hierarchy with few interfaces and classes, rather than a proliferation of special-case classes or adornments to interfaces.

The helper classes `GiftOptions`, `Status`, `PaymentTerms`, `ShippingOptions`, and `ShippingRegions` encapsulate information about items. Tables 5-3 through 5-8 show the properties of the `GiftSettings`, `ItemStatus`, `PaymentTerms`, `ShippingPayment`, and `ShippingOptions` classes, respectively.

Table 5-3. Properties of the GiftOptions Class

Property	Purpose
GiftExpressShipping	If true, the seller is offering to ship the item via an express shipping method (named in the item description).
GiftIcon	If true, a generic gift icon appears in the item's listing.
GiftShipToRecipient	If true, the seller is offering to ship to the gift recipient, not the buyer, when payment clears.
GiftWrap	If true, the seller is offering to gift wrap the item (and possibly include a card) as described in the item description.

Table 5-4. Properties of the Status Class

Property	Purpose
Adult	Indicates that the item is an adult-only item, only visible to those who agree to eBay's Mature Category agreement.
BindingAuction	When true, indicates that buyer and seller intend to follow through on the transaction. Used by real estate auctions.
BinLowered	If true, indicates that the Buy It Now price has been lowered. Used by eBay Motors auctions.
CheckoutEnabled	If true, checkout is enabled for this item.
ReserveLowered	If true, the seller has lowered the reserve price for the item. Used by eBay Motors auctions.
ReserveMet	If true, the item's reserved price has been met. This is null for International Fixed Price items.

Table 5-5. Properties of the PaymentTerms Class

Property	Purpose
AmEx	When true, the seller accepts American Express.
CashOnPickupAccepted	When true, the seller accepts payment on pickup of the item.
CCAccepted	When true, the seller accepts credit card payment.
COD	When true, the seller accepts cash-on-delivery payment.
Discover	When true, the seller accepts the Discover card.
Escrow	Specifies escrow options, as described by the EscrowEnum enumeration.
MOCashiers	When true, money orders and cashier's checks are accepted.
ModifiedProperties	Lists the names of modified properties.
MoneyXferAccepted	When true, the seller accepts a money transfer.
MoneyXferAccepted InCheckout	When true, the seller accepts a money transfer at checkout time by users who have their bank account information on file with eBay.
Other	When true, the seller accepts other forms of payment as described in the item's description.
OtherPaymentsOnline	When true, the seller accepts other non-eBay forms of online payment.

Table 5-5. Properties of the PaymentTerms Class (continued)

Property	Purpose
PayPalAccepted	When true, the seller accepts PayPal payments.
PayPalEmailAddress	Contains the PayPal address of the seller, returned when calling GetItem.
PersonalCheck	When true, the seller accepts personal checks.
SeeDescription	When true, the acceptable payments are listed in the item description.
VisaMaster	When true, the seller accepts Visa and Mastercard.

Table 5-6. Properties of the ShippingPayment Class

Property	Purpose
ModifiedProperties	Lists the names of modified properties
SeeDescription	Specifies shipping terms in item description
WhoPays	Represents an element of the WhoPaysShipping enumeration to indicate who is responsible for paying shipping

Table 5-7. Properties of the ShippingRegions Class

Property	Purpose
Africa	When true, the seller will ship the item to Africa.
Asia	When true, the seller will ship the item to Asia.
Caribbean	When true, the seller will ship the item to the Caribbean.
Europe	When true, the seller will ship the item to Europe.
LatinAmerica	When true, the seller will ship the item to Latin America.
MiddleEast	When true, the seller will ship the item to the Middle East.
ModifiedProperties	Lists the names of modified properties.
NorthAmerica	When true, the seller will ship the item to North America.
Oceana	When true, the seller will ship the item to Pacific islands other than those in Asia.
SouthAmerica	When true, the seller will ship the item to South America.

Table 5-8. Properties of the ShippingSettings Class

Property	Purpose
ShippingPayment	Shipping options described by a ShippingPayment object.
ShippingRange	Where the seller will ship the item as described by a ShippingRangeEnumerator.
ShippingRegions	When ShippingRange is ShippingRangeEnum.SiteAndRegions, this field contains a ShippingRegions object.

Representing Fees for Listing Items with the eBay.SDK.Model.Item.Fees Class

At the heart of eBay's business model is charging fees for carrying items for auction. eBay charges a variety of listing fees when you list an item for auction, depending on the marketing tools you choose to use to help promote your auction on the eBay site where you list an item when you list that item. To help your application present these fees to your customers, use the Fees class and its IFees interface. Table 5-9 shows the properties of the Fees class and its interface.

Table 5-9. Properties of the Fees Class

Property	Purpose
AuctionLengthFee	The fee for a ten-day auction.
BoldFee	The fee for listing the auction's title in bold.
BuyItNowFee	The fee for adding a Buy It Now option to the item's listing.
CategoryFeaturedFee	The fee for having the item featured in its category.
CurrencyId	The seller's currency ID.
FeaturedFee	The fee for having the item featured at the top of item listings.
FeaturedGalleryFee	The fee for having the item featured in its gallery.
FixedPriceDurationFee	The fee for listing a fixed-price item for a specific duration.
GalleryFee	The fee for having the item included in the gallery.
GiftIconFee	The fee for including a gift icon in the listing.
HighLightFee	The fee for having the item listing highlighted.

Table 5-9. Properties of the Fees Class (continued)

Property	Purpose
InsertionFee	The fee for listing the item on the eBay service.
ListingFee	The total fee for listing the item. Includes the basic fee, InsertionFee, plus any specialty listing features.
PhotoDisplayFee	Fee for using the eBay Photo Hosting feature.
PhotoFee	Fee for associating 1–6 photos with the item.
ReserveFee	Fee for placing a reserve on an item.
SchedulingFee	Fee for scheduling an item to be listed at a later time.

The Fees class is a container for *all* of the fees that may be charged at item insertion time. The base fee, stored in the InsertionFee property, shows the base fee for listing the item for auction. Other properties provide itemized fees for other listing options, while the ListingFee provides the total cost for listing an option so that your application doesn't need to calculate the sum of all fees.

Serializing eBay.SDK.Model.Item Helper Classes

Several of the classes in the eBay.SDK.Model.Item namespace have accompanying serializing helpers, which let you convert between a class object and its representation as a hash table (a System.Collections.Hashtable object). The eBay SDK provides serializing helpers for the ListingFeatures, PaymentTerms, ShippingPayment, and ShippingRegions classes with the ListingFeaturesSerializer, PaymentTermsSerializer, ShippingPaymentSerializer, and ShippingRegionsSerializer classes. Each of these have two methods:

- The FromHashtable method constructs an instance of the class the serializing helper assists from the hash table that you provide.

- The ToHashtable method constructs a hash table from an instance of the class the serializing helper assists that you provide.

Tables 5-10 through 5-13 list the properties of each of the helper classes.

Table 5-10. Properties of the ListingFeaturesSerializer Class

Property	Purpose
ListingFeatures	The ListingFeatures associated with this object
ModifiedOnly	If true, serializes only modified properties

Table 5-11. Properties of the PaymentTermsSerializer Class

Property	Purpose
PaymentTerms	The PaymentTerms associated with this object
ModifiedOnly	If true, serializes only modified properties

Table 5-12. Properties of the ShippingPaymentSerializer Class

Property	Purpose
ShippingPayment	The ShippingPayment associated with this object
ModifiedOnly	If true, serializes only modified properties

Table 5-13. Properties of the ShippingRegionsSerializer Class

Property	Purpose
ShippingRegions	The ShippingRegions associated with this object
ModifiedOnly	If true, serializes only modified properties

Examining the eBay SimpleList Sample Application

When learning a new platform, it's always important to remember that there's more than one way to do something. In this spirit, let's take a look at the SimpleList example that accompanies the eBay SDK. Here, I'll examine the C# implementation, because the Perl implementation is straightforward: Prompt the user using console input/output for the item characteristics and then use an AddItemCall object to add the item to the service. The C# version, on the other hand, uses the extensive support of the Microsoft Windows GUI found in the .NET Framework to provide a simple GUI for listing items on eBay. Figures 5-1 and 5-2 show some of the GUI for the C# SimpleList application.

BORDERS

Merchandise presented for return, including sale or marked-down items must be accompanied by the original Borders store receipt. Returns must be completed within 30 days of purchase. The purchase price will refunded in the medium of purchase (cash, credit card or gift card). Items purchased by check may be returned for cash after 10 business days.

Merchandise unaccompanied by the original Borders store receipt, presented for return beyond 30 days from date of purchase, must carried by Borders at the time of the return. The lowest price offered the item during the 12 month period prior to the return will be refunded via a gift card.

Opened videos, discs, and cassettes may only be exchanged replacement copies of the original item.
Periodicals, newspapers, out-of-print, collectible and pre-owned items may not be returned.
Returned merchandise must be in saleable condition.

BORDERS

Merchandise presented for return, including sale or marked-down items must be accompanied by the original Borders store receipt. Returns must be completed within 30 days of purchase. The purchase price will refunded in the medium of purchase (cash, credit card or gift card). Items purchased by check may be returned for cash after 10 business days.

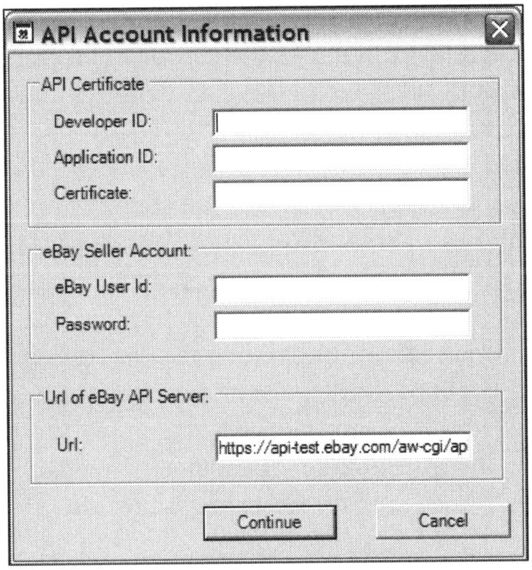

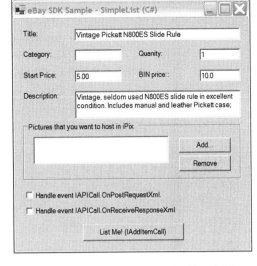

Figure 5-1. Authenticating your account in SimpleList

Figure 5-2. Listing your item in SimpleList

Authenticating the User

Figure 5-1 shows a more traditional user login screen than you've seen in the examples I provide elsewhere in this book. The SimpleList application prompts you for your eBay developer keys, as well as the seller's login and password. This is the exact opposite approach than taken in the examples you've seen, but is equally valid. This form is implemented in the AccountForm class; the only eBay-specific code is in mBtnContinue_Click. Listing 5-1 shows this method.

Listing 5-1. The mBtnContinue_Click Method of the AccountForm Class

```
1: private void mBtnContinue_Click( object sender,
2:                                      System.EventArgs e)
3: {
4:    mApiSession = new ApiSession();
5:
6:    mApiSession.LogCallXml = true;
7:    mApiSession.Application = mTxtApplicationId.Text;
8:    mApiSession.Developer = mTxtDeveloperId.Text;
9:    mApiSession.Certificate = mTxtCertificate.Text;
10:   mApiSession.RequestUserId = this.mTxtUser.Text;
11:   mApiSession.RequestPassword = this.mTxtUserPass.Text;
12:   mApiSession.Url = mTxtUrl.Text;
13: }
```

Pretty anticlimactic, wouldn't you say? The AccountForm class is essentially the same as the Config class for the sample applications in this book (which you can see in its entirety in the Appendix), prompting users for their account information and storing them in the eBay IAPISession for the application.

To implement a more modal-oriented login slip that actually authenticates the user, you can use the method that stores the session data to issue an eBay API call to verify the account and password. Two good choices are GeteBayOfficialTimeCall and GetLogoUrlCall. The former call returns the official time of the eBay clock, and you can use the result to determine the clock offset between the application host and eBay—good for when you need to precisely time events with the eBay service. The other, GetLogoUrlCall, returns the URL of the eBay logo your application can show in cobranding with eBay. This is an especially good choice if your application has an About box or similar information available from its main screen, because you can then update your application interface to meet any changes in content provided by eBay.

Whether to authenticate a user at the time the application is launched or when the application first issues an eBay API regarding application data depends on the nature of your application and the sensitivity of the data it maintains. Many applications, especially consumer applications, would do well to prompt for your credentials on first launch via a configuration wizard or the like, and then defer credential verification until you actually try to perform something meaningful with the eBay service. This reflects the current thinking in application design, minimizing the amount of interaction your application requires. Vertical applications, however, especially those used by more than one person, may well want to require an initial credential check via an eBay SDK API invocation before accessing application data to ensure data security and integrity.

Listing an Item

The SimpleList application uses the FormSimpleList class to list an item on eBay. Like the AccountForm class, the FormSimpleList class collects all of your user input, letting you describing the item to list and only interacting with eBay when you actually submit the item for sale. This is good design practice; it postpones application latency for as long as possible, while still holding the number of Web transactions with eBay to a minimum. (In the next chapter, you will learn about how the eBay Integration Library can also help you control application latency by *caching* eBay Web transactions via an intermediary database.) The interaction with eBay occurs in two methods, FillItemFields and BtnListItem_Click. Both are shown in Listing 5-2.

Listing 5-2. The FillItemFields and BtnListItem_Click Methods

```
1: private IItem FillItemFields()
2: {
3:    IItem item = new Item();
4:
5:    // Generate a unique UUID.
6:    item.Uuid = new eBay.SDK.Model.Uuid(true);
7:
8:    // If using other than 0 (US), make sure
9:    // LibraryManager.InternationUrl is defined and valid.
10:    item.SiteId = SiteIdEnum.US;
11:
12:    item.Title = mTitle.Text;
13:    item.Type = ItemTypes.Auction;
14:    item.Description = mDescription.Text;
15:    item.Currency = CurrencyEnum.USDollar;
16:    item.Location = "San Jose, CA";
17:    item.Country = "us";
18:    item.CategoryId = Int32.Parse(mCategory.Text);
19:    item.Quantity = Int32.Parse(mQuantity.Text);
20:    item.StartPrice = Decimal.Parse(mMinimunBid.Text);
21:    item.Duration = 3;
22:    item.BuyItNowPrice = Decimal.Parse(mBINPrice.Text);
23:    item.ReservePrice = 0;
24:    item.ListingFeatures.BoldTitle = true;
25:    item.PaymentTerms.SeeDescription = true;
26:    item.ShippingOptions.ShippingRange =
27:       ShippingRangeEnum.SiteOnly;
28:    item.ShippingOptions.ShippingPayment.WhoPay =
29:       WhoPayShippingEnum.BuyerPaysActual;
30:    return item;
31: }
32:
33: private void BtnListItem_Click( object sender,
34:                                 System.EventArgs e)
35: {
36:    // Now let's start listing the item.
37:    // Define your Item.
38:    IItem item = FillItemFields();
39:
40:    // Make AddItemCall from ebay SDK API.
41:    IAddItemCall api = new AddItemCall(mApiSession);
42:    api.ItemToAdd = item;
```

```
43:    api.ErrorLevel = ErrorLevelEnum.BothShortAndLongErrorStrings;
44:
45:    // Install event handlers.
46:    if( this.chkbOnPostRequestXml.Checked )
47:      api.OnPostRequestXml +=
48:        new FilterXmlHandler(this.HandleOnPostRequestXml);
49:
50:    if( this.chkbOnReceiveResponseXml.Checked )
51:      api.OnReceiveResposeXml +=
52:        new FilterXmlHandler(this.HandleOnReceiveResponseXml);
53:
54:    // Add all pictures that we selected for this item.
55:    // These pictures will be uploaded and hosted in iPix.
56:    //
57:    // iPix support is a feature of AddItemCall class,
58:    // not Item class.
59:    // Setting AddItemCall.PictureFiles will cause Item.PhotoUrl
60:    // and Item.PhotoCount to be ignored by AddItemCall.
61:
62:    foreach( string imgFile in ListBoxPictures.Items )
63:      api.PictureFiles.Add(imgFile);
64:
65:    // Always use Try/Catch to guard API calls.
66:    try
67:    {
68:      // IFees is returned with details of fee information.
69:      IFees ife = api.AddItem();
70:
71:      // If there's an error an exception will be thrown.
72:      // So when we get to here everything is OK.
73:      MessageBox.Show(
74:        "AddItem succeeded! The new item id is: " + item.ItemId);
75:    }
76:
77:    catch(APIException ex)
78:    {
79:      MessageBox.Show(
80:        "APIException - AddItem call failed: " + ex.Message);
81:    }
82:    catch(Exception ex)
83:    {
84:      MessageBox.Show(
85:        "Exception - AddItem call failed: " + ex.Message);
86:    }
87: }
```

The first method, FillItemFields, is straightforward, save line 6, which shows how to use the Uuid interface to create a new unique ID for an item to be added to eBay. After line 6, the remainder of the method simply copies data from the appropriate user interface objects and populates the newly created Item object (created on declaration on line 3). If you're new to C#, be sure to note the Parse method of classes such as Int32 and Decimal (lines 18, 19, and 20), which you can use to convert between a String object and an object of another class.

The heavy lifting of the SimpleList sample application is done by BtnListItem_Click, which creates an AddItemCall to add the item, uses FillItemFields to create and populate a new Item based on your user input, and then uses the AddItemCall.AddItem method to add the item to eBay. Starting on line 38, the method uses FillItemFields to create a unique ID for the item and gather its description and other characteristics from the application user interface. Next, on lines 41–43, the application creates and initializes api, the AddItemCall object. Lines 46–52 create *event handlers* for the outgoing and incoming XML; I discuss this in detail in the next section, "Intercepting the eBay API XML."

Lines 62–63 add the pictures of the item you select to the AddItemCall.PictureFiles property, instructing eBay to host the pictures on your behalf. By doing this, not only does the eBay server ignore the Item.PhotoUrl and Item.PhotoCount properties of the associated item, but it will upload the files named in the PictureFiles collection, making it easy for an Item to simultaneously submit pictures of an item for listing.

Lines 66–75 issue the AddItem call, contained within the obligatory try block that protects your application from embarrassing runtime failures because the Internet path to eBay is down or something else goes awry on the network. The eBay-written catch expressions on lines 77–86 are a little more descriptive than what I've shown you; they differentiate between generic .NET Framework Exception objects and API-generated exception objects, denoted by the APIException type.

Intercepting the eBay API XML

The eBay.SDK.API interfaces include the OnPostRequestXml and OnReceiveResponseXML properties through their common superclass APICall, which can store event handlers that the eBay SDK invokes when the underlying eBay API XML is composed or the eBay API XML response is received, respectively. These are fully qualified event handlers, and you may chain these event handlers as you would other .NET event handlers by simply adding new event handlers to the property using += (lines 46–52).

Using one of these event handlers, you can intercept the outgoing or incoming XML, delivered to your event handler in an FilterXmlEventArgs object. This class has one public property, the Xml property, which contains the outgoing or incoming XML. You can mutate this XML by assigning new XML to this property, although the most common use for this property is to simply view it for debugging purposes.

When first studying the underlying eBay API (see Chapters 8 and 9), I found it handy to dump the contents of this property to the console to check the XML I was using to invoke eBay API methods directly over HTTPS.

Representing Feedback with the Feedback Class and Its Collection, the FeedbackCollection Class

The eBay.SDK.Model.Feedback namespace contains two classes: the Feedback class and the FeedbackCollection class. Together, they let your application collect individual feedback items from specific transactions, or leave feedback for buyers of your products. Table 5-14 shows the properties of the Feedback class.

Table 5-14. Properties of the Feedback Class

Property	Purpose
AppData	A generic object to store application data. Not shared with the eBay service.
CommentingUserId	The user ID of the user who is leaving the feedback.
CommentingUserScore	The user feedback score of the user leaving the feedback.
CommentText	The comment text of the feedback entry.
CommentType	The type of feedback (an element of the CommentTypes enumeration, either Positive, Negative, or Neutral).
FeedbackRole	Indication of whether the user leaving feedback is leaving feedback ToBuyer or ToSeller.
Followup	The text left by the commenting user in response to the Response.
ItemId	The item pertaining to the feedback.
Response	The text left by the feedback recipient in response to the CommentText.
TimeOfComment	The time and date that the user left the comment entry.
TransactionId	The transaction to which this feedback pertains.

As you can see from Table 5-14, an exchange of feedback has at least two and at most four components:

- The CommentingUserScore, indicating the user score the commenting user gives the receiving user, a numeric value. A feedback item must have this value.

- The CommentText, a short note regarding the transaction. A feedback item must have this value.

- The Response, an optional text message left by the receiving user regarding the transaction.

- The Followup, an optional text message left by the commenting user in response to the Response.

The FeedbackCollection is simply a collection of Feedback objects, and you can treat it just as you would any other collection (see Chapter 3 for an example using the CategoryCollection, which shares the same base class and interface).

The eBay SDK API provides two classes that manipulate Feedback objects. The first, GetFeedbackCall, lets you obtain the history of feedback left for a specific user. The feedback is returned by *pages,* so that a single query doesn't necessarily return every feedback item left for a specific user. By breaking the query response into pages, you can optimize network access between your application and the server. The example in the next section shows you how to use GetFeedbackCall.

The other call, LeaveFeedbackCall, lets you leave feedback for a specific user with a specific Feedback object. In addition to filling its Comment field, you must specify the recipient of the feedback using the TargetUser field before invoking eBay.SDK.API.LeaveFeedbackCall.LeaveFeedback.

Key Points

In this chapter, you learned the following key points about how to manage items and user feedback with the eBay SDK.

- The eBay Item class and its IItem interface encapsulate the notion of an eBay item for sale.

- An eBay item is best thought of as an item for auction: Some auctions can have many discrete items, but still refer to only one Item object.

- The eBay.SDK.Model.Item namespace has a plethora of helper classes that encapsulate data for presentation via the Item object and its properties.

- When creating Item objects for listing via eBay, be sure to set its Uuid property to a freshly allocated eBay.SDK.Model.Uuid object.

- You can leave new feedback for a buyer or seller using the Feedback class and its IFeedback interface and the LeaveFeedbackCall.

- You can view the feedback exchanged between buyer and seller using the Feedback class and its IFeedback interface and GetFeedbackCall.

CHAPTER 6

Introducing the eBay Integration Library

IN THE LAST TWO CHAPTERS, you've learned how to directly access the eBay service via the eBay SDK. For many applications, the eBay SDK is ideal: It provides you with a data model and a slew of individual eBay SDK API calls to invoke specific operations on the eBay service on behalf of your application. For other applications, you may need to use the SDK in conjunction with an existing or new database to cache eBay content. Another tool atop the eBay SDK, the eBay Integration Library, lets you integrate your application with either a new or legacy database. Through the eBay Integration Library, your application downloads all pertinent information about your application's sellers, separates the data into the appropriate eBay data model objects, and stores them in the database. In turn, your application uses the eBay SDK via the Integration Library to fetch its data from the database, rather than making Internet requests to satisfy eBay API calls. In addition, the eBay Synchronization Library manages regular synchronization operations between your application's local database and the eBay service, ensuring that your application has access to an accurate snapshot.

In this chapter, I introduce the eBay Integration Library, and help you understand when you would want to design your application around it. You'll learn what you can do with the eBay Integration Library, what it requires from your application, and how to use it in general terms. As the chapter closes, you'll see two samples using the Integration Library: The first lets you manipulate categories stored in the Integration Database, and the other lets you peruse items associated with a specific eBay user.

Choosing the Integration Library

The Integration Library sits between your application, the eBay SDK, and the eBay service. Figure 6-1 shows a deployment diagram that describes the relationship between these parts.

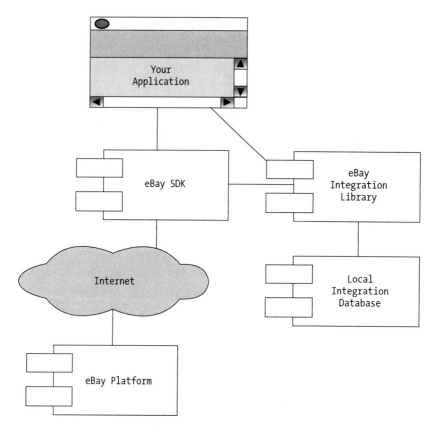

Figure 6-1. The relationship between your application, the Integration Library, the eBay SDK, and the eBay service

At a high level, you can think of the Integration Library as a cache that sits between your application and the eBay service. By using the Integration Library, you can batch your Web transactions to the eBay service, limiting the amount of latency your application users encounter when using eBay. Because the Integration Library stores all of the data pertaining to each of your application's selling users, the majority of data that they need is available locally. Moreover, your application uses the Integration Library to synchronize data between the local database and eBay, ensuring timely updates of the information.

This synchronization is a key aspect of the Integration Library. Many application developers new to Web services make an erroneous assumption: that because they can get the latest information from the application service, it's crucial that their application does so. Unfortunately, with few exceptions (such as stock or commodity transactions), this is seldom the case. Consider scenarios like these:

- Listing items for a hundred individual auctions

- Collecting the eBay categories for your application's user interface

- Leaving feedback for the buyers of your items

- Collecting the sales history of the items you've listed

- Collecting your eBay account activity and invoice so that you can reimburse eBay for their services

> **WARNING**   *Even though you're using the eBay Integration Library, you should be aware that the API calls it issues on your application's behalf still count against the allotment of API calls for your class of application.*

In all of these scenarios, although you require up-to-date and accurate information, you don't need to have information from eBay updated at the time you request the information, because it's highly unlikely that the data will change substantially between the time you synchronize the Integration Library database with eBay and the time you need the information. Moreover, if it does, odds are that the exact value at a specific instant in time (say, a high bid before an auction has closed) probably isn't relevant to your users, because what they need are rough estimates of true values. To balance up-to-date data with user expectations, you can tune your application's use of synchronization to ensure that the database has a relatively timely snapshot of the information you need.

> **TIP**   *In almost every application you write that uses eBay, you'll need some kind of cache to store intermediate results that don't change often. Sometimes, this cache need only persist while the application is running; when this is the case, in-memory structures are often adequate. Other applications require a cache that persists between application invocations. Why not consider using the Integration Library to provide that cache?*

There's a second reason you may choose to use the Integration Library. If you're developing an application that integrates the eBay service with a legacy database within your (or your customer's) organization, you can leverage the Integration Library to provide an interface from your application to that database. Unlike when you use the Integration Library with the database that's provided by eBay (see "Configuring a Database for the Integration Library" later in the chapter), you'll need to implement the glue that binds your database to the Integration Library (see "Integrating the eBay Integration Library with Your Legacy Database" later in the chapter). Although this sounds like a lot of work, it's not, and doing this gives you the advantage of being able to use eBay's robust data model framework, rather than needing to reinvent the wheel and come up with your own encapsulations for common eBay concepts such as users, items, categories, and accounts. The eBay SDK graciously provides a mind-bogglingly large amount of code that's already been carefully implemented and tested.

With the Integration Library, you can perform essentially the same transactions you would using the eBay data model objects I showed you in the last two chapters. Because in your application you use *interfaces* to eBay data model objects, rather than their underlying class implementation, it's often a simple thing to migrate an existing eBay application to use the Integration Library (or go the other way, making parts of your application bypass the Integration Library and interact with eBay directly).

It's quite likely that your application should leverage the Integration Library for much of its functionality, especially if you're deploying it to large-scale customers such as companies with an existing inventory database, or those customers who regularly move hundreds of items through eBay's auctions.

Understanding the eBay Integration Library Data Model

The eBay Integration Library uses a set of interfaces separate from the eBay SDK. To help keep these concepts separate, the engineers at eBay created a new namespace, eBay.SDK.Integration. This namespace contains the interfaces and classes specific to the Integration Library, so when using the library, you need to either reference the library objects you use within the namespace or include the namespace in your program with the using directive, depending on the language you use.

The namespace contains a host of interfaces, the most important of which are the following:

- IDataStore, which represents the database within the Integration Library and manages the database configuration.

- IEnvironment, which encapsulates your user's and application's credentials for accessing eBay. It's similar to the IApiSession the eBay SDK itself uses, but more robust, and is where you set your eBay developer keys, the URL for the eBay server to use, and so on.

- IAppUser, which represents a seller using the application and Integration Library to communicate with eBay.

- IEBaySession, which provides the working session to eBay that lets you manage items, sales, feedback, and such. The IEBaySession provides methods that let you synchronize items between the database and eBay.

Using the eBay Integration Library

As you've doubtlessly learned by now, there's no such thing as a free lunch. Although eBay doesn't charge for the Integration Library (the terms of use are the same as they are for the eBay SDK), using the Integration Library does require you to make some changes to your application and provide a database the Integration Library can use. This isn't hard, and the investment you make up front can pay great dividends in your application, especially if you *need* to integrate with an existing database anyway.

Configuring a Database for the Integration Library

The easiest way to use the Integration Library is with the presupplied Microsoft Access or Microsoft SQL Server, databases provided by the SDK, which you can find in the eBay SDK's Database directory. (If you're using Microsoft SQL Server, you need to import the eBay database schema into your database server by following the instructions in the Database directory in the file SQL Server/Readme.txt.) If you're using a legacy database, you can skip the following information and read the next section.

> **NOTE** *You may be tempted to use the Integration Library with another database that's compliant with OLEDB, ODBC, or ADO. If you do, bear in mind that you will need to initialize the database with the same tables you find in the sample databases provided by eBay in the SDK.*

Once you've installed the database where it belongs, you must configure it using the eBay Database Configuration Wizard. This is an easy process; simply launch the wizard, select whether you want to configure a Microsoft Access or a Microsoft SQL Server database, enter your database's login credentials, and the wizard does the rest. Once it's done, it presents a screen that indicates the successful configuration of the eBay SDK and creates a file called eBaySales.exe.config, which contains the configuration information the Integration Library needs to access the database. The key entity in this file you'll need is the DBConnection field, which looks something like this:

```
1: <add key="DbConnection"
2:     value="Provider=Microsoft.Jet.OLEDB.4.0;
3:     Data Source=C:\Program Files\eBay\SDK\Database\eBaySdk.mdb;
4:     Persist Security Info=False;
5:     Jet OLEDB:Database Password=SecretKey;
6:     Jet OLEDB:Encrypt Database=True" />
```

> **WARNING**   *I've broken up the* value *string in this listing at semicolons to help make it more readable for you. When you access this file,* don't *add carriage returns!*

This string defines the connection to the database the eBay Integration Library will use. The wizard creates this string on your behalf when you specify the kind of database to use (Microsoft Access or Microsoft SQL Server), the security information, and whether or not the database should be kept encrypted.

In all but the most special cases, you probably won't need a detailed view into the schema of the eBay Integration Library database. The organization is actually quite simple. There's an intuitive pairing between data model items and database tables as described here:

- `AppData` (which isn't shared with the eBay service), which contains the `AppData` fields of each item stored in the database. Unlike when you use the eBay SDK alone, this field contains additional Integration Library information, so you shouldn't overwrite it.

- `AppUsers`, which contains the application's users (each an eBay seller with an associated `IUser` object).

- `Categories`, which contains the `ICategory` interfaces.

- `Feedbacks`, which contains the various feedback messages left for eBay users.

- `Items`, which contains information about each of the items managed by the users. This table relies on the `ItemImages` table, which contains item images, and the `ItemPropertiesMapping` table, which maps records in the `Properties` table with individual records in the `Items` table.

- The `Sales` table, which contains information about the sales of items on eBay.

- The `Users` table, which contains information about eBay users, both the application users referenced in the `AppUsers` table and other users the application users interact with in the course of an auction.

Moreover, the data model for Integration Library is as follows:

- All `IItem` objects are standard among objects that belong to certain users.

- Each `IItem` object may have one or multiple `ISale` objects associated with it.

- Each ISale object is associated with one item and one buyer.

- Optionally, each ISale object can have up to two IFeedback objects associated with it: one for the buyer and one for the seller.

One thing to consider when using the Integration Library is that there's no
reason why your application can't add additional tables to the database for its
own purposes. For example, one of the eBay samples adds a Resources table to the
database to store application-specific resources. Something else worth thinking
about as you develop your application is that while the Integration Database is
local, it doesn't have to reside on the same machine as your application. For
example, if your application is to help medium-sized businesses sell their products
on eBay, you can choose to use a single database for the entire company, and
have your application interact with eBay via that central server. In other words,
the word *local* really pertains to the fact that the Integration Library's database
resides outside of eBay, not necessarily meaning that it's on the same computer
as that which executes your eBay application. This fact gives you as the developer
a great deal of latitude when designing the deployment environment for your
application.

Integrating the eBay Integration Library with Your Legacy Database

Using the Integration Library with a legacy database is a bit more difficult because
the Integration Library has no knowledge of your database or its schema.
Consequently, it's up to you to provide the connections between data model objects
and your database. Typically, this is an exercise in *serialization,* the process of
converting a memory-resident object to a format appropriate for storage in your
database. In doing so, you'll replace methods such as IEBaySession.SaveItem, which
saves an IItem to the database, with code that saves an IItem to your database in
whatever format you require.

In addition, you're responsible for providing the code that synchronizes
your database with the eBay service. This functionality, provided by the
IEBaySynchronizer, is required because without it, your application can communicate to your database and to eBay via the SDK, but once your application
places objects in your database, you still need to synchronize them with eBay.
Moreover, the synchronization interface can speed your application's performance,
precaching information during synchronization that your application will use
later as it executes.

Using the eBay Integration Library in Your Application

Once you've resolved the choice of using an eBay-provided database or your own, the next thing is to add the eBay Integration Library to your application. The process is actually quite simple.

1. Include the eBay.Model.Integration namespace in your application with a using directive.

2. On application initialization, create an IDataStore instance.

3. Using the freshly created IDataStore, call its Connect method to establish a connection to the database with a valid connection string.

4. Obtain your application's environment variable to connect to the database using the IDataStore.LoadEnvironment method. You'll want to verify that its fields are correctly populated; if not, prompt the user for corrections and save the results using IDataStore.SaveEnvironment.

5. Use the resulting IEnvironment.UserManager to fetch an IAppUser instance.

6. Call IDataStore.GetEBaySession to obtain an IEBaySession instance.

7. If you've just created a new user, you should synchronize its representation from eBay by calling IEBaySession.EBaySynchronizer.SynchronizeCategories. You should also call ImportItemsFromEBay and GetFeedbacksFromEBay to bring the IItems and Feedback that pertain to the new user into the local database.

These steps are shown in pseudocode modeled in C# syntax in Listing 6-1; I'll show you the Perl syntax a little later in this section.

Listing 6-1. Initializing the Integration Library in Your Application (C#)

```
1: private void startup
2: {
3:    eBay.SDK.Integration.DataStore dataStore;
4:    eBay.SDK.Integration. Environment environment;
5:    try
6:    {
7:       int myEnv = (int)eBay.SDK.Integration.EnvironmentEnum.SANDBOX;
8:       dataStore = new eBay.SDK.Integration.DataStore ();
```

```
 9:      dataStore.Connect( this.DBConfiguration);
10:      environment = dataStore.LoadEnvironment( myEnv );
11:      this.UserManager = environment.UserManager;
12:      this.User = this.UserManager.LoadUser(
13:         this.CurrentUserAppId );
14:      this.EBaySession = dataStore.GetEBaySession( this.User );
15:   }
16:   catch{ Exception e }
17:   {
18:     // Do something useful.
19:     Close (); // Close the application if needed.
20:     dataStore.Disconnect();
21:   }
22: }
```

This pseudocode assumes that the application has already gotten its connection preferences (which you generate using the eBay Database Configuration Wizard) from the registry or a configuration file, and placed the database's connection info in the DBConfiguration property, and the current user's application ID (see "Moving Data Between Your Application and the Database: The IEBaySession Interface" later in this chapter) in the property CurrentUserAppId.

As is always the case, the eBay code is wrapped in a try/catch block (lines 5–15), so that if the eBay SDK fails to establish a connection to your database, it doesn't crash your entire application. The code begins by connecting to the database (line 9). If this is successful, the application gets a reference to the data store's IEnvironment on line 10 so that it can use its UserManager (lines 11–13) to load the local representation of the current eBay user and store it in the User property (lines 12–13). Finally, the code uses the freshly obtained user to get a reference to the EBaySession for the application.

Now here's Listing 6-2, which shows the Perl syntax for adding the Integration Library to your application.

Listing 6-2. Initializing the Integration Library in Your Application (Perl)

```
1: sub InitIntegrationLibrary
2: {
3:   my $appuserid = shift;
4:
5:   $datastore = Win32::OLE->new(
6:      "eBay.SDK.Integration.DataStore" );
7:   $datastore->Connect( $dbConfiguration );
8:   my $result = Win32::OLE->LastError();
```

```
 9:    die $result if $result;
10:
11:    $environment = $datastore->LoadEnvironment(
12:       EnvironmentEnum_SANDBOX );
13:
14:    $appuser = $environment->{UserManager}->LoadUser(
15:       $appuserid );
16:    $result = Win32::OLE->LastError();
17:    die $result if $result;
18:
19:    $session = $datastore->GetEBaySession( $appuser );
20:    my $result = Win32::OLE->LastError();
21:    die $result if $result;
22: }
```

This code is essentially the same as the C# version, of course. The function begins by setting aside the incoming application user ID (needed to obtain the eBay session for the user) on line 3. After that, it establishes a connection to the database using a new eBay.SDK.Integration.DataStore object on lines 3–9. Next, on lines 11–12, you specify the environment you want to use (in this case, the eBay Sandbox), which you use on lines 14–17 to load the specified user. Finally, on lines 19–21, you get the eBay session.

Whether you use C# or Perl, the EBaySession object is your primary entry point to access eBay data using the Integration Library. It provides several key pieces of functionality to synchronize access rules and categories, import a seller's item list, list new items, and perform end of auction processing:

- You can load an item or details about an item, or save an item or items to the database.

- You can obtain information about the sale of an item on eBay.

- You can get information about the buyer of an item in an auction on eBay.

- You can review user feedback or leave feedback for buyers given a specific sale ID for an item.

- You can list or relist items on eBay by creating the item in the database and synchronizing the item with eBay.

With each of these functions, the results are data model objects, letting you focus on the data model for your application, relying on the work done by eBay engineers in designing the data model for eBay.

Working with Synchronization

When using the Integration Library, it's crucial to remember that the changes you make to objects are stored in the *local* database, not the eBay service. To make changes to objects that persist on the eBay service, you must *synchronize* your application database with the eBay service. You do this using two interfaces: the IEBaySession interface and the IEBaySynchronizer interface. The former provides an interface between your application and the Integration Library's database; it's analogous to the IAPICall interfaces you encountered in previous chapters. You use the latter interface to synchronize between the Integration Library's database and the eBay service.

Synchronization is a two-way process, although the methods let you select whether you're moving application data from your local application or database to its remote destination on the eBay service, or the reverse. The key to selecting which method to use is the inclusion of the words *Load*, *Save*, *FromEBay*, or *ToEBay* in the method name. Generally, *Load* indicates that the method takes a datum from the database and passes it to your application, while *Save* does the reverse. Similarly, *From* indicates that the datum comes from eBay, while *To* packages your datum from your database and sends it to eBay.

Moving Data Between Your Application and the Database: The IEBaySession Interface

The IEBaySession interface lets you move data between your application and the local Integration Database. Table 6-1 shows the methods of the IEBaySession database.

Table 6-1. A Summary of Methods of the IEBaySession Interface

Method	Purpose
CalculateListingFees	Determines the listing fees for an item. Uses eBay.SDK.API.VerifyAddItem.
CloneItem	Makes a copy of an existing Item in the database.
DeleteFeedbackToBuyer	Deletes an unsynchronized feedback to a buyer.
FindFeedback	Searches the Feedbacks table of the database for feedback by user, role, and item.
FindSale	Finds the sale record for a given user and item.
GetAppItemIDList	Returns the IDs of all items in the database that match the given status.

Table 6-1. A Summary of Methods of the IEBaySession Interface (continued)

Method	Purpose
GetBuyerIdList	Returns the eBay user ID of all buyers in the database.
GetItemsCount	Returns the number of items in the database with the specified status.
GetPendingItemsCount	Returns a count of the unsynchronized items in the database.
GetSaleIdList	Gets a list of the IDs of all sales in the database.
LeaveFeedbackToBuyer	Leaves feedback to the buyer of an item in a sale.
LoadBothFeedbacks	Loads feedback from seller to buyer and the reverse from the database.
LoadBuyer	Loads a specified buyer from the database.
LoadBuyers	Loads a collection of buyers from the database.
LoadFeedback	Loads feedback from buyer or seller from the database.
LoadItem	Loads an item from the database.
LoadItemDetails	Selectively loads IItem properties from the database.
LoadItems	Loads items matching the specified criteria.
LoadItemSales	Loads all sales of an item by application ID specific to the database.
LoadItemSalesByEBayId	Loads all sales of an item given the item's eBay ID.
LoadItemSet	Loads items with specified application IDs.
LoadSale	Loads a sale.
LoadSales	Loads sales belonging to an application user.
RelistUnsoldItem	Relists an unsold item.
SaveBuyer	Saves an eBay user as a buyer.
SaveFeedback	Saves feedback to the database.
SaveItem	Saves an item to the database.
SaveItems	Saves a list of items to the database.
SaveSale	Saves a sale to the database.
SetItemStatus	Sets the AppStatus field in a list of application item IDs to the specified value.

Even a quick glance at Table 6-1 shows a proliferation of IDs: sales, users, buyers. Items all have their own IDs, as you might imagine, just as they do on the eBay service. But what about the new kid on the block, the application ID? This is simply the ID of an item in the database assigned *before* the item is synchronized with the eBay service. It's the primary key for an item—you use it when referring to items created locally. While it's admittedly a bit of a headache to juggle two IDs for the same conceptual thing, it's not as bad as it sounds, and it's a very reasonable way to solve the problem of assigning new items unique IDs without actually interacting with the eBay service.

> **TIP**   *If you need to find the unique ID of a data model object such as an* IItem *you're working with that originated with the application library, you can get it by casting its* AppData *property to the appropriate* AppData *object (such as* ItemAppData*) and accessing its ID field (such as* AppItemId*).*

Although the library provides collections for most objects, some of the methods use the .NET Framework DataSet class to represent in memory a snapshot of a search result, such as a collection of buyers. The DataSet class, a keystone in the ADO.NET architecture, contains a collection of objects that represent each of the tables in a relational database. Using a DataSet object, you can obtain XML representations of the object's schema and data as well as slice and dice the data much as you would if it were in an SQL database, only more conveniently in your implementation.

In all but a few cases, instead of needing to deal with a DataSet object, Integration Library collections use the same ICollection interface you encountered in the last three chapters. This includes the IAppUserCollection, IItemImageCollection, IPropertyCollection, and IIntCollection collections, among others. The last collection, IIntCollection, is used to provide collections of integer IDs for application database objects; it's the same as other collections, save that it provides a type-safe mechanism for collecting integers.

> **TIP**   *Because the* IEBaySession *interface is responsible for communications between your application and the local database, you don't need to use it if you're working with an existing database. You can, however, model your application's legacy database interface after the* IEBaySession *interface, which eases your design burden by modeling after a well-documented and functional interface to the local database. In fact, if you implement the interface exactly, you can switch between an eBay-provided database and the legacy database during testing, making quality assurance and upgrades easier too!*

Moving Data Between Your Database and the eBay Service: The IEBaySynchronizer Interface

The IEBaySession interface does little for your application without the ability to move data to and from the eBay service. This functionality is provided by the IEBaySynchronizer interface, which, as its name suggests, synchronizes records in the local database with the eBay service. Table 6-2 shows the methods of this interface.

> **NOTE** *You must remember that while the Integration Library synchronizes data between your local database and the eBay service via the IEBaySynchronizer interface, it does so* only *at your application's behest! It's imperative that you include the triggers for database synchronization in your application's design; otherwise, as you implement your application, you're left with a local database that doesn't communicate with eBay, and you would have to shoehorn in the necessary synchronization sessions.*

Table 6-2. Methods of the IEBaySynchronizer Interface

Method	Purpose
GetFeedbacksFromEbay	Retrieves the feedback from eBay associated with an eBay user.
ImportItemsFromEBay	Retrieves the items associated with a specific user from eBay.
LeaveFeedbacksToEBay	Sends feedback in the database to eBay.
ListItemsToEBay	Lists items in the database not previously listed with eBay on eBay.
RelistItemsToEBay	Relists items in the database not previously relisted with eBay on eBay.
SynchronizeCategories	Updates the categories in the database with those on eBay.
SynchronizeClock	Determines the clock offset between eBay and the system clock, and uses the offset in subsequent local database interactions.
UpdatePricesFromEBay	Updates prices for sold items, but does no end auction processing.
UpdateSalesFromEBay	Updates the sales information for items in the database.
UpdateUserDetailsFromEBay	Updates user information from eBay.

The question of *when* to synchronize is actually far more difficult than *how* to synchronize, because to a large extent it depends on the nature of your application. Some applications, like those that run continually, interacting with a database as if they were running on a mainframe system, would do well to simply synchronize periodically or when they detect a certain number of local changes to objects. This is also likely to be the case with server-oriented applications, such as those that provide a Web front end to a seller's database of items and transactions. Smaller applications may choose to *schedule* synchronizations, waking a synchronization component at times when the user's system is otherwise idle, to reduce the latency of network interaction. Perhaps the simplest mechanism for your application is the most effective: user-initiated synchronization, once the user has finished interacting with the objects in the local database. The path you choose depends entirely on your user interface.

Using the Integration Library with Items in C#

Arguably the best sample that accompanies the eBay SDK is the MiniEBay application, which you can find in the folder SDK/Samples/VB.NET/IntegrationLibraryDemo. It's in Visual Basic .NET, not C#, however.

To help you see how to use the Integration Library, I present the IntegrationDemo, which offers the basic functionality necessary to log in as a user of the eBay Integration Library, list items pending for sale, at auction, or sold on eBay, and add new items to list on eBay. The application has three user interface elements, shown in Figures 6-2, 6-3, and 6-4, as well as a host of ancillary error dialog box messages presented by exception handlers.

Figure 6-2 shows the login form of the application. The first time you launch the application, you can enter an existing eBay account name, e-mail address, and password to log in. Once you do, the form memorizes—saves for future use—the user information and adds the eBay account to the list on the left-hand side, so that in subsequent sessions, you can log in by picking an eBay account name and clicking the Login button.

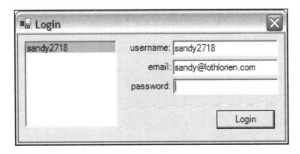

Figure 6-2. Logging in to the IntegrationDemo sample application

Figure 6-3 shows the main form of the application, which is dominated by the large ListView control in the center, enumerating each of the items you listed. Along the bottom are buttons to let you create a new item to list, update the categories in the eBay Integration Library database, configure the application keys, and log out (returning to the form shown in Figure 6-2).

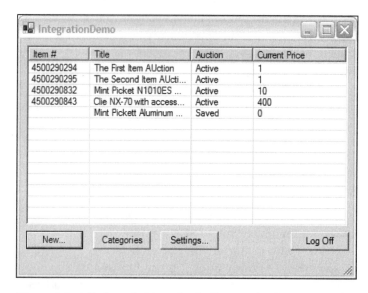

Figure 6-3. A listing of objects in the IntegrationDemo sample application

Figure 6-4 shows the new item form, which lets you enter the bare information necessary to add an item first to the eBay Integration Library database and from there to eBay to list a new item.

Figure 6-4. Creating a new item in the IntegrationDemo sample application

As you use the application, it interacts with both the eBay Integration Library database *and* the eBay service at critical points:

- When you first log in, if you are logging in as a user who hasn't used the application before, it loads all items associated with your eBay account into the database. Otherwise, it simply updates the synchronization library with any changes.

- When you click the button named Categories, the application synchronizes the eBay Integration Library categories with the eBay service.

- When you create a new item, the application saves it in the database.

- When you log off, the application sends new items to the eBay service to be listed as new items for auction.

Initializing the eBay Integration Library

The responsibility of initializing the eBay Integration Library belongs to the main form, SampleApp. This form has two properties to facilitate initializing the eBay Integration Library and accessing the library from the application's other forms:

- The Environment property returns the eBay IEnvironment.

- The AppUser property returns the eBay IAppUser for the user currently used by the eBay session.

The Environment property is initialized by LoadEnvironment, which the SampleApp constructor invokes. Listing 6-3 shows the LoadEnvironment method.

Listing 6-3. The LoadEnvironment Method

```
 1: private void LoadEnvironment()
 2: {
 3:    // Create the integration datastore.
 4:    dataStore = new eBay.SDK.Integration.DataStore ();
 5:    // Connect it to the default database.
 6:    try
 7:    {
 8:      dataStore.Connect( dbConfig );
 9:      // Load the database's environment.
10:      environment = dataStore.LoadEnvironment(
11:        (int)eBay.SDK.Integration.EnvironmentEnum.SANDBOX );
12:    }
```

```
13:    catch
14:    {
15:      MessageBox.Show( this,
16:        "Could not connect to the Integration Database.",
17:        "Error"  );
18:      this.Close ();
19:        dataStore.Disconnect();
20:    }
21: }
```

The method first attempts to connect to the database using the SampleApp field dbConfig; the LoadKeys method initializes from an element of the ebayrc file. (See the Appendix for a detailed description of the sample application framework, including how it manages the ebayrc file.) Both the attempt to connect to the database (line 8) and the subsequent initialization of the environment variable on lines 10–11 (which other classes access via the Environment property) are wrapped in the obligatory try/catch block to ensure that in the event of an error, the application notifies the user with a meaningful error message before aborting the application (lines 15–18).

With the IEnvironment in hand, the application needs to create an IEBaySession in order to access the eBay Integration Library. In order to obtain this, you must first provide a valid user of the eBay service. Obtaining this information is the responsibility of the LoginForm class, which prompts you to enter a user; when you click the Login button, it creates an IAppUser instance with the entered user credentials and uses the application's AppUser property to finish the startup process. Listing 6-4 shows login_Click, which does the work of creating an IAppUser object.

Listing 6-4. The login_Click Method of the LoginForm Class

```
1: private void login_Click(object sender, System.EventArgs e)
2: {
3:    int i;
4:    IAppUser appUser;
5:    bool found = false;
6:
7:    if ( username.Text == null || username.Text.Length == 0 ||
8:        email.Text == null || email.Text.Length == 0 ||
9:        password.Text == null || password.Text.Length == 0 )
10:      return;
11:
12:    // First, if the user's not in the user array, add it.
13:    for ( i = 0; i < userID.Count; i++ )
14:    {
15:      if ( userID[i].ToString() == username.Text )
```

```
16:     {
17:         found = true;
18:         break;
19:     }
20:   }
21:
22:   if ( found )
23:   {
24:       appUser = App.LoadUser(userAppId[ i ] );
25:   }
26:   else
27:   {
28:     appUser = App.NewUser( username.Text,
29:                     password.Text,
30:                     email.Text);
31:     userID.Add( username.Text );
32:     userPassword.Add( password.Text );
33:     userEmail.Add( email.Text );
34:     userAppId.Add( appUser.AppUserId.ToString() );
35:   }
36:
37:
38:   // Next, set the application's user ID field.
39:   App.AppUser = appUser;
40:
41:   // Finally, close the login form.
42:   this.Close();
43:   // And tell the user interface to log in to eBay.
44:   App.Login( true );
45: }
```

After declaring the necessary locals, the method performs some simple sanity checking on lines 7–10, ensuring that you didn't enter only part of the necessary eBay access information. The form itself keeps the list of user account information in a trio of arrays, backed by a file on disk accessed by the methods LoadUsers and SaveUsers (which I omit here for brevity). Lines 13–20 search the arrays to determine whether the user credentials you entered are for a previously accessed user; if they are, the eBay application user ID will be available, or if not, the application must create a new IAppUser for the information you entered.

If the application recognizes the user credentials you entered (lines 22–26), it creates the application user object by using the UserManager.LoadUser method of the application's EBayEnvironment. Because this method takes an application user ID, it's imperative that your application store it somewhere. In this application, you choose to store it in a flat text file; by comparison, the eBay MiniEBay sample application uses a separate table in the eBay database, and accesses the information using a database query. If, on the other hand, you entered information for a new user, the application must create a new IAppUser object (lines 28–37). After creating the user using the application's NewUser helper method, it updates the form's arrays with the new user account name, e-mail address, and password, and updates the file with the new user information. Regardless, the method then sets the application's AppUser with the newly created IAppUser object.

Loading an existing user is trivial; in fact, the LoginForm could do it on its own with the interfaces offered by SampleApp, as you can see in Listing 6-5.

Listing 6-5. The LoadUser Method of the SampleApp Class

```
 1: public IAppUser LoadUser( string id )
 2: {
 3:    IAppUser result = null;
 4:
 5:    try
 6:    {
 7:      result = environment.UserManager.LoadUser(
 8:        int.Parse( id ) );
 9:    }
10:    catch
11:    {
12:      result = null;
13:    }
14:    return result;
15: }
```

No surprises here: The LoadUser method just returns the AppUser it obtains from the IEnvironment's UserManager, or null in the event of any errors.

Creating the new user isn't hard, either; the application does it in a few lines with the NewUser method, which you can see here in Listing 6-6.

Listing 6-6. The NewUser Method

```
 1: public IAppUser NewUser( string id,
 2:                 string password,
 3:                 string email )
 4: {
 5:    IAppUser ebayUser = new AppUser( EBayEnvironment );
 6:    ebayUser.EBayUserId = id;
 7:    ebayUser.Password = password;
 8:    ebayUser.Email = email;
 9:
```

```
10:  try
11:  {
12:     EBayEnvironment.UserManager.SaveUser( ebayUser );
13:     bNewUser = true;
14:     return ebayUser;
15:  }
16:  catch
17:  {
18:     return null;
19:  }
20: }
```

This method just calls SaveUser on the application's environment (line 12), after creating the new AppUser instance on entry (line 5) and initializing it with its incoming arguments. I originally debated placing SaveUser in the LoginForm class, except that when you create a new AppUser instance, after initializing the IEBaySession with the new AppUser instance, you need to use the session to obtain a one-time image of the user's existing items. After you log in, the application checks the bUser flag when updating the eBay Integration Library.

Fetching Data from eBay

The last thing that happens when you log in, on line 52 of Listing 6-3, is that the LoginForm class instance invokes the application's Login method, responsible for obtaining the latest items for you from eBay and placing the results in the eBay Integration Library Database. Listing 6-7 shows the Login method.

Listing 6-7. Logging In to eBay Using the Login Method of the SampleApp Class

```
1: public void Login( bool bSyncEBay )
2: {
3:    // Update the contents from eBay.
4:    if ( bSyncEBay )
5:    {
6:       DownloadUser();
7:       DownloadItems();
8:
9:       // Now update the user interface.
10:      UpdateItemView();
11:   }
12:
13:   itemView.Show();
```

```
14:    newItemButton.Show();
15:    updateCategoriesButton.Show();
16:    loginButton.Text = "Log Off";
17: }
```

Login takes a single argument, a flag named bSyncEBay, indicating whether
the application should synchronize or not when you first log in. If this flag is true,
the application first updates the user information by calling the application's
DownloadUser method on line 6 and then updates individual item data by calling the application's DownloadItems on line 7. Once it does this, it updates the
user interface by placing each of the items in the database associated with the
user using UpdateItemView on line 10, and then updates the status of each of the
buttons and changes the label of the login button on lines 13–16.

DownloadUser is straightforward; it only downloads information about new
users, as you can see from Listing 6-8.

Listing 6-8. Updating a New User's Data in DownloadUser

```
1: public void DownloadUser()
2: {
3:    // Set the cursor to busy.
4:    Cursor.Current = Cursors.WaitCursor;
5:
6:    // Update the status line.
7:    try
8:    {
9:      // Update the user info.
10:      session.EBaySynchronizer.UpdateUserDetailsFromEBay();
11:      user = session.LoadBuyer(appUser.EBayUserId);
12:
13:      if ( bNewUser)
14:      {
15:        session.EBaySynchronizer.ImportItemsFromEBay( );
16:        session.EBaySynchronizer.GetFeedbacksFromEBay(
17:          eBay.SDK.Model.SiteIdEnum.US );
18:      }
19:    }
20:    catch
21:    {
22:      Logoff( false );
23:      MessageBox.Show( this,
24:                       "Could not connect to eBay.",
25:                       "Error" );
```

```
26:    }
27:    bNewUser = false;
28:
29:    // Set the cursor to normal.
30:    Cursor.Current = Cursors.Default;
31: }
```

The routine begins by setting the cursor to `WaitCursor` on line 4, to indicate that the application is busy, even though in most cases it doesn't take very long. Next, it updates the local database with your user information by calling `UpdateUserDetailsFromEBay`, a method of the synchronizer (recall that all methods that communicate between the service and the database are methods of the `IEBaySynchronizer` interface). Next, it calls `LoadBuyer`, to update the application's notion of the current user with the latest information from the database, replacing the `IAppUser` instance created during the login process with the resulting `IAppUser` object.

If you logged in with a new eBay account, the application must download the items and feedback relating to you (lines 17–19). It's imperative that you *only* do this for a new user, because this is an expensive operation, and can significantly slow your application if a user has a large number of objects or feedbacks. (In fact, unnecessarily invoking either `ImportItemsFromEBay` or `GetFeedbacksFromEBay` can cause your application to fail eBay logo certification, because of the load these methods can incur on eBay servers.)

If anything goes wrong, the application ends the user session by calling its `Logoff` method (which I discuss later in the section "Sending Data to eBay") and displaying a simple error message to the user on lines 20–26.

You can see `DownloadItems`, the application method that is the item analogue of `DownloadUser`, in Listing 6-9.

Listing 6-9. The DownloadItems Method

```
1: public void DownloadItems()
2: {
3:    // Set the cursor to busy.
4:    Cursor.Current = Cursors.WaitCursor;
5:
6:    // Do the sync.
7:    try
8:    {
9:      session.EBaySynchronizer.UpdatePricesFromEBay();
10:     session.EBaySynchronizer.UpdateSalesFromEBay();
11:   }
12:   catch
13:   {
```

```
14:      Logoff( false );
15:      MessageBox.Show( this,
16:                          "Could not connect to eBay.",
17:                          "Error" );
18:   }
19:
20:   // Set the cursor to normal.
21:   Cursor.Current = Cursors.Default;
22: }
```

This method is a little simpler. After setting the cursor to indicate that the application is busy (line 4), it updates the prices for items at auction on eBay (line 9), and updates the data for any items that have sold since the last update (line 10). As with DownloadUser, these calls are wrapped in a try/catch block, and the application forces the end of the user session if either fail. Finally, the method restores the cursor on line 21 before returning control to the user.

Once Login completes, you can peruse the ListView of items at your leisure, or click the button labeled New to create a new item and save it in the Integration Database.

Enumerating Items Cached by the eBay Integration Library

To fill the ListView, the application obtains IItemCollections from the eBay Integration Library for active (items at auction), sold, pending, and saved items, and adds each item in each collection to the ListView. Listing 6-10 shows UpdateItemView, which does this.

Listing 6-10. Updating the ListView with Items

```
1: public void UpdateItemView()
2: {
3:    IItemCollection activeItems = null;
4:    IItemCollection soldItems = null;
5:    IItemCollection pendingItems = null;
6:    IItemCollection savedItems = null;
7:
8:    itemView.Items.Clear();
9:
10:   // First, snag the data from eBay Integration Library.
11:   try
12:   {
```

```
13:     activeItems = session.LoadItems( AppStatusEnum.Active );
14:     soldItems = session.LoadItems( AppStatusEnum.Sold );
15:     pendingItems = session.LoadItems( AppStatusEnum.PendingAdd );
16:     savedItems = session.LoadItems( AppStatusEnum.Saved );
17:   }
18:   catch
19:   {
20:     MessageBox.Show( this,
21:       "Could not connect to the Integration Database.", "Error" );
22:   }
23:   try
24:   {
25:     // Now, populate the ListView.
26:     foreach( IItem item in pendingItems )
27:     {
28:       ListViewItem viewItem =
29:         new ListViewItem( item.ItemId.ToString(), 0);
30:       viewItem.SubItems.Add( item.Title );
31:       viewItem.SubItems.Add( "Pending" );
32:       viewItem.SubItems.Add( item.CurrentPrice.ToString() );
33:       itemView.Items.Add( viewItem );
34:     }
35:
36:     foreach( IItem item in activeItems )
37:     {
38:       ListViewItem viewItem =
39:         new ListViewItem( item.ItemId.ToString(), 0 );
40:       viewItem.SubItems.Add( item.Title );
41:       viewItem.SubItems.Add( "Active" );
42:       viewItem.SubItems.Add( item.CurrentPrice.ToString() );
43:       itemView.Items.Add( viewItem );
44:     }
45:
46:     foreach( IItem item in soldItems )
47:     {
48:       ListViewItem viewItem =
49:         new ListViewItem( item.ItemId.ToString(), 0 );
50:       viewItem.SubItems.Add( item.Title );
51:       viewItem.SubItems.Add( "Sold" );
52:       viewItem.SubItems.Add( item.CurrentPrice.ToString() );
53:       itemView.Items.Add( viewItem );
54:     }
55:
56:     foreach( IItem item in savedItems )
```

```
57:     {
58:       ListViewItem viewItem =
59:         new ListViewItem( item.ItemId.ToString(), 0 );
60:       viewItem.SubItems.Add( item.Title );
61:       viewItem.SubItems.Add( "Saved" );
62:       viewItem.SubItems.Add( item.CurrentPrice.ToString() );
63:       itemView.Items.Add( viewItem );
64:     }
65:   }
66: }
67: catch
68: {
69:   MessageBox.Show( this,
70:     "Could not enumerate items.", "Error" );
71: }
```

The routine begins by clearing the ListView itemView on line 8, after declaring the IItemCollections that store the results from the local database. On lines 11–22, the code simply loads each item in the Active, Sold, PendingAdd, and Saved categories. LoadItems returns an IItemCollection of all the items associated with the current user that match the specific state.

> **NOTE** *If you want to load a single item, use* LoadItem. *Unlike* LoadItems, *however, you must first initialize an* Item *and pass it to* LoadItem. *In turn,* LoadItem *populates the fields of the* Item *you provided with the fields from the database for the item you seek.*

The loops on lines 27–35, 37–45, 47–55, and 57–65 add each item in each of the states to the itemView by creating a new ListViewItem and setting its fields to the item's Title, the state of the item (a compile-time string based on the result of the query), and the CurrentPrice and adding the newly created ListViewItem to the itemView's Items collection.

The try/catch blocks around these loops provide error handling in case the ListViewItem creation fails, or if the returned item can't be converted to a string.

eBay Pagination with the Integration Library

Just as this book went to press, eBay added *pagination* to the Integration Library interfaces, letting you obtain a subset of items. If an application is being used by a large seller that deals with large numbers of items, it may not be a good idea to load all items, buyers, or sales into memory at one time, since doing so may consume too much memory. To solve this issue, IEBaySession includes methods to handle a large volume of items, buyers, or sales by paginating the data.

1. GetAppItemIdList returns a list of only the IDs of all items that have a specified status. Call LoadItem or LoadItemDetails respectively for each AppItemId. Another method, LoadItemSet, lets you specify an array of item IDs that you want to load and return the loaded item instances for you.

2. GetSaleIdList and LoadSale help handle the pagination of sales data.

3. GetBuyerIdList and LoadBuyer help handle pagination of buyer data.

I discuss the general notion behind pagination in more detail in Chapter 9.

Creating New Items

When you click the button titled New, the application opens a new NewItemForm instance as shown here:

```
1: private void newItemButton_Click( object sender,
2:                                       System.EventArgs e)
3: {
4:    NewItemForm newItemForm = new NewItemForm();
5:
6:    newItemForm.App = this;
7:    newItemForm.ShowDialog( );
8: }
```

The newItemForm does all of the work of creating a new item in the aptly named NewItem method, which you can see here in Listing 6-11.

Listing 6-11. Creating a New Item with the Integration Database

```
1: private void NewItem()
2: {
3:    Item item = new Item();
```

```
 4:    ItemAppData appData = new ItemAppData();
 5:
 6:    appData.AppUserId = App.AppUser.AppUserId;
 7:    item.AppData = appData;
 8:
 9:    // Always, always set the status to PendingAdd or Save!
10:    appData.AppStatus = AppStatusEnum.PendingAdd;
11:
12:    // Now populate its fields.
13:    item.SiteId = SiteIdEnum.US;
14:    item.Type = ItemTypes.Auction;
15:    item.Title = title.Text;
16:    item.Description = description.Text;
17:    item.Currency = CurrencyEnum.USDollar;
18:    item.Location = "Santa Cruz, CA";
19:    item.Country = "us";        // two-character country code
20:
21:    item.CategoryId = int.Parse( category.Text);
22:    item.Quantity = 1;
23:    item.Duration = 5;
24:
25:    item.MinimumToBid = decimal.Parse( openingPrice.Text);
26:    item.ReservePrice = 0;
27:    item.PaymentTerms.SeeDescription = true;
28:    item.ShippingOptions.ShippingRange =
29:      ShippingRangeEnum.SiteOnly;
30:    item.ShippingOptions.ShippingPayment.SeeDescription = true;
31:    item.Uuid = new Uuid(true);
32:
33:    try
34:    {
35:      App.Session.SaveItem( item );
36:    }
37:    catch
38:    {
39:      MessageBox.Show( this,
40:              "Could not connect to the Integration Database.",
41:              "Error"  );
42:    }
43:    App.UpdateItemView( );
44: }
```

It's easy to create a new item, but if you don't include all of the necessary fields, the eBay Integration Library won't let you send the item to eBay, so it's important you take care to do it right. When creating a new item, you must include at least the following fields:

- `AppData`, an `IItem.AppData` instance.

- The `Item.AppData AppStatus` property, which indicates the item's state in the eBay database. If you set it to `AppStatusEnum.Save`, it is saved in the database and not sent to eBay during synchronizations; if you set it to `PendingAdd`, the item will be added to a new auction after the next synchronization.

- `SiteId`, indicating on which site the item should be listed.

- `Type`, indicating the type of item auction for which the item should be listed.

- `Title`, indicating the title of the auction.

- `Description`, describing the item.

- `Currency`, indicating the currency of the item's price information while at auction.

- `Location`, indicating the location of the seller.

- `Country`, indicating the country of the seller.

- `CategoryId`, indicating the item's category.

- `Quantity`, indicating how many physical items are for auction for this item's auction.

- `Duration`, indicating the number of days the item's auction should last.

- `PaymentTerms` for the item.

- `ShippingOptions` for the item, indicating to where you'll ship the item and how the seller should pay for shipping.

- `Uuid`, the item's unique item ID.

The `NewItem` method fills these properties on lines 6–31, using a combination of data from the form's input elements and reasonable defaults. In a real application, defaults such as the location (lines 18–19) should come from application preferences, not source code, of course.

Line 35 saves the item to the database. The application will synchronized the new item with eBay later, when you log out.

Sending Data to eBay

Updating the eBay service with the changed contents of the eBay Integration Library's database is the same in principle as what happens when you log in, except that instead of fetching items, the application sends items. All of this is triggered when you log off, in the application's Logoff method, shown here in Listing 6-12.

Listing 6-12. The Logoff Method

```
 1: public void Logoff( bool bSyncEBay)
 2: {
 3:    if ( bSyncEBay )
 4:    {
 5:      // Update items to eBay.
 6:      UploadItems();
 7:    }
 8:    itemView.Hide();
 9:    newItemButton.Hide();
10:    updateCategoriesButton.Hide();
11:    loginButton.Text = "Log In";
12:    loginForm.ShowDialog();
13:    dataStore.Disconnect();
14: }
```

If the method is invoked with the value true, the method will send any changes to the database to eBay using the UploadItems method (lines 3–7). After that, it simply updates the state of itemView, newItemButton, and updateCategoriesButton, respectively. Listing 6-13 shows the UploadItems method, which looks a lot like DownloadItems.

Listing 6-13. Sending Item Updates to the eBay Service

```
 1: public void UploadItems()
 2: {
 3:    // Set the cursor to busy.
 4:    Cursor.Current = Cursors.WaitCursor;
 5:
 6:    try
 7:    {
```

```
8:        session.EBaySynchronizer.ListItemsToEBay();
9:    }
10:   catch
11:   {
12:     MessageBox.Show( this,
13:                "Could not connect to eBay.", "Error" );
14:   }
15:
16:   // Set the cursor to normal.
17:   Cursor.Current = Cursors.Default;
18: }
```

The method first sets the cursor to WaitCursor, customary for network actions, and then uses the EBaySynchronizer's ListItemsToEBay method. When it's done, you see the obligatory error message presented on lines 12–13 if an error occurs; otherwise, the application restores the cursor.

Getting Status from the eBay Synchronization Library

The IntegrationDemo application doesn't have much by way of status notification—in fact, except for switching the cursor from Default to WaitCursor and back during network operations, there's no status notification at all unless an error occurs. This is a limitation of this application, not the eBay Integration Library. The eBay Integration Library can provide status to your application through a function it periodically invokes; you must simply register a function (in C#, a delegate; in other languages, it's a function pointer or a reference to a function) for the Integration Library to invoke. The application does this when setting the AppUser property, as you can see in Listing 6-14.

Listing 6-14. Creating and Registering a StatusListener to Obtain eBay Integration Library Status

```
1: public IAppUser AppUser
2: {
3:   set
4:   {
5:     this.appUser = value;
6:     try
7:     {
8:       session = dataStore.GetEBaySession( appUser );
9:
```

```
10:        // Create a new status listener.
11:        IStatusListener l = new StatusListener();
12:              l.RegisterStatusUpdate(
13:           new StatusListener.StatusUpdateDelegate(UpdateStatus) );
14:        session.StatusPublisher.AddListener( l );
15:      }
16:    catch
17:    {
18:      session = null;
19:    }
20:  }
21:  // Get follows, ommitted for brevity.
22: }
```

After saving aside the incoming value, the method begins on line 8 by initializing the class's `session` to a session with the given `appUser`. It then creates a new `StatusListener` instance, setting the notification function to the application's `UpdateStatus` method on lines 11–13. Finally, it adds the listener function to the `session`'s list of functions to receive notification.

The eBay Integration Library invokes the notification function you register with a string and a percentage complete. The `UpdateStatus` method simply prints the status message to the console (Listing 6-15).

Listing 6-15. Showing eBay Integration Library Status

```
1: void UpdateStatus( string message, int percent)
2: {
3:   System.Console.WriteLine( message );
4: }
```

Even if your application doesn't include more detailed status reporting, just as this one doesn't, logging status messages to the console or a file gives you a way to look under the hood and debug what the eBay Integration Library is doing on your behalf. If you'd like to provide more status reporting, you can use the `percent` argument to plot a progress bar or provide other feedback to the user.

Using the Integration Library with Categories in Perl

In Chapter 3, I promised you an opportunity to see how to access eBay categories in Perl using a Tk::TreeView control. The categories.pl sample, shown in Figure 6-5, does just that.

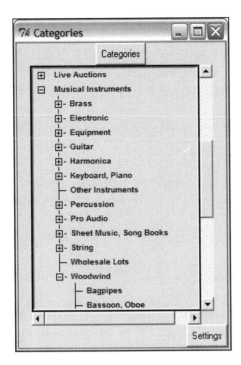

Figure 6-5. The categories.pl sample application

The application itself is simple: The Categories button at the top of the interface synchronizes the Integration Library's table of categories with the eBay categories, and you can navigate the hierarchy of eBay categories using the tree view control that occupies the bulk of the interface. As always, the Settings button at the bottom of the application lets you enter your eBay SDK keys, required by eBay Integration Library applications just as any other eBay SDK application.

Initializing the eBay Integration Library

As you can see from Listing 6-16, initializing the eBay Integration Library in Perl is essentially the same as initializing it in C#.

Listing 6-16. Initializing the eBay Integration Library

```
1: sub InitIntegrationLibrary
2: {
3:   my $self = shift;
4:   $self->Busy( 1 );
5:
```

```
 6:    # Create the data store.
 7:    $app->{DATASTORE} = Win32::OLE->new(
 8:       "eBay.SDK.Integration.DataStore" );
 9:    $app->{DATASTORE}->Connect( $app->{DATABASEINFO} );
10:    my $result = Win32::OLE->LastError();
11:    if($result)
12:    {
13:       print $result;
14:       return;
15:    }
16:
17:    $app->{ENVIRONMENT} = $app->{DATASTORE}->LoadEnvironment(
18:       EnvironmentEnum_SANDBOX );
19:
20:    $self->Busy( 0 );
21: }
```

This method, part of the Perl application framework I describe in Appendix A,
uses two application properties, DATASTORE and ENVIRONMENT, to store the resulting
IDataStore and IEnvironment objects. The code begins by displaying a busy cursor
(line 4) and creating a new DataStore object on line 7. This DataStore instance is
connected to the database via the configuration string $app->{DATABASEINFO}, loaded
from the application's ebayrc file (lines 8–9). If an error occurs, the user is notified on the console and the routine exits (lines 10–15), or else the application
obtains an Environment instance that can communicate with the eBay Sandbox
on lines 17–18.

The categories.pl application invokes this method and sets the user during
its initialization. Even though the application doesn't do anything specific with
application users, the eBay Integration Library must still have a valid application
user to obtain an EBaySynchronizer. The application framework handles setting
the current application user in its AppUser method, shown here in Listing 6-17.

Listing 6-17. Obtaining the IEBaySession by Setting the AppUser in Perl

```
 1: sub AppUserId
 2: {
 3:    my $self = shift;
 4:    $self->{APPUSERID} = shift if ( @_ );
 5:
 6:    if ( $self->{APPUSERID}   )
 7:    {
 8:       $app->{APPUSER} =
 9:          $app->{ENVIRONMENT}->{UserManager}->LoadUser( 1 );
10:       my $result = Win32::OLE->LastError();
11:       if($result)
```

```
12:    {
13:       print $result;
14:       return;
15:    }
16:
17:    $app->{SESSION} =
18:       $app->{DATASTORE}->GetEBaySession( $app->{APPUSER} );
19:    my $result = Win32::OLE->LastError();
20:    if($result)
21:    {
22:       print $result;
23:       return;
24:    }
25:  }
26:  return $self->{APPUSERID};
27: }
```

This method saves aside the incoming user ID for the current application user (line 4), loads the user from the eBay Integration Database (lines 6–15), and gets the session for the current application user (lines 17–25).

Synchronizing the eBay Integration Library Categories

In order for the eBay Integration Library to possess the eBay service categories, the application must synchronize them from eBay. Doing this in Perl is the same as in C#, as you see in Listing 6-18.

Listing 6-18. Synchronizing eBay Categories in Perl

```
1: sub Categories_Click
2: {
3:    $application->Busy( 1 );
4:
5:    $application->{SESSION}->{EBaySynchronizer}->
6:       SynchronizeCategories( $application->SiteIDEnum_US, 0 );
7:    my $result = Win32::OLE->LastError();
8:    if($result)
9:    {
10:    print $result;
11:    return;
12:    }
13: }
```

This method invokes the EBaySynchronizer's SynchronizeCategories method. The first argument specifies the site to which the database should synchronize, while the second argument, if true (nonzero), indicates that *all data*, not just updates to the categories, should be synchronized.

> **WARNING** *Synchronizing all categories is a lengthy process, as you doubtless noticed the first time you invoked* SynchronizeCategories *on an empty database. Needlessly invoking* SynchronizeCategories *with the second argument* true *not only wastes your application users' time, but can result in your failing eBay certification because of the number and size of requests your application makes of the eBay service.*

Obtaining the eBay Integration Library Categories

Before you can browse the categories using the tree view, the application must load the categories from the eBay Integration Library Database. This is done during application startup in categories.pl. Listing 6-19 shows the code that obtains the list from the database and initializes the top level of the ScrollTree control.

Listing 6-19. Obtaining a List of eBay Categories from the eBay Integration Database in Perl

```
 1: $categories = $application->{ENVIRONMENT}->
 2:   LoadAllCategories( $application->SiteIDEnum_US );
 3:
 4: my $result = Win32::OLE->LastError();
 5: if($result)
 6: {
 7:   print $result;
 8:   return;
 9: }
10:
11: for ( $i = 0; $i < $categories->ItemCount(); $i ++ )
12: {
13:   if ( $categories->ItemAt($i)->{CategoryName} &&
14:       $categories->ItemAt($i)->{CategoryId} ==
15:       $categories->ItemAt($i)->{CategoryParentId} )
16:   {
17:     $tree->add( $categories->ItemAt($i)->{CategoryId},
18:                   -text => $categories->ItemAt($i)->{CategoryName} );
19:     $tree->setmode( $categories->ItemAt($i)->{CategoryId},
20:             -d $categories->ItemAt($i)->{CategoryLeaf} ?
```

```
21:                    "none" : "open" );
22:    }
23: }
```

Fetching the categories is easy, as you can see from lines 1–9. The application calls LoadAllCategories, which returns a CategoryCollection of *all* of the categories in the database. The application then enumerates this collection with the loop beginning on line 11. As you recall from Chapter 3, a category is a top-level category if its ID is the same as its parent's ID; the comparison on lines 13–15 tests this, and if the condition is true, adds the item to the $tree's list of items on lines 17–18. (Note that to facilitate finding subitems, the application uses the tree's text property to store the item's human-readable name, and the path of items consists of '/'-delimited category IDs.) Next, the code sets the new item's mode to indicate if the category is a collection of subcategories or a leaf on lines 19–21.

When you click a category item in the tree view, Perl/Tk invokes the openCmd of $tree, which executes the routine shown in Listing 6-20.

Listing 6-20. Opening a Category of the Tree

```
 1: sub opencmd
 2: {
 3:    my( $tree, $path ) = @_;
 4:    my $currentId = (split( "/", $path ))[-1];
 5:
 6:    $application->Busy( 1 );
 7:    # For each category, if it has a name and
 8:    # its parent is the current ID and it's not its parent
 9:    # add it to the current node as a subitem.
10:    for ( $i = 0; $i < $categories->ItemCount(); $i ++ )
11:    {
12:       if ( $categories->ItemAt($i)->{CategoryName} &&
13:          $categories->ItemAt($i)->{CategoryParentId} == $currentId &&
14:          $categories->ItemAt($i)->{CategoryId} !=
15:          $categories->ItemAt($i)->{CategoryParentId} )
16:       {
17:          my $id = $categories->ItemAt($i)->{CategoryId};
18:          my $name = $categories->ItemAt($i)->{CategoryName};
19:          my $leaf = $categories->ItemAt($i)->{LeafCategory};
20:          $tree->add("$path/$id", -text => $name );
21:          $tree->setmode( "$path/$id", !$leaf ? "open" : "none" );
22:       }
23:    }
24:    $application->Busy( 0 );
25: }
```

The routine begins on line 4 by obtaining the ID of the currently selected item, which is the last item of the '/'-delimited category ID path. Next, the application indicates that it will be busy for a bit on line 6, because enumerating the category list takes time. Enumerating the category list is the work of the loop on lines 10–23, which tests each item to see if its parent is the currently selected item (line 13), and if the item itself is not a top-level category (lines 14–15). If it isn't, it obtains the category's ID, name, and whether or not it's a leaf node (with no subcategories), and uses the Tk function additem to actually add the item to the tree as a new item under the current path.

> **NOTE** *Of course, you could initialize the entire $tree with all of the categories and subcategories at application launch time. The only reason I didn't show you this in this sample is because it could have detracted from your understanding of how the categories and subcategories are organized, and how you access them in Perl. That concern aside, preinitializing the entire category list would certainly make expanding list items faster.*

Key Points

In this chapter, you learned the following things about the eBay Synchronization Library:

- The Integration Library gives you a collection of interfaces and data model objects to work with eBay users, items, feedback, and sales locally, only periodically exchanging data with the eBay service.

- The Integration Library requires a local database in which to store items that have not been exchanged with eBay, as well as those items retrieved from eBay.

- eBay provides template databases for the Integration Library in both Microsoft Access and Microsoft SQL Server formats that you can use in your application.

- The Integration Library provides the IEBaySession interface for your application to interact with the local database and the eBay site your application uses.

- You can use the Integration Library with your existing database by providing serialization methods akin to those implemented by the IEBaySession interface.

- The Integration Library provides the IEBaySynchronizer interface for your application to move data between the local database and the eBay service.

CHAPTER 7

Reviewing Internet Programming

IN THE LAST SIX CHAPTERS, you've learned how to use the eBay service via the eBay SDK, a framework that provides a traditional object-oriented metaphor for working with eBay concepts such as items, users, and their transactions. One of the eBay SDK's great strengths is that it hides the notion of Internet programming, letting you concentrate on building your application and not on the minutia of making Internet requests of eBay servers and parsing the results. At times, however, it's necessary to set aside the abstractions and see how things work. Perhaps you're just curious about what goes on behind the curtain of the eBay SDK, or you're looking to bring your eBay application to platforms such as Linux where the eBay SDK isn't available. Regardless, you should understand the fundamentals of Internet programming, upon which the eBay API—the underpinning of the eBay SDK—is based.

In this chapter, I review the basic fundamentals you need to understand how to craft Internet applications. I review the difference between a traditional application and a networked application, how modern network applications use the HyperText Transfer Protocol (HTTP) to carry data between hosts, and how applications use the eXtensible Markup Language (XML) as the *lingua franca* for exchanging data. After reading this chapter, you'll have the knowledge you need to better understand how the eBay SDK works or to create an eBay application that uses the eBay API directly.

Looking Inside an Internet Application

When you write a traditional computing application, you divide application functionality up in terms of objects and the methods they can perform (or perhaps just methods, if you tend to think in terms of procedural programming). In an Internet application, such as one that uses the eBay service, you do the same—except that some of the code runs on other hosts. Instead of passing the data that represents your objects around in memory, an Internet application may well pass some data over the Internet. Figure 7-1 shows a deployment diagram for an Internet application that lists items on eBay. This deployment diagram is typical of many Internet applications.

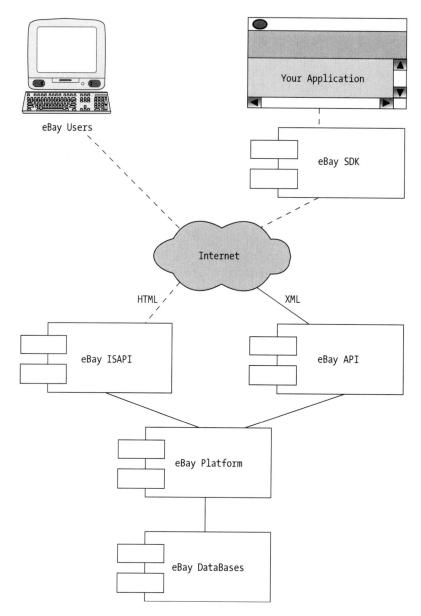

Figure 7-1. A typical Internet application deployment diagram

Although Internet applications share common elements with traditional applications in that they both use persistent storage to store between-instance data and memory to store images of data during program execution, there are two key differences. First, the application actually runs on two different hosts: the *client*, which originates the request to list a new item on eBay; and the *server*, which handles this request. Second, the application uses a network (the Internet) to perform this request and receive the response.

Most network applications follow this basic topology, with the client initiating requests and the server responding. Some applications may include multiple tiers of client and server, such as Internet applications in which you use a Web browser to access your eBay application, which in turn accesses the eBay service directly. Figure 7-2 shows a deployment diagram that clarifies the roles of each component of an application such as this.

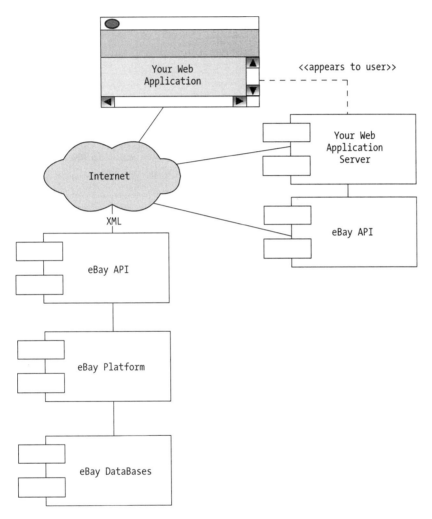

Figure 7-2. An Internet application with multiple clients and servers

In Figure 7-2, the Web browser is a client of the Web application server. The Web application server is a server with respect to the Web browser, but a client with respect to the eBay service.

In this diagram, both the Web client you use to access the application and the application itself are clients of eBay; it's common to refer to the application itself as a server with respect to your Web browser and as a client with respect to eBay. As with many other things, the notion of client and server is a relative one.

Moving Data with the HyperText Transfer Protocol

HTTP is an application-level protocol that has fast become the workhorse of the Internet, moving data not just for Web browsers but also for countless applications. Originally developed at CERN by Tim Berners-Lee and others in the early nineties, it was created to carry text and images between workstations for scientific collaboration. From there, the protocol blossomed first into a vehicle for exchanging files of all kinds across the World Wide Web. Now it serves many other purposes, including transferring files for file sharing (as the WebDAV protocol), news (by carrying Real Simple Syndication, or RSS, feeds between Web sites and RSS readers), and application-specific data for applications via services such as those offered eBay and other companies.

At its heart, the HTTP protocol is strikingly simple. As with all client-server protocols, a client computer initiates a request on the network, which is received by a server, which then transmits a response. These requests and responses are human-readable messages, consisting of either a *request body* or a *response body*, and an *object body*. The request (or response body) begins with an opening line that specifies the request (or response status), followed by *headers* that describe the request. Listing 7-1 shows a typical HTTP request for a Web document.

Listing 7-1. A Typical HTTP Request

```
1: GET /index.html HTTP/1.1
2: Host: www.lothlorien.com
3: Accept: text/html
4: Accept-Language: en
5: Accept-Charset: ISO-8859-1
6: User-Agent: Mozilla/4.0 (compatible; MSIE-5.01; Windows NT 5.0)
7: Connection: Close
8:
```

The first line is the request itself. In Listing 7-1, the client is requesting the document named index.html, located at the server's root. The remaining lines (lines 2–7) are the request's headers, and they describe various attributes of the request, including the name of the server the client is trying to contact (line 2, www.lothlorien.com), what formats of data the client will accept (line 3, HyperText Markup Language), what natural language the client prefers (line 4, en for English), the character set the server should use to encode the response (line 5, ISO-8859-1, which is ASCII), the kind of client (line 6), and that the server should close the connection at the end of the request (line 7). The end of the request is indicated by a blank line. In response to the request, the server will send a message such as what you see in Listing 7-2.

Listing 7-2. A Typical HTTP Response

```
 1: HTTP/1.1 200 OK
 2: Date: Wed, 20 Sep 2003 03:18:25 GMT
 3: Server: Apache/1.3.12 (Unix) PHP/4.0.1pl2
 4: Last-Modified: Wed, 16 Oct 2003 03:15:22 GMT
 5: Connection: close
 6: Content-Type: text/html
 7:
 8: <html>
 9: <body>
10: <p>
11:    Hello world!
12: </p>
13: </body>
14: </html>
```

The first line of the response is the response code. It has three parts: the version of the protocol (version 1.1, in this case), the response code, a three-digit integer, and finally a human-readable response. The code 200 indicates success, as does the terse string OK. Lines 2–6 comprise the response headers, which describe the response contents. The first, line 2, indicates the date at which the response object was served to the client. Line 3 indicates the kind of server that answered the request (in this case, the Apache server with the optional PHP scripting language). Line 4 indicates the last time the desired object was changed, whereas line 5 indicates that the server will close the request after delivering the desired object. Finally, line 6 indicates the format of the data.

After the response headers comes a blank line, and then the response itself. In this case, it's a simple HTML document. However—and this is the beauty of HTTP—the objects exchanged by HTTP for the request and response can be *anything*. In fact, for most Web applications, the request uses the HTTP POST instruction to send a bit of XML (which I discuss toward the end of this chapter in the section "Representing Data with XML") to the server, describing what the application wants the server to do (such as perform a search or list an item). The server accepts the XML in the HTTP message, parses it, performs the desired operation, and then sends the response as another XML document. In turn, the client application then parses the XML to obtain the results.

HTTP provides a number of kinds of requests, but the two you'll see most often are GET and POST. You use the GET request to obtain an object from the remote server, whereas you use the POST request to send an object to the remote server. That said, in the early days of HTTP, there was no POST request. Instead, to send data to the server, you'd append it to the URL you pass to the server after a question mark (?) symbol. The World Wide Web Consortium quickly found this to be inefficient for a number of reasons, and introduced the more useful POST request.

If all of this sounds a little complex, don't worry: In almost every case you're likely to want to use HTTP, the platform you're developing on has already implemented an HTTP interface for you. In most cases, all you need to do is create the request's object body, set options indicating any desired HTTP header values, and then make the request. The underlying library handles the implementation of the HTTP protocol for you, and returns the resulting HTTP response, either synchronously or asynchronously, with an interface that lets you determine the value of the response headers.

Although simple, the HTTP protocol has an obvious drawback: It's not secure. When you make an HTTP request, anybody on the network between your computer and the remote server can monitor the packets on the network and determine the contents of the HTTP request. Moreover, there's no way to be sure that the server you contact is really who it claims to be, or that (from the server's perspective) the client is who it claims to be. While acceptable in many cases (nobody really worries about whether or not somebody's snooping when they casually read BBC or Slashdot, and spoofing a Web server takes a reasonable amount of work), for most cases that relate to business applications, a more secure alternative is necessary.

Enter HTTPS: the secure flavor of HTTP, which uses HTTP over the Secure Sockets Layer (SSL), sometimes referred to as Transport Layer Security (TLS). HTTPS uses a bag of public-key cryptographic tricks to ensure that the client and server are who they say they are before permitting an interaction to take place, and then encrypts the transaction to keep the contents of the request and response hidden from prying eyes. If you've ever bought a book on Amazon.com, made a bid on eBay, made a payment on PayPal, or performed any one of millions of other financial transactions on the Web, it's likely that it was protected by HTTPS. As with HTTP, many platforms now include support for HTTPS, so making an HTTPS request isn't any harder than making an HTTP request.

Because of the sensitive nature of eBay's transactions, they must be secure. Your users must be sure that they're actually interacting with the eBay service, and not an impostor. Moreover, information such as their transaction account balance, item listings, and the like, must also be protected from prying eyes. Consequently, *all* interactions with eBay interfaces such as the eBay API use HTTPS to protect the contents of the messages being exchanged.

If you're looking to bring your eBay application to a platform other than Microsoft Windows, you need to use the eBay API, which requires that you use HTTPS. To get a feel for how to do this, in the next two chapters I show you how to use the eBay API in both C# and Perl. In the following sections here, I show you both C# and Perl's support for HTTP (including HTTPS).

Using HTTP in C#

In the next two chapters, you'll learn how to use the eBay API to perform the same sorts of tasks you've already performed using the eBay SDK. To do this, you'll need to have access to an HTTP implementation. Fortunately, .NET includes the HTTPWebRequest and HTTPWebResponse classes in the System.Net namespace, which let you make HTTP requests, including those secured using SSL.

> **NOTE** *Of course, if you're developing your eBay application using C# and .NET, you'll probably just want to use the eBay SDK instead of the eBay API. That's exactly what you* should *do. The reason I'm using C# and .NET with the eBay API here is to show you how to use the API in an environment familiar to you.*

Using these classes is easy, as you can see from Listing 7-3.

Listing 7-3. Pseudocode Demonstrating How to Use an HTTPWebRequest Object in C#

```
1: using System;
2: using System.Net;
3: using System.IO;
4:
5: namespace com.lothlorien.ebaysdkbook
6: {
7:     class SampleHttpRequest
8:     {
9:         static void Main()
10:         {
11:             HttpWebRequest   request;
12:             HttpWebResponse  response;
13:             Uri              requestUri;
14:             StreamReader     bodyreader;
15:             string           bodytext = "";
16:             string           line;
17:             Stream           responsestream;
18:             requestUri = new Uri("http://www.apress.com/");
19:             request = (HttpWebRequest)
```

```
20:                    WebRequest.Create(requestUri);
21:
22:              // You can fill in the properties of the request
23:              // here if you want. All properties are optional.
24:
25:              // Now get the response.
26:              response = (HttpWebResponse)request.GetResponse();
27:
28:              // Get a stream to read the requested document.
29:              responsestream = response.GetResponseStream();
30:              if (responsestream != null)
31:              {
32:                  bodyreader = new StreamReader(responsestream);
33:                  while((line=bodyreader.ReadLine())!=null)
34:                  {
35:                      bodytext+=line+"\r\n";
36:                  }
37:                  bodyreader.Close();
38:              }
39:              response.Close();
40:              Console.WriteLine( bodytext );
41:          }
42:      }
43: }
```

First, the routine creates a unique Uniform Resource Indicator (URI), stored in a new Uri object on line 18. The application uses the WebRequest class factory method Create to create a new HttpWebRequest subclass on lines 19–20. If you like, you can initialize the various properties of the new HttpWebRequest, as the comment on lines 22–23 indicates, but for the purposes of this example, don't bother; instead, choose to use the defaults, which include settings that indicate making a conventional HTTP GET request. Line 26 makes the request using the GetResponse method. The result is represented as a stream, which the routine obtains on line 29, and then reads the data from the stream into a string on lines 30–37. Once the response has been read, the routine closes the stream and the HttpWebResponse (which closes and frees the underlying network interfaces) on lines 37–39. Finally, the code prints the object body returned by the server to the console on line 40.

Using HTTP in Perl

Making an HTTP request in Perl is easy, too, with the help of the Library for WWW access for Perl (LWP). The LWP module provides classes that encapsulate HTTP requests and responses, in much the same way as the HttpWebRequest and HttpWebResponse classes do in the Microsoft .NET Framework. In addition, there's a related class, the *user agent* class, which is responsible for using the request object to actually make the HTTP request. Listing 7-4 presents pseudocode in Perl demonstrating how to use these classes.

Listing 7-4. Pseudocode Demonstrating How to Use an HTTPWebRequest Object in Perl

```
 1: use LWP;
 2: use LWP::UserAgent;
 3:
 4: # The user agent actually makes the request.
 5: $ua = new LWP::UserAgent;
 6:
 7: # Create a request.
 8: my $request = new HTTP::Request(
 9:   GET => 'http://www.apress.com'
10:   );
11:
12: # Configure the request here if you want.
13:
14: my $result = $ua->request($request);
15:
16: # Check the outcome of the response.
17: if ($result->is_success)
18: {
19:   print $result->content;
20: }
```

The routine begins by requiring the presence of the LWP and LWP::UserAgent modules (typically part of a default Perl installation). The routine first creates a UserAgent object on line 5, which is responsible for actually fulfilling the HTTP request on behalf of the example. Next, on lines 8–9, the routine creates a new HTTP::Request object, initialized to perform an HTTP GET to the URL http://www.apress.com/. Line 14 uses the UserAgent object's request method to make the request, storing the result in $result. This result is an object, with properties including is_success, which indicates whether the transaction succeeded or failed. Lines 17–20 print the content that the server returned if the transaction succeeded.

TIP *In order to make HTTPS requests, you must have installed the Crypt:SSLeay module for Perl, which adds SSL support to Perl for use with the LWP module. If you want to try the examples in the next two chapters, be sure to install Crypt:SSLeay first. If you're using ActiveState Perl, take a peek at* http://aspn.activestate.com/ASPN/Mail/Message/ppm/1817334 *for the not-so-gory details. Otherwise, head on over to* http://www.cpan.org/ *and search for Crypt:SSLeay.*

Representing Data with XML[1]

XML has become the de facto standard for representing data between applications over the Internet.

As with other markup languages, XML uses tags (which are formally known as *elements*) interspersed with your content to denote meaning. You write XML tags as text between angle brackets ‹ and › (the greater than and less than symbols). Opening tags are written like ‹this›, while closing tags are written like ‹/this›. Tags without content—so-called *empty tags*—are written using a trailing solidus, like this: ‹empty/›. Tag names must begin with a letter or an underscore (_), and may contain letters, digits, underscores, hyphens, and periods. XML tags are case sensitive, so ‹request› is *not* the same as ‹REQUEST› (or ‹Request› for that matter!).

It's important to realize that XML describes the syntax by which you create tags, but doesn't define tags per se. Instead, the responsibility for creating tags falls upon the application developer who creates tags that have special meaning for the application at hand. For example, as you'll see in the next chapter, the eBay API defines tags including ‹RequestUserId› and ‹RequestPassword›. Most of what you do when you use the eBay API is to format the arguments for eBay API calls inside of XML tags like these. Once you do that, all you need to do is send the resulting XML to eBay, and when the response comes back, interpret the XML in the response.

XML has a few special tags, too, which you've already seen. The ‹?xml?› tag identifies an XML document, whereas the ‹!DOCTYPE› tag identifies the kind of XML document, such as XHTML.

Any tag may have one or more attributes. An *attribute* is a name/value pair that provides additional information about a tag. The name follows the same rules as a tag name: Begin with an alphabetic character or an underscore, and follow with letters, numbers, hyphens, underscores, and periods. Attribute values are always strings contained between double quotes. For example, in the XML line

```
1: <?xml version="1.0"?>
```

the word version is an attribute of the xml tag, with the value 1.0.

XML defines four entities to represent special characters that XML reserves for its own use. Table 7-1 shows these entities.

---

1. This section was adapted from another of my books, *Wireless Web Development with PHP and WAP* (Berkeley, CA: Apress, 2001).

Table 7-1. XML Entities

Entity	Character	Note
&amp;	&	Ampersand
&lt;	<	Less than symbol
&gt;	>	Greater than symbol
&quot;	"	Double quote

You can include comments in your XML, too, by enclosing the comments within the `<!--` and `-->` characters. You can't put comments before the `<?xml?>` declaration, however, or within a tag itself. You can also use white space wherever you like, except between characters of a tag or attribute.

XML provides the notion of the *well-formed* XML document, which XML parsers must be able to interpret. Well-formed XML documents have the following properties:

- The `<?xml?>` declaration must be the first thing in the document.

- The document should contain exactly one tag that encloses all other tags.

- Tags may be nested but may not overlap other tags.

- Tags that contain content must have matching start and end tags.

- Tags that don't contain content must end in `/>`.

- Attribute values must be quoted using `""`.

By following these rules, any XML document can be represented as a *tree*. A tree is a data structure that has connected nodes, beginning with a single node called the *root*. In turn, the root connects to one or more nodes, called *children*, which themselves may have children.

In the examples in the next two chapters, I show you how to use the eBay API in both C# and Perl. To do this, I'll use the XML facilities present in these two languages. If you're not familiar with these facilities already, read on to see how they can help you manage XML.

Creating XML in C# and Perl

Through framework classes (modules in Perl, .NET Framework classes in C#), both C# and Perl support XML creation. Although these framework classes can be very useful when crafting applications with complex XML requirements, it's often far easier to simply use templates of the desired XML, and fill them in on-the-fly using bits of string replacement code. Doing this has two advantages: It's simple to update the XML if the eBay API changes and you need to update the XML (because you can keep the XML in an external resource), and it's more likely to be closer to how you'd have to do it on other platforms, such as in C on a mobile device, where typically you don't have the luxury of robust application frameworks.

> **NOTE** *While simple, the template approach can break down rather quickly if you're constructing complex XML. In practice, I find that it works well with things like creating eBay API requests, but not for things like representing a complex in-memory object on disk.*

For example, Listing 7-5 has a snippet of XML for a typical eBay SDK request to get a list of categories. In the format you see in the listing, things the application will want to change are enclosed in caret (^) characters. (Don't worry about the actual XML tags in the listing; you'll learn all about them in the next chapter.)

Listing 7-5. A Template for Fetching Categories Using the eBay API

```
 1: <?xml version="1.0" encoding="utf-8"?>
 2: <request>
 3:    <RequestUserId>^userid^</RequestUserId>
 4:    <RequestPassword>^password^</RequestPassword>
 5:    <DetailLevel>1</DetailLevel>
 6:    <ErrorLevel>1</ErrorLevel>
 7:    <SiteId>0</SiteId>
 8:    <Verb>GetCategories</Verb>
 9:    <CategoryParent>^parent^</CategoryParent>
10:    <LevelLimit>^limit^</LevelLimit>
11: </request>
```

If you load this into a string, you can easily use string replacement commands to create the desired XML for a specific category request. For example, Listing 7-6 shows a snippet of C# that will do this.

Listing 7-6. Using the Template in Listing 7-5 to Create a GetCategories API Call in C#

```
1: // Template has the actual XML template
2: template = template.Replace( "^userid^", "sandy2718" );
3: template = template.Replace( "^password^", "magic" );
4: template = template.Replace( "^parent^", "2" );
5: template = template.Replace( "^limit^", "1" );
```

Pretty simple stuff. Listing 7-7 shows the same trick in Perl.

Listing 7-7. Using the Template in Listing 7-5 to Create a GetCategories API Call in Perl

```
1: # $xml contains the desired XML.
2: $xml =~ s/\^userid\^/sandy2718/g;
3: $xml =~ s/\^password\^/magic/g;
4: $xml =~ s/\^parent\^/2/g;
5: $xml =~ s/\^limit\^/1/g;
```

Using templates with string replacement like this also has the advantage of being self-documenting.

Parsing XML in C#

One of the key advantages of the .NET Framework is its support classes for parsing XML. The .NET Framework has a bevy of XML parsers, the simplest of which merely reports the type and contents of each XML item (tag, entity, character data—what have you), and more complex ones that generate an entire well-formed tree from an XML document.

These XML parsers all take a stream that you can obtain from a file or a string. Let's see how to parse XML using the XML created from Listing 7-5 and Listing 7-6. Listing 7-8 shows a simple application that does the trick using the .NET Framework XmlTextReader class.

Listing 7-8. Parsing XML in C#

```
1: using System;
2: using System.IO;
3: using System.Xml;
4:
5: namespace com.lothlorien.ebaysdkbook
6: {
```

```
 7:    /// <summary>
 8:    /// Summary description for Class1.
 9:    /// </summary>
10:    class XMLExample
11:    {
12:      [STAThread]
13:      static void Main(string[] args)
14:      {
15:        string xml = // The XML template from Listing 7-5.
16:        StringReader reader;
17:        XmlTextReader parser;
18:        string result;
19:
20:        xml = xml.Replace( "^userid^", "sandy2718" );
21:        xml = xml.Replace( "^password^", "magic" );
22:        xml = xml.Replace( "^parent^", "2" );
23:        xml = xml.Replace( "^limit^", "1" );
24:
25:        System.Console.WriteLine( xml );
26:
27:        reader = new StringReader( xml );
28:        parser = new XmlTextReader( reader );
29:
30:        while( parser.Read() )
31:        {
32:          if ( parser.NodeType == XmlNodeType.Element )
33:          {
34:            result = parser.Name + ":";
35:            parser.Read();
36:            result += parser.Value;
37:            System.Console.WriteLine( result );
38:          }
39:        }
40:        System.Console.ReadLine();
41:        parser.Close();
42:      }
43:    }
44: }
```

The code begins by creating the XML document string, using the template you saw in Listing 7-5 (omitted for brevity on line 15 of Listing 7-8) on lines 20–23. For posterity, the code prints the resulting XML to the console on line 25.

Next, it creates a StringReader class instance using the contents of the string xml, which the XmlTextReader will use to parse the XML on line 27. The new XmlTextReader reads one token at a time from the XML stream in the loop on lines 30–39, stopping if the token is an XML tag on line 32. If it is, the next token will be the contents of the tag, and it prints both the name of the tag and the contents of the tag to the console, delimited by a colon and line break.

Once the loop finishes, the application pauses to show the output (handy if you're running the code in the debugger) and then cleans up the parser and exits.

Parsing XML in Perl

Like C#, Perl has a bevy of XML parsers. My personal favorite is XML::Simple (included with most Perl distributions), which interprets an XML document and makes it a hash, with each XML tag a key and each attribute's contents the value of that key in the hash. Consider Listing 7-9, which uses the template XML you first saw in Listing 7-5, creates an XML document, and then interprets it using XML::Simple.

Listing 7-9. Parsing XML in Perl

```
 1: use XML::Simple;
 2: use Data::Dumper;
 3:
 4: my $xml = <<TEMPLATE;
 5: <?xml version="1.0"?>
 6: <request>
 7:   <RequestUserId>^userid^</RequestUserId>
 8:   <RequestPassword>^password^</RequestPassword>
 9:   <DetailLevel>1</DetailLevel>
10:   <ErrorLevel>1</ErrorLevel>
11:   <SiteId>0</SiteId>
12:   <Verb>GetCategories</Verb>
13:   <CategoryParent>^parent^</CategoryParent>
14:   <LevelLimit>^limit^</LevelLimit>
15: </request>
16: TEMPLATE
17:
18: # $xml contains the desired XML.
19: $xml =~ s/\^userid\^/sandy2718/g;
20: $xml =~ s/\^password\^/magic/g;
21: $xml =~ s/\^parent\^/2/g;
22: $xml =~ s/\^limit\^/1/g;
23:
24: my $result = XMLin( $xml );
25:
26: print Dumper( $result );
```

The routine begins by storing the template in the variable $xml using the here-notation with TEMPLATE on lines 4–16. Lines 18–22 use Perl's regular expression substitution to insert the correct values for the eBay user ID, eBay password, category parent, and level limit, respectively. Line 24 uses the XML::Simple method XMLin to parse the XML, returning a reference to a hash stored in $result. Finally, the code prints the contents of the hash on line 26. You can see the resulting output in Listing 7-10.

Listing 7-10. The Hash Created by the Code in Listing 7-9

```
 1: {
 2:             'RequestPassword' => 'magic',
 3:             'ErrorLevel' => '1',
 4:             'CategoryParent' => '2',
 5:             'SiteId' => '0',
 6:             'Verb' => 'GetCategories',
 7:             'RequestUserId' => 'sandy2718',
 8:             'DetailLevel' => '1',
 9:             'LevelLimit' => '1'
10:         };
```

Key Points

In this chapter, you reviewed the following important points about programming over the Internet:

- Programs that involve the Internet divide their functionality across multiple machines, using the Internet to carry data between one computer and another. The computer originating a request is called the *client,* whereas the computer responding to the request is called the *server.*

- Many of today's Internet applications use HTTP to carry their data between a client application and a server application.

- For secure applications such as accessing eBay with the eBay API, you must use HTTPS (HTTP with SSL) to protect your data.

- Many applications, including the eBay SDK, use XML to encapsulate application data.

- You can use a template and string substitutions to create XML in your application.

CHAPTER 8

Using the eBay API

IN CHAPTERS 3, 4, 5, AND 6 of this book, you learned how to access the eBay service using the high-level eBay SDK, which provides an abstraction that lets you treat the remotely hosted resources of the eBay service as local to your machine through a robust environment of data model objects and API classes available via the Component Object Model (COM) and the .NET Framework. Although the eBay SDK is the logical method of choice for many of your applications to access the eBay service, as a developer you have another choice: the eBay API itself. Unlike the eBay SDK, the eBay API doesn't provide an abstraction layer residing on the application host. Instead, the eBay API consists of the raw eXtensible Markup Language (XML) requests and responses your application exchanges with the eBay service via HTTPS. The lack of an abstraction layer is an asset in some applications, because using the eBay API you can write applications that interact with the eBay service on any platform that has access to HTTPS.

In this chapter, I show you how to apply the fundamentals of Web programming I reviewed in the previous chapter to using the eBay API in your applications. First, I explain the benefits and costs of using the eBay API, comparing it with the eBay SDK. Next, I take you step-by-step through the process of making a request and handling a response with the eBay API. Finally, I show you how to use the eBay API by re-creating the ValidateUser example you first saw in Chapter 2 using the eBay API in both C# and Perl.

Choosing to Use the eBay API

The eBay API predates the eBay SDK: It's the lowest-level interface that third-party developers such as you and I have to the eBay service. Using XML and HTTPS, it provides a down-to-the-metal network applications development environment for integrating your applications with eBay. As such, it offers some concrete benefits over the eBay SDK, but these benefits come with a cost.

Because the eBay API uses XML and HTTPS to talk directly to the eBay service, there are virtually no platform requirements for applications that use the cBay API—unlike the eBay SDK, which takes advantage of powerful technologies present on today's Microsoft Windows platform, including COM and the underlying framework Microsoft provides when building COM objects. Thus, the eBay SDK requires that your application execute on a system that provides support for COM running on the Intel processor platform: a version of Microsoft Windows such as Microsoft NT 4.0 or Microsoft Windows XP. Although this is appropriate for a large number of consumer and business applications, and even many Web-based applications, other developers may want to target non-Microsoft platforms, such as the Palm Powered Platform, Linux, or another UNIX-style operating system like Mac OS X, or even a smart phone platform such as QUALCOMM BREW or Nokia's Series 60. You simply can't do this with the eBay SDK, but you can with the eBay API, which only requires you have a network stack that includes support for HTTPS and XML creation and parsing. You can easily provide the last two items yourself in any high-level language, as I showed you in the previous chapter,

So one obvious reason to choose the eBay API over the eBay SDK is you may have no other choice. In rare cases—and this is increasingly rare as eBay enhances both the eBay API and SDK simultaneously—you may find an eBay API you need to use that has no corresponding component in the eBay SDK. If this is the case, you can use the eBay API for the missing interface you need in conjunction with the eBay SDK, or you can write your entire application using the eBay API.

One good reason why you *don't* want to choose the eBay API over the eBay SDK is performance. Although the eBay API resides below the eBay SDK, selecting the eBay API in the hopes of obtaining better runtime or memory performance for your application is a bad decision, because the eBay SDK adds little overhead above the API. (In fact, the bulk of *any* network application's execution, be it eBay or any other, is often spent waiting for the underlying network to bear requests and responses between your application and the remote service.) Moreover, the added benefits of the eBay SDK are its robust data model, the ability to use a debugged network layer that sits atop the eBay API, and the fact that the eBay SDK implementation is written by eBay engineers in ways that optimize the use of eBay resources. These benefits make it an excellent choice for most applications.

Making a Request with the eBay API

At the heart of using the eBay API is the client-server (request-response model) popularized in distributed computing in the late eighties and early nineties that continues today in the implementation of the HTTP protocol that powers the World Wide Web. Using an eBay API is different from making a traditional API request (calling a function). Instead, it's the same as making a Web request to receive the contents of a resource from a remote host on the network.

1. First, you must construct the eBay API request: an XML document that specifies who you are, your credentials that permit you to access eBay, and the nature of the eBay API request that you wish eBay to carry out.

2. Next, you must use HTTPS to send this XML document to eBay for processing in the form of an HTTPS POST request.

3. Once the eBay service has received this request, it validates your credentials and the request document. If you are allowed to request the action you specified, the eBay service carries out your request.

4. Once the eBay service has carried out your request (or has determined that your request is in error), it encodes the response as an XML document and returns it to you as the object body of the response of your HTTPS POST request.

5. Your application interprets the XML document that the eBay service returns to you and acts on the contents.

The eBay service requires that you use HTTPS, and not the less secure HTTP, because doing so ensures that your application is communicating with the eBay service and not a third party impersonating eBay, and the encryption provided by HTTPS ensures that third parties can't eavesdrop on the transactions your application shares with eBay.

Understanding the Contents of the eBay API Request and Response

The request and response messages you exchange with eBay are encoded in XML, which I reviewed in the previous chapter. The eBay API defines a small set of common nodes required by *all* eBay API request and response messages, along with a slew of other nodes specific to individual eBay API transactions.

All eBay API requests must be contained in an XML document with an XML root node <request>. Within this request are the nodes that define the request, as you can see from Listing 8-1. The XML should be encoded as either UTF-8 or iso-8859-1, and the encoding scheme you use indicated in the <?xml?> preamble; if you omit the encoding scheme, the default is iso-8859-1.

Listing 8-1. An eBay API Request

```
1: <?xml version="1.0" encoding="iso-8859-1"?>
2: <request>
3:   <RequestUserId>sandy2718</RequestUserId>
4:   <RequestPassword>secret</RequestPassword>
5:   <ErrorLevel>1</ErrorLevel>
6:   <DetailLevel>0</DetailLevel>
7:   <SiteId>0</SiteId>
8:   <Verb>GetLogoURL</Verb>
9: </request>
```

All eBay API requests must include at least the following nodes:

- The RequestUserId node (line 3) contains the eBay user ID of the user making the request.

- The RequestPassword node (line 4) contains the password of the eBay user making the request.

- The ErrorLevel node (line 5) contains an integer indicating how detailed errors from the response should be reported. (Higher numbers indicate greater levels of detail.)

- The DetailLevel node (line 6) contains an integer indicating the desired level of detail for the response. (Higher numbers indicate greater levels of detail, and not all requests support varying levels of detail.)

- The SiteId node (line 7) contains an integer identifying the site to which the request pertains. Table 8-1 shows some eBay sites and their corresponding SiteId value.

- The Verb node (line 8) contains the name of the eBay API the eBay service is to execute.

> **NOTE**   *The eBay API also defines a* RequestToken *node, which can take the place of the* RequestUserId *and* RequestPassword *items in the XML. This node contains a token provided by eBay that identifies a user ID and a password for a session. In the examples that follow, for simplicity I stick to using the* RequestUserId *and* RequestPassword *nodes.*

Table 8-1. eBay Site Identifiers

eBay Site	SiteId Value
United States	0
Canada	2
United Kingdom	3
Australia	15
Austria	16
Belgium (French)	23
France	71

Table 8-1. eBay Site Identifiers (continued)

eBay Site	SiteId Value
Germany	77
Italy	101
Belgium (Dutch)	123
Netherlands	146
Spain	186
Switzerland	193
Taiwan	196
eBay Motors	100

As you'll see in the section "Understanding the Contents of the eBay API," many eBay API requests have additional arguments, such as an item or category ID. These are represented as additional per-request XML elements.

The structure of a response from the eBay service is similar, as you see in Listing 8-2, which shows the response to the call shown in Listing 8-1.

Listing 8-2. An eBay API Response

```
 1: <?xml version="1.0" encoding="iso-8859-1"?>
 2: <eBay>
 3:   <EBayTime>2003-11-27 22:25:27</EBayTime>
 4:   <Logo>
 5:     <Height>60</Height>
 6:     <URL>
 7:       https://scgi.sandbox.ebay.com/saw/pics/api/ebay_market_144x60.gif
 8:     </URL>
 9:     <Width>144</Width>
10:   </Logo>
11: </eBay>
```

The eBay service returns its response in an XML document whose root node is named eBay. Inside this node the eBay service always includes the EBayTime node, which contains the eBay canonical time at which the request was serviced.

> **NOTE** *It's important that you be aware of the time returned by* EBayTime, *because it's the official clock at eBay by which all eBay actions, such as auctions, are measured.*

As you can see in Listing 8-3, errors are reported using the `Errors` node.
Listing 8-3 shows a typical error response when the `ErrorLevel` is set to 1.

Listing 8-3. The eBay API Response Indicating an Error

```
 1: <?xml version="1.0" encoding="iso-8859-1"?>
 2: <eBay>
 3:   <EBayTime>2003-11-28 02:13:26</EBayTime>
 4:   <Errors>
 5:     <Error>
 6:       <Code>35</Code>
 7:       <ErrorClass>RequestError</ErrorClass>
 8:       <SeverityCode>1</SeverityCode>
 9:       <Severity>SeriousError</Severity>
10:       <Line>0</Line>
11:       <Column>0</Column>
12:       <ShortMessage>
13:         <![CDATA[Invalid user name or password.]]>
14:       </ShortMessage>
15:       <LongMessage>
16:         <![CDATA[Invalid user name or password.
17:                  The username/password pair specified
18:                  for the user is not valid. You may
19:                  not use an email address as a username
20:                  if the member has a User ID.]]>
21:       </LongMessage>
22:     </Error>
23:   </Errors>
24: </eBay>
```

The `Errors` node contains one or more `Error` nodes, each with the details of a specific error, such as incorrect eBay user ID, bad eBay certificate information, or information about a malformed eBay API request. Note that you can get an Errors node with valid responses, too. In that case, the text you receive in each `Error` node is a warning regarding how you're using the API.

> **TIP** *The errors reported by the eBay API, especially those in the* LongMessage *node, have enough detail that they're appropriate for you to show to your users in the event of an error. I find it helpful as a developer to leave the* ErrorLevel *set to 1 and print error messages to the console or log file while debugging, and then to turn off the logging when I ship my application, and use the error messages in my user interface.*

Populating the HTTP Headers in a Request

In addition to supplying request information in the body of your HTTPS POST, you must also provide some information to the eBay service in the HTTPS headers for your request. The HTTP headers you must provide are the following:

- X-EBAY-API-COMPATIBILITY-LEVEL, which specifies the version of the eBay API that your application is using.

- X-EBAY-API-SESSION-CERTIFICATE, which contains your eBay application's developer key, application key, and certificate, each separated by semi-colon (;) characters. This is case and space sensitive; don't add spaces or change the case of the keys, or your request will be denied.

- X-EBAY-API-DEV-NAME, which contains the developer key that eBay issued to you. This is case and space sensitive; don't add spaces or change the case of the keys, or your request will be denied.

- X-EBAY-API-APP-NAME, which contains the application key that eBay issued to you. This is case and space sensitive; don't add spaces or change the case of the keys, or your request will be denied.

- X-EBAY-API-CERT-NAME, which contains the certificate that eBay issued to you. This is case and space sensitive; don't add spaces or change the case of the keys, or your request will be denied.

- X-EBAY-API-CALL-NAME, which contains the name of the eBay API your request invokes. This must match the contents of the Verb you pass to eBay in your request.

- X-EBAY-API-SITEID, which contains the site ID of the site your request accesses. This must match the contents of the SiteId tag in your request.

- X-EBAY-API-DETAIL-LEVEL, which contains the detail level your request requires. This must match the contents of the DetailLevel node in your request.

- Content-Type, which should contain text/xml indicating that the object body of your request is an XML document.

You should also include the optional but encouraged Content-Length header, which contains the size of the object body of your request in bytes.

> **WARNING**   *Neglecting to set one of these headers (except the* Content-Length
> *header, which is encouraged but not required) will cause your API request to
> fail. A common mistake developers new to the API make is to forget the*
> X-EBAY-API-CALL-NAME *header, which must contain the same API as your
> request invokes. Failure to include this header can result in somewhat cryptic
> error messages, so if you find that the eBay service is returning errors from
> a request that you think is correct, stop and check the headers: You may have
> forgotten to specify the* X-EBAY-API-CALL-NAME *header, or mistakenly set its
> contents to an incorrect value. When all else fails, be sure to carefully check
> the case and spacing of each of the header values you send, and compare
> those values with the values in your request.*

The X-EBAY-API-COMPATIBILITY-LEVEL header deserves additional explanation.
At times, eBay makes changes to the eBay API. To ensure that applications can
continue to use the eBay API without needing constant changes, eBay assigns
a compatibility level to a specific package of APIs that the eBay service supports
at any given time (as of this writing, that compatibility level is 327). When you
write your application, you must take note of the API version you're using, and
include that version information in this header. As the eBay service accepts your
request, it has the option to deny requests that predate a specific API version,
allowing them to deprecate eBay APIs over time. (In a similar vein, using a compatibility level greater than the current eBay compatibility level is an error.)

You may find it odd that some of the information in your eBay API request is
duplicated in your request's HTTPS headers, such as the X-EBAY-API-CALL-NAME
header, which must be the same as the <Verb> node in your request. By including
this information in the header, the server can make initial decisions about how
to handle your request (possibly offloading it to another server or directing it to
a specific cache) without taking the overhead of actually interpreting the XML in
your request.

Making the Request

Once you create the request XML and a request object with the appropriate headers, you simply send the XML document to the eBay service at the URL for the
Sandbox or production service using an HTTPS POST request. Of course, how you
actually make this request will differ depending on which language your application
is written in, and the interface that language provides to an HTTPS implementation.
Chapter 7 gives examples for both C# and Perl; other languages such as Java and
PHP are quite similar.

Using the eBay API

Although using the eBay API is admittedly more work than using the eBay SDK, it isn't hard, especially if you've had previous experience developing Web-based applications. In this section, I re-create the ValidateUser example you first saw in Chapter 2, using the eBay API instead of the eBay SDK.

Validating a User in C#

There's little point in using C# to implement an eBay API-based application such as ValidateUser, because there's the easier-to-use eBay SDK class ValidUserCall instead. That said, presenting the ValidateUser application using the eBay API lets you see how to use the API in a high-level language with C-like syntax, something you don't get when you look at the example in Perl in the next section. Listing 8-4 shows the ValidateUser example in C#.

Listing 8-4. The ValidateUser application in C# Using the eBay API

```
 1: // Dependencies
 2: using System;
 3: using System.IO;
 4: using System.Net;
 5: using System.Text;
 6: using System.Xml;
 7:
 8: namespace com.lothlorien.ebaysdkbook
 9: {
10:    class ValidateUser
11:    {
12:      private static string devID;
13:      private static string appID;
14:      private static string crtID;
15:
16:      static void Main(string[] args)
17:      {
18:        const string ebayAPIUrl =
19:                    "https://api.sandbox.ebay.com/ws/api.dll";
20:        const string detailLevel = "0";
21:        const string siteId = "0";
22:        const string verb = "ValidateTestUserRegistration";
23:        const string compatLevel = "327";
```

```
24:        Uri requestUri. new Uri( ebayAPIUrl );
25:        HttpWebRequest  request;
26:        HttpWebResponse response = null;
27:        string userid, password;
28:        string xmlRequest;
29:        StreamWriter writer;
30:        XmlTextReader parser;
31:        string result;
32:
33:
34:        xmlRequest = "<?xml version=\"1.0\"?><request>" +
35:          "<RequestUserId>^userid^</RequestUserId>" +
36:          "<RequestPassword>^password^</RequestPassword>" +
37:          "<ErrorLevel>1</ErrorLevel>" +
38:          "<DetailLevel>^detaillevel^</DetailLevel>" +
39:          "<Verb>^verb^</Verb>" +
40:          "<SiteId>^siteid^</SiteId>" +
41:          "</request>";
42:
43:      // Create the Web client object.
44:      request = (HttpWebRequest) WebRequest.Create( requestUri );
45:      // CAUTION: This is case sensitive!
46:      request.Method = "POST";
47:
48:      // Get the eBay keys.
49:      getKeys();
50:
51:      // Find out which account we should validate.
52:      Console.Write( "Enter eBay User ID of " );
53:      Console.Write( "the seller account: ");
54:      userid = Console.ReadLine();
55:
56:      Console.Write( "Enter password to the " );
57:      Console.Write( "seller account: " );
58:      password = Console.ReadLine();
59:
60:      // Create the request XML.
61:      xmlRequest = xmlRequest.Replace( "^userid^", userid );
62:      xmlRequest = xmlRequest.Replace( "^password^", password );
63:      xmlRequest = xmlRequest.Replace( "^detaillevel^",
64:                                        detailLevel );
65:      xmlRequest = xmlRequest.Replace( "^verb^", verb );
66:      xmlRequest = xmlRequest.Replace( "^siteid^", siteId );
67:
```

```
68:        // Create the API Request HTTP Headers.
69:        request.ContentType = "text/xml";
70:        request.ContentLength = xmlRequest.Length;
71:        request.Headers.Set( "X-EBAY-API-COMPATIBILITY-LEVEL",
72:                              compatLevel );
73:        request.Headers.Set( "X-EBAY-API-SESSION-CERTIFICATE",
74:          devID + ";" + appID + ";" + crtID );
75:        request.Headers.Set( "X-EBAY-API-DEV-NAME" , devID );
76:        request.Headers.Set( "X-EBAY-API-APP-NAME", appID );
77:        request.Headers.Set( "X-EBAY-API-CERT-NAME" , crtID );
78:        request.Headers.Set( "X-EBAY-API-CALL-NAME" , verb );
79:        request.Headers.Set( "X-EBAY-API-SITEID", siteId );
80:        request.Headers.Set( "X-EBAY-API-DETAIL-LEVEL",
81:                              detailLevel );
82:
83:        // Create the request.
84:        writer = new StreamWriter( request.GetRequestStream() );
85:        writer.Write( xmlRequest );
86:        writer.Close();
87:
88:        // Issue the call.
89:        Console.Write( "Issuing ValidateTestUserRegistration " );
90:        Console.WriteLine( "API call..." );
91:        try
92:        {
93:          response = (HttpWebResponse)request.GetResponse( );
94:
95:          // Parse XML.
96:          parser = new XmlTextReader(
97:            response.GetResponseStream() );
98:
99:          result = "Congratulations! " +
100:            "The user has been validated successfully!";
101:
102:          while( parser.Read() )
103:          {
104:            if ( parser.NodeType == XmlNodeType.Element )
105:            {
106:              if ( parser.Name == "LongMessage" )
107:              {
108:                parser.Read();
109:                result = parser.Value;
110:              }
```

```
111:                 }
112:             }
113:             parser.Close();
114:             Console.WriteLine( result );
115:         }
116:         catch( Exception e )
117:         {
118:           Console.Write( "**Error**: " );
119:           Console.Write( e.Message );
120:         }
121:
122:         // Show the results.
123:         Console.ReadLine();
124:     }
125:
126:     /*
127:      * Fetches the eBay developer keys from either
128:      * a dotfile or from the input line if the dotfile
129:      * isn't available.
130:      */
131:     static void getKeys( )
132:     {
133:         // Omitted; see the implementation in Appendix A.
134:     }
135:   }
136: }
```

This example is purposely monolithic, encapsulating both its console-based user interface and the interaction with eBay in a single function, the application's entry point. After declaring a bevy of variables (lines 18–31), you initialize a template the actual parameters of the request. Lines 43–46 create a .NET Framework `WebRequest` object to the eBay service URL `https://api.sandbox.ebay.com/ws/api.dll`, indicating that the request should use the `POST` method (line 46) when sending data to the URL.

Line 49 reads your application keys from a configuration file using the same getKeys implementation you first saw in Chapter 3 and discussed in Appendix A.

Lines 51–58 comprise the application's feeble user interface; the code prompts the user for the eBay user to validate, getting first the user's ID (lines 51–54), and then the user's password (lines 56–58). (I break each of the prompt lines across two lines of code in this example to better format the listing for this book; of course you wouldn't need to do that.)

Lines 60–66 create the eBay API request, using the template initialized on lines 33–41 and the trick I showed you in Chapter 7 in the section "Creating XML in C# and Perl." Using a succession of `Replace` method invocations on the XML template, the code replaces each of the special tokens in the template (such as "^userid^")

with values the application obtains from you or from the constants declared on lines 20–23.

Lines 68–81 set each of the request's HTTPS headers using the request's Set method of the request's Headers property. As with the XML, the values for the headers are largely programmatically defined, coming from the contents placed in the request on lines 60–66, or the various keys previously obtained using the getKeys function on line 49.

The C# HTTP implementation uses the StreamWriter interface to pass data from your application to the HTTPS connection; lines 83–86 pass the contents of the eBay API request in xmlRequest to the request via a StreamWriter instance.

Lines 89–124 issue the request and parse the resulting XML. The bulk of this code is wrapped in an expansive try/catch block to handle errors that might arise either from the Web request or from parsing the resulting XML. The line that actually makes the request is line 93, which blocks until the HTTP request completes and data is available on the underlying socket for the application to read.

Lines 96–97 begin reading this data using an XmlTextReader instance, reading each node in the loop that spans lines 102–112. This example cheats—on line 99–100 it sets the result assuming that the request completed successfully—and looks for a node indicating that an error occurred. If one occurred, the comparison on line 106 will be true, and lines 108–109 get the value of the error returned by the eBay service. Regardless of success or failure, line 114 shows the value of result, giving you feedback as to the success or failure of the request. The exception handler on lines 116–120 simply print the message associated with the exception in the event of an error.

Finally, line 123 simply pauses the display until you press the Enter key, giving you the opportunity to read the output if you execute the application from the Microsoft Windows Explorer.

Validating a User in Perl

If you prefer to develop applications on a platform other than Microsoft Windows, you've either read the previous seven chapters with amazing patience, or skipped it all to read the code that follows. This example, ValidateUser written in Perl with the eBay API, runs on any platform that has Perl, including Linux and Mac OS X. As such, it delivers on the promise of platform agnosticism made by the eBay API. Listing 8-5 shows ValidateUser in Perl.

Listing 8-5. The ValidateUser Application in Perl Using the eBay API

```
1: # Dependencies
2: use LWP::UserAgent;
3: use HTTP::Request;
```

```
 4: use HTTP::Headers;
 5: use XML::Simple;
 6: use Data::Dumper;
 7:
 8: sub getKeys;
 9:
10: # Constants
11: use constant True => 1;
12: use constant False => 0;
13: use constant COMPATIBILITY_LEVEL => 335
14: use constant EBAY_API_URL =>
15:    'https://api.sandbox.ebay.com/ws/api.dll';
16: use constant DEBUG => 0;
17: use constant SITE_ID => '0';
18: use constant DETAIL_LEVEL => '0';
19: use constant VERB => 'ValidateTestUserRegistration';
20:
21: # Variables
22: my $input;
23: my $siteid = SITE_ID;
24: my $detaillevel = DETAIL_LEVEL;
25: my $verb = VERB;
26: my $xml = <<TEMPLATE;
27: <?xml version="1.0"?>
28: <request>
29:    <RequestUserId>^userid^</RequestUserId>
30:    <RequestPassword>^password^</RequestPassword>
31:    <ErrorLevel>1</ErrorLevel>
32:    <DetailLevel>^detaillevel^</DetailLevel>
33:    <Verb>^verb^</Verb>
34:    <SiteId>^siteid^</SiteId>
35: </request>
36: TEMPLATE
37:
38:
39: # Create the user agent object.
40: print "Creating user agent object...\n";
41: my $useragent = LWP::UserAgent->new;
42:
43: # Get the eBay keys.
44: my ( $devKey, $appKey, $crtKey ) = getKeys();
45:
46: # Find out which account we should validate.
47: print "Enter eBay User ID of the seller account: ";
```

```
48: chomp($input = <>);
49: my $userid = $input;
50:
51: print "Enter password to the seller account: ";
52: chomp($input = <>);
53: my $password = $input;
54:
55: # Create the request XML.
56: $xml =~ s/\^userid\^/$userid/g;
57: $xml =~ s/\^password\^/$password/g;
58: $xml =~ s/\^detaillevel\^/$detaillevel/g;
59: $xml =~ s/\^verb\^/$verb/g;
60: $xml =~ s/\^siteid\^/$siteid/g;
61:
62:
63: # Create the API Request HTTP Headers.
64: my $header = HTTP::Headers->new;
65: $header->push_header( 'X-EBAY-API-COMPATIBILITY-LEVEL' =>
66:                       COMPATIBILITY_LEVEL );
67: $header->push_header( 'X-EBAY-API-SESSION-CERTIFICATE' =>
68:                          "$devKey;$appKey;$crtKey");
69: $header->push_header( 'X-EBAY-API-DEV-NAME' => $devKey );
70: $header->push_header( 'X-EBAY-API-APP-NAME' => $appKey );
71: $header->push_header( 'X-EBAY-API-CERT-NAME' => $crtKey );
72: $header->push_header( 'X-EBAY-API-CALL-NAME' => VERB );
73: $header->push_header( 'X-EBAY-API-SITEID' =>  SITE_ID );
74: $header->push_header( 'X-EBAY-API-DETAIL-LEVEL' => SITE_ID );
75: $header->push_header( 'Content-Type' => 'text/xml' );
76: $header->push_header( 'Content-Length' => length( $xml ) );
77:
78: print $xml, "\n" if DEBUG;
79:
80: # Create the request.
81: my $request = HTTP::Request->new( "POST", EBAY_API_URL,
82:                                   $header, $xml);
83:
84: # Issue the call.
85: my $response = $useragent->request($request);
86:
87: # Handle transport errors first.
88: die "Network error contacting eBay." if $response->is_error;
89:
90: print $response->content(), "\n" if DEBUG;
```

```
91: # Parse the result.
92: my $result = XMLin( $response->content() );
93: print Dumper( $result ), "\n" if DEBUG;
94:
95: # Show the result.
96: if( $result->{Errors} )
97: {
98:    print "**Error**:",
99:    $result->{Errors}->{Error}->{LongMessage}, "\n";
100: }
101: else
102: {
103:    print "Congratulations! ";
104:    print "The user has been validated successfully!\n";
105: }
106: print "\n";
107: <>;
108:
109: # Fetches the eBay developer keys from either
110: # a dotfile or from the input line if the dotfile
111: # isn't available.
112: sub getKeys
113: {
114:    # omitted for brevity; see the implementation in Appendix A.
115: }
```

The example begins by importing the various modules on which it depends, including LWP for Web access, HTTP for Web access and HTTP Header management, XML::Simple for XML parsing, and Data::Dumper for debugging. Lines 11–19 define a plethora of constants the script uses later, such as the URL of the eBay service (lines 14–15), whether or not to run the script with debugging (line 16), and attributes of the eBay request itself (lines 17–19). Lines 22–36 initialize several local variables, including the XML template for the eBay API request.

Line 41 creates the $useragent that provides the HTTPS protocol, whereas line 44 obtains the application's eBay credentials using the getKeys method developed for the purpose and shown in Appendix A.

Lines 46–53 prompt you for the eBay user ID and password of the user to validate.

Lines 55–60 populate the XML template with the request data using Perl's regular expression search-and-replace operator s///g and ~=, which replaces the first argument with the second throughout the string. Lines 63–76 complete creating the request by creating the headers required by eBay.

Lines 81–82 create the request, indicating by the arguments to the new operator that the request is a POST request to the eBay service URL with the headers initialized in lines 63–76, and with the object body in $xml. Line 85 uses the resulting $request to send the eBay API request to the eBay service, storing the result in the $response structure. This is a synchronous call; the LWP module performs the request and reads the entire response, returning it as the result value $response, a hash that contains both the result data and a success or failure notification. Line 88 ends the script with an error if the request failed, checking the $response's is_error field.

Line 92 parses the XML using the XML::Simple module, converting the returned XML from a string of XML nodes to a Perl hash. Lines 96–100 look for any indication of error, whereas lines 103–104 print a success message if the eBay service didn't return an error.

Key Points

In this chapter, you learned the following key points about the eBay API:

- The eBay API provides a low-level interface between applications and the eBay service using XML and HTTPS. All applications that use eBay use the eBay API, including those you build with the eBay SDK.

- To use the eBay API, your target platform need only have a network implementation capable of supporting HTTPS.

- You can write applications using the eBay API on platforms that don't support the eBay SDK, letting you develop for platforms such as Linux, flavors of UNIX such as Mac OS X, or even handheld and telephony platforms such as the Palm Powered Platform or Nokia's Series 60.

- You must use HTTPS to exchange requests and responses with the eBay service to ensure the security of your application. The eBay service doesn't support the less secure HTTP protocol.

- When making an eBay API request, you must encode the request in XML and include your eBay keys and other information in the request's HTTPS headers.

- The eBay service responds to your request with an XML document that contains the results of your request or an <Errors> node that enumerates the errors that your request may have encountered.

CHAPTER 9

Using the eBay API Within a Web Site

IN THE LAST TWO CHAPTERS, you learned that under the eBay SDK resides the eBay API, a Web service interface to the eBay service. In the last chapter you learned how to access this interface in both C# and Perl, demonstrating the basics of using the eBay API in your application.

In this chapter, I build on that knowledge to show you how you can use the eBay API when crafting your Web site, and include a sample Web application in Perl that lets you search the eBay Sandbox for items currently up for auction. First, I discuss how the eBay service can enhance your Web presence. Next, I take you through the most commonly used eBay API interfaces, one at a time, so that you'll understand what facilities are available to you within the eBay API (whether you intend to use it in a Web application or as part of a stand-alone application). Finally, I close the chapter with the aforementioned sample application, demonstrating how to search the eBay service from a Web site powered by Perl using the eBay API.

Understanding How the eBay Service Fits with Your Web Site

There are myriad reasons why you might want to integrate the eBay service with a Web site. Perhaps it's to provide a Web-based interface on a local intranet that unifies your product inventory with your eBay store, or maybe you'd like to offer a turnkey package to small businesses that lets them list and sell items on their Web site via eBay. Regardless, the eBay service works as well with Web-hosted services as it does for stand-alone applications.

Although I can't hope to cover the entire gamut of writing a Web application from scratch here, it's important to note that using the eBay API or SDK within your Web application is really no different than using it from a stand-alone application. In either case, you define your business logic, decide where the eBay service fits, and then use either API or SDK calls to interact with eBay. The challenges inherent in writing a Web application, such as providing security and session management (or ensuring that your relationship with your clients is sessionless, something that's getting harder and harder to do every day as users expect more from Web applications), aren't affected by the eBay interfaces. The converse is true, too: The eBay interfaces don't do much to help you in those situations, because that's beyond their purview.

One thing you'll need to consider when integrating eBay in your application is how the application running on the server should cache data from eBay, such as category data, item query results, and so forth. If you're using the eBay SDK and the eBay Integration Library, you're all set: You can use these with a back-end database such as Microsoft Access or Microsoft SQL Server. If you're using the eBay SDK alone, however, or simply the eBay API, you'll have more work to do because you'll need to use a database (or mimic your own with files) to store the data your Web application must cache. Regardless, this is a consideration you should tackle up front so that your design can include the interaction with the local cache of eBay data.

This brings up an important point that I've not stated directly: Just because this chapter talks about both the eBay API and Web sites, that certainly doesn't mean that you can *only* integrate your Web site with the eBay service using the eBay API. If you're developing a Web site using the .NET Framework, you should definitely be using the eBay SDK and the eBay Integration Library! If, on the other hand, you're targeting a deployment on Linux or a UNIX variant, you'll need to use the eBay API.

> **TIP** *If you're new to building and deploying Web sites and services, you should step back and learn what you need to do. In today's high-bandwidth world, it's often not quite as simple as hanging a Linux box off the end of a DSL line, or writing a few Web pages and posting them on your local Web hosting provider. Check out a book such as* PHP MySQL Website Programming: Problem—Design—Solution *by Mike Buzzard, Chris Lea, Dilip Thomas, and Jessey White-Cinis (Berkeley, CA: Apress, 2003) for traditional Web-based development or* Wireless Web Development with PHP and WAP *by your humble author (Berkeley, CA: Apress, 2001).*

Understanding the Contents of the eBay API

This section describes the most common eBay API interfaces you're likely to encounter when developing your application. To help you learn these APIs, I've broken them up into a few broad categories. For a detailed list of all of the eBay APIs sorted by alphabetical order, check the documentation available at eBay's developer Web site, http://developer.ebay.com.

In the discussion of each eBay API, I show only those argument entity tags that are appropriate for a specific eBay API call. When crafting your eBay API XML, don't forget the required tags you learned in the section "Understanding the Contents of the eBay API Request and Response" in the previous chapter. In addition, the Verb attribute you pass is the same name as the call itself; for example, if you are invoking the GetAPIAccessRules API, the Verb in your request should be GetAPIAccessRules.

Understanding General eBay API Calls

The interfaces in this section pertain to general operating aspects when using the eBay interfaces, such as enumerating categories, determining shipping rates, and so forth.

The GetAPIAccessRules Interface

The GetAPIAccessRules interface provides your application with a way to determine the access rules and usage statistics for each API call. Through this API, your application can measure how it uses the eBay service, and your application users can meter application use. The GetAPIAccessRules method has no arguments.

Your application likely won't reveal the access rules to its users, but you can use this API to track how much of your quota for API access your application has used, and inform users when they're running low on specific API calls over a time interval through the use of warning messages.

The return value for the GetAPIAccessRules interface is contained within the APIAccessRules tag, with a single APIAccessRule tag for each eBay API that has an access rule. Within the APIAccessRule tag are the access rules for a specific API; Table 9-1 shows the tags you'll find within the APIAccessRule tag.

Table 9-1. Tags Returned by GetAPIAccessRules

Tag	Purpose
CallName	Name of the API call.
CountMode	Indicator of whether the rule is counted toward the application aggregate limit. Returns a value of true (1) if the rule is counted.
DailyHardLimit	Number of calls per day that your application may make before a call is refused.
DailySoftLimit	Number of calls per day that your application may make before you receive a warning.
DailyUsage	Number of calls that your application has already made today.
EnforceURL	Indicator of whether URL pooling for this call is currently being enforced. Returns a value of true (1) if pooling is being enforced.
HourlyHardLimit	Number of calls per hour that your application may make before a call is refused.

Table 9-1. Tags Returned by GetAPIAccessRules (continued)

Tag	Purpose
HourlySoftLimit	Number of calls per hour that your application may make before you receive a warning.
HourlyUsage	Number of calls that your application has already made this hour.
ModTime	Last time that values for RuleCurrentStatus, RuleStatus, URL, or EnforceURL changed.
RuleCurrentStatus	Your application's current status with regards to the access rule. Possible values are 0: Not set 1: Your application has exceeded its hourly limit 2: Your application has exceeded its daily limit 3: Other
RuleStatus	Status of the access rule. Possible values are -1: The rule is turned off. No rule validation was performed. 0: The application cannot make requests for the specified CallName. 1: The rule is enabled. Rule validation was performed.
URLModTime	Last time that values for URL or EnforceURL changed.

The GetCategories Interface

The GetCategories interface lets you enumerate over eBay's categories, providing a way to determine the name of a category for a specific ID, as well as determine the relationship between a parent category and its children. Table 9-2 shows the argument tags to the GetCategories interface, whereas Table 9-3 shows the tags returned by the eBay service.

Table 9-2. Tags Passed to GetCategories

Tag	Purpose
CategoryParent	Specifies the ID of the parent category for the child categories that you want to return. Not specifying a CategoryParent defaults to the root category.
CategorySiteId	Indicates the eBay site from which you are requesting categories. Should be the same as the mandatory SiteId argument.

Table 9-2. Tags Passed to GetCategories (continued)

Tag	Purpose
LevelLimit	Specifies which levels of categories to return. By specifying a value in LevelLimit, you'll retrieve all category nodes with a CategoryLevel less than or equal to the LevelLimit value. Use LevelLimit with DetailLevel set to 1.
ViewAllNodes	Specifies whether to return only leaf categories (0 is false) or leaf and container categories (1 is true). Default is 1.

Table 9-3. Tags Returned by GetCategories

Tag	Purpose
CategoryId	Distinct numeric ID for each returned category.
CategoryLevel	Level where each returned category fits into the category hierarchy.
CategoryName	Textual name for each category returned. Retrieved as character data.
CategoryParent	Distinct numeric ID for the parent category of each returned category. Should always be the same as the category ID specified in the CategoryParent input argument.
IsExpired	Indicator of whether a category is no longer available. Applications shouldn't allow users to list items in expired categories.
IsVirtual	Indicator of whether a category is virtual. Applications shouldn't allow users to list items in virtual categories. (Used by eBay Motors listings.)
LeafCategory	Indicator of whether a category is a leaf (1) or a container (0) category with subcategories.
CategoryCount	Total number of category nodes returned.
UpdateGMTTime	Date and time the category set was last updated, in GMT. (Same as UpdateTime, but in GMT.) Use the UpdateTime with DetailLevel set to 0 to determine if a full GetCategories call is necessary.
UpdateTime	Date and time the category set was last updated, in Pacific standard time. Use UpdateTime with DetailLevel set to 0 to determine if a full GetCategories call is necessary.
Version	Version number assigned to the current rendition of the category hierarchy and category group divisions.

As you may recall from Chapter 3, eBay categories are kept in a hierarchical tree, with some categories being parents of other categories. The CategoryParent tag, used by both the request and the response, indicates the parent of a specific category.

Downloading the entire category tree using GetCategories is an expensive operation resulting in the transfer of over a megabyte of data between eBay and your application. For that reason, you should cache the result of the GetCategories interface, and only obtain updates when the Version tag shows that your category cache is out of sync with eBay. You can do this by determining the current category set's version by invoking GetCategories with a value of 0 for both the DetailLevel and ViewAllNodes tags; the return value will provide the current version without sending a new image of the category data. If the category version isn't equal to the version you cached (eBay reserves the right to both increment *and* decrement the category version!), you should download a new category tree using GetCategories, and again cache both the version and all of the category information. Although category data seldom changes more than once a month, eBay suggests that you perform this check and resynchronize at least once a day.

> **WARNING**   *You must cache the results from calling* GetCategories, *rather than calling it repeatedly to determine the same category information. Moreover, you should only call* GetCategories *to update your application's cache of categories once a day per eBay's recommendation. Failure to follow these guidelines—invoking* GetCategories *more often than necessary—will result in your application failing to receive eBay certification.*

The GeteBayOfficialTime Interface

The GeteBayOfficialTime interface returns the current time used by eBay with respect to all auctions. It takes no arguments, and returns the current eBay time in the EBayTime tag. The returned date and time is passed as a string in the format YY-MM-DD HH:MM:SS in Greenwich mean time.

The GetLogoURL Interface

The GetLogoURL interface returns the URL where your application can obtain the eBay logo that your application must show in conjunction with other application credits. The method takes one argument, the Size argument, for which you may include one of the following values:

- Specify a value of Small for an image that is no larger than 44 pixels high and 108 pixels across.

- Specify a value of Medium for an image that is no larger than 60 pixels high and 144 pixels across.

- Specify a value of Large for an image that is no larger than 79 pixels high and 182 pixels across.

The response contains the URL you use to obtain the logo image, along with two additional parameters: Height, which specifies the height of the image in pixels; and Width, which specifies the width of the image in pixels.

> **WARNING** *Your application must cache and show the eBay logo provided by this interface somewhere within its user interface if your application displays data from eBay. Your application should cache the returned image, periodically refresh it, and show it in a place such as your application's About box.*

The GetShippingRates Interface

The GetShippingRates interface lets your application directly access the eBay shipping calculator. Your application can use it anytime to provide you with estimated shipping costs, such as when first listing an item. Table 9-4 shows the argument tags you may pass to the GetShippingRates interface, whereas Table 9-5 summarizes the response tags you can expect.

Table 9-4. Tags Passed to GetShippingRates

Tag	Purpose
PriceSold	Value of the item. Used to calculate value returned in InsuranceFee field.
QuantitySold	Number of objects sold in the auction to a single buyer that would be shipped together. Default is 1.
ShipFromZipCode	Zip code from which the seller is shipping the item.
ShippingIrregular	An item that can't go through the stamping machine at the shipping service office (a value of 1) and requires special or fragile handling.

Table 9-4. Tags Passed to GetShippingRates (continued)

Tag	Purpose
ShippingPackage	Size of the package to be shipped. Valid values are 0: None 1: Letter 2: Large envelope 3: USPS flat-rate envelope 4: Package/thick envelope 5: USPS large package/oversize 1 6: Very large package/oversize 2 7: UPS letter
ShippingService	Shipping carrier for the item. Valid values are 3: UPS Ground 4: UPS 3rd Day 5: UPS 2nd Day 6: UPS Next Day 7: USPS Priority 8: USPS Parcel 9: USPS Media 10: USPS First Class 11: USPS Express Mail
ShipToZipCode	Zip code that the seller is shipping to.
WeightMajor	Weight of the item(s): Number of units for shipping weight unit of measure specified by WeightUnit.
WeightMinor	Weight of the item(s): Fractional number of units for shipping weight unit of measure, either pounds or fractions of a kilogram, depending on WeightUnit.
WeightUnit	Unit of measure for shipping weight. Default value is 1. Valid values are 1: WeightMajor specifies pounds, WeightMinor specifies ounces 2: WeightMajor specifies kilograms, WeightMinor specifies fractions of a kilogram

Table 9-5. Tags Returned by GetShippingRates

Tag	Purpose
ShippingRates	Container node for the one or more shipping rates returned.
ShippingRate	Each ShippingRate contains the detail data for one shipping rate. If no shipping service was specified in the ShippingService input argument, result includes shipping rate data for all available shipping services.
InsuranceFee	Insurance fees associated with shipping the item(s). Calculated from the value in the PriceSold argument. If no PriceSold is specified, InsuranceFee returns zero.
ShippingFee	Shipping costs for the item. (Doesn't include any seller packaging or handling fees.)
ShippingRateErrorMessage	Container of any error message associated with the attempt to calculate shipping rates. If there was no error, returns No Error.
ShippingService	Carrier and service for shipping the item. Possible values are 3: UPS Ground 4: UPS 3rd Day 5: UPS 2nd Day 6: UPS Next Day 7: USPS Priority 8: USPS Parcel 9: USPS Media 10: USPS First Class 11: USPS Express Mail
ShippingType	Indicator of whether shipping costs are flat rates or calculated rates. Possible values are 1: Flat shipping rate 2: Calculated shipping rate

The GetStoreDetails Interface

The GetStoreDetails interface lets you obtain the custom categories—which eBay calls *departments*—for the stores maintained by the specified eBay user. To use GetStoreDetails, pass the eBay ID of the owner of the eBay store auction in question. (Users can only own one store at a time, so there's no possible issue with store details being returned for multiple stores.). Table 9-6 summarizes the response tags you can expect.

Table 9-6. Tags Returned by GetStoreDetails

Tag	Purpose
CustomCategories	Contains Category tags and the Count tags. This provides a list of the custom categories defined by the store.
Category	Container for CategoryNumber and Name tags.
CategoryNumber	Number of the returned category within the Category tag.
Name	Name of the category returned as character data within the Category tag.
Count	Number of Category tags returned within the CustomCategory tag.
StoreName	Name associated with the seller's eBay store.

Although this interface doesn't offer the same versioning as GetCategories, you can query the interface once and cache the results during your application's execution.

Understanding eBay API Calls for Users

The interfaces in this section give your application access to information about eBay users, such as their account, feedback, specific user interface choices when using the Web services, and the transactions a seller must manage.

The GetAccount Interface

The GetAccount interface returns the account information for the currently logged-in user, enumerating transactions either by time period or as an invoice for recent activity. Note that the GetAccount tag can only return account information for the user indicated by the RequestUserId tag in the request. Table 9-7 shows the argument tags you may pass to the GetAccount interface, whereas Table 9-8 summarizes the response tags you can expect within the Account tag (which contains both an account summary in the Summary tag as well as information about each account in one or more Entry tags) returned by the eBay service.

Table 9-7. Tags Passed to GetAccount

Tag	Purpose
PageNumber	For paginated result sets, specifies the subset ("page") of items to return. Default is 1 to return the first page.
AccountPageType	Specifies the report type, period, or invoice. Allowed values are 0: View by period or date/range (default) 1: View by invoice
Period	Specifies the time period for a period report. This argument only required if AccountPageType is 0. Possible values are 0: Since last invoice (the default value) 1: For the last day 2: For activity between dates (BeginDate and EndDate) 3: Ever since the user joined eBay 7: For the last week 14: For the last two weeks 30: For the last month 60: For the last two months
BeginDate	Start date for a period report. Use with EndDate to define a date range. This argument is only required if Period is 2. Date format is YYYY-MM-DD.
EndDate	End date for a period report. Use with BeginDate to define a date range. This argument is only required if Period is 2. Date format is YYYY-MM-DD.
InvoiceMonth	Month of the eBay invoice to return as a report. Use with InvoiceYear to uniquely identify the invoice. This argument is only required if AccountPageType is 1. Allowed values are 0: Since last invoice (the default value) 1: January 2: February 3: March 4: April 5: May 6: June 7: July 8: August 9: September 10: October 11: November 12: December

Table 9-7. Tags Passed to GetAccount (continued)

Tag	Purpose
InvoiceYear	Year of the eBay invoice to return as a report. Use with InvoiceMonth to uniquely identify the invoice. Specify year in four-digit format, YYYY. This argument is only required if AccountPageType is 1. If InvoiceMonth is 0, don't specify a value for InvoiceYear.
Currency	ID for the currency for the account report. The currency for the user's associated eBay site is used as default.
Summary	Indicator of whether to include account summary information in the returned report.

Table 9-8. Tags Returned by GetAccount

Tag	Purpose
PageNumber	Number of the page returned.
TotalPages	Total number of pages in the account.
Currency	ID of currency in which monetary values are returned.
Summary	Container node for account summary leaf nodes if requested.
AccountId	ID for the account if requested.
AccountState	State of the account returned in the Summary tag. Possible values are Active: The account is active. Pending: The account is awaiting confirmation. Inactive: The account has been terminated.
BillingCycleDate	Indicates the billing cycle in which eBay sends a billing invoice to the specified user returned in the Summary tag. Possible values are 0: On the last day of the month 15: On the 15th day of the month
PaymentType	Indicates the method the specified user selected for paying eBay returned in the Summary tag. The values for PaymentType vary for each site ID.
CCInfo	Last four digits of the user's credit card selected as payment type returned in the Summary tag. Empty string if no credit is on file.

Table 9-8. Tags Returned by GetAccount (continued)

Tag	Purpose
CCExp	Expiration date for the credit card selected as payment method, in GMT returned in the Summary tag. Empty string if no credit card is on file or if account is inactive (even if there is a credit card on file).
CCModifyDate	Last date credit card or credit card expiration date was modified, in GMT, returned in the Summary tag. Empty string if no credit card is on file.
BankAccountInfo	First four digits of the debit card for the account returned in the Summary tag. Empty string if no debit card is on file.
BankModifyDate	Last date BankAccountInfo or BankRoutingInfo was modified, in GMT. Empty string if no debit card is on file. Returned in the Summary tag.
PastDue	Indicator of whether the account has past due amounts outstanding. Returned in the Summary entity. Possible values are 1: Account is past due 0: Account is current
AmountPastDue	Amount past due. Returned in the Summary tag.
LastPaymentDate	Date of last payment by specified user to eBay, in GMT. Empty string if no payments posted. Returned in the Summary tag.
LastAmountPaid	Amount of last payment posted. Returned in the Summary tag.
CurrentBalance	User's current balance, returned in the Summary tag. Can be 0.00, positive, or negative.
LastInvoiceDate	Date of last invoice sent by eBay to the user, in GMT. Empty string if this account hasn't been invoiced yet. Returned in the Summary tag.
LastInvoiceAmount	Amount of last invoice. 0.00 if account not yet invoiced. Returned in the Summary tag.
EmailAddress	E-mail address to which eBay invoices are sent. Returned as character data.
InvoiceDate	Invoice date, in GMT.
InvoiceBalance	Invoice amount.
AdditionalAccounts Count	Number of additional accounts (AdditionalAccounts nodes returned) the specified user has or 0 if no additional accounts. Returned in the Summary tag.

Table 9-8. Tags Returned by GetAccount (continued)

Tag	Purpose
AdditionalAccount	Container of leaf nodes with information about each additional account. Returned in the Summary tag.
AdditionalId	ID for an additional account. Returned in each AdditionalAccount tag.
AdditionalCurrency	ID for the currency in which additional account monetary amounts are returned. Returned in each AdditionalAccount entry.
AdditionalBalance	Balance for an additional account. Returned in each AdditionalAccount tag.
Entry	Container node for leaf nodes containing data about each account entry.
EntryCount	Number of detail nodes in the response within the Entry tag.
ItemNumber	Item number for the transaction. Returned in each Entry tag.
Number	eBay reference number for an account entry. Returned in each Entry tag.
Date	Date entry was posted, in GMT. Returned in each Entry tag.
Type	Integer code for account details entry type. See the eBay API documentation for details. Returned in each Entry tag.
Memo	Memo line for an account entry, can be empty string. Returned as character data. Returned in each Entry tag.

The GetAccount interface provides a *paged* metaphor to the returned data: The interface returns a subset of the data available based on a page number you specify. Each request may return up to 500 records for either the period or invoice view of the account data. When making a request, specify the page number of the data to fetch using the PageNumber tag; the return value also contains the same attribute noting the page number of the returned data.

To get an invoice report itemizing each transaction that occurs during an interval in time, pass 1 in the AccountPageType tag, and pass the month and year in question in the InvoiceMonth and InvoiceYear arguments. The return Account tag will contain Entry tags for each transaction that affected the user account.

To get a period report, pass 0 in the AccountPageType tag, and pass the period of interest in the Period tag. Set other tags, such as BeginDate and EndDate as described in Table 9-7, and the response's Summary tag will contain the account balance over the specified period.

The GetFeedback Interface

The GetFeedback interface lets your application obtain detailed feedback information for a user. Like GetAccount, the GetFeedback call provides a paged metaphor within its requests and responses. When issuing a GetFeedback call, you must also provide the StartingPage tag, which tells eBay on which page to start, and the ItemsPerPage tag, which indicates how many feedback items to place on a page. The returned XML contains the FeedbackDetailItemTotal tag to let you know how many items are available, letting you create multiple requests to iterate across all entries.

The DetailLevel tag lets you select whether you want only a summary of the user's feedback within a FeedbackScoreSummary tag (set DetailLevel to 0) or individual feedback items enumerated within a FeedbackDetail tag (set DetailLevel to 1).

Table 9-9 summarizes the response tags you can expect.

Table 9-9. Tags Returned by GetFeedback

Tag	Purpose
FeedbackDetail	Parent node for all FeedbackDetailItem nodes. Only returned with a DetailLevel of 1.
FeedbackDetailItem	Parent node for all attribute leaf nodes describing one feedback. There may be multiple FeedbackDetailItem nodes in a result set page. Returned within a FeedbackDetail tag when DetailLevel is 1.
CommentText	Text message left by user specified in CommentingUser. Used to provide a more in-depth description of the user's opinion of their transaction with the user about whom they left feedback. Returned as character data in the language that the comment was originally left in. Returned within the FeedbackDetailItem tag.
CommentType	Type of feedback. Can be Praise, Complaint, or Neutral. Returned within the FeedbackDetailItem tag.
CommentingUser	eBay user ID for the user who left the feedback. Returned within the FeedbackDetailItem tag.
CommentingUserScore	Feedback score of the user indicated in CommentingUser. Returned within the FeedbackDetailItem tag.
FeedbackRole	Indicator of whether the user who the feedback is being retrieved for was a buyer or a seller for that transaction. Returned within the FeedbackDetailItem tag. (A value of B represents a buyer, whereas a value of S represents a seller.)

Table 9-9. Tags Returned by GetFeedback (continued)

Tag	Purpose
Followup	Explanation a user can give to a response. Returned within the FeedbackDetailItem tag.
ItemNumber	Item number for the item sold in the auction on which the feedback is based. Returned within the FeedbackDetailItem tag.
Response	Textual comment that the user targeted by feedback may leave in response or rebuttal to the feedback. Returned within the FeedbackDetailItem tag.
TimeOfComment	Date and time (in GMT) that the feedback was submitted to eBay. Returned within the FeedbackDetailItem tag.
TransactionId	Unique identifier of the feedback transaction. This is *not* the same as the TransactionId of the corresponding purchase that led to this feedback record. Returned within the FeedbackDetailItem tag.
FeedbackDetail ItemTotal	Total number of feedback entries.
FeedbackScoreSummary	Parent node for all feedback summary information leaf nodes.
BidRetractionCountINT1	Count of bid retractions for the preceding seven days. Returned within the FeedbackScoreSummary tag.
BidRetractionCountINT2	Count of bid retractions for the preceding month. Returned within the FeedbackScoreSummary tag.
BidRettractionCountINT3	Count of bid retractions for the preceding six months. Returned within the FeedbackScoreSummary tag.
NegativeFeedbackCount	Total count of negative feedback entries.
NegativeFeedbackCountINT1	Count of negative feedback entries for interval 1. Returned within the FeedbackScoreSummary tag.
NegativeFeedbackCountINT2	Count of negative feedback entries for interval 2. Returned within the FeedbackScoreSummary tag.
NegativeFeedbackCountINT3	Count of negative feedback entries for interval 3. Returned within the FeedbackScoreSummary tag.
NeutralCommentCount	Total count of neutral feedback entries. Returned within the FeedbackScoreSummary tag.

Table 9-9. Tags Returned by GetFeedback (continued)

Tag	Purpose
NeutralCommentCountFrom SuspendedUsers	Total count of neutral feedback entries from suspended users. Returned within the FeedbackScoreSummary tag.
NeutralFeedbackCountINT1	Count of neutral feedback entries for interval 1. Returned within the FeedbackScoreSummary tag.
NeutralFeedbackCountINT2	Count of neutral feedback entries for interval 2. Returned within the FeedbackScoreSummary tag.
NeutralFeedbackCountINT3	Count of neutral feedback entries for interval 3. Returned within the FeedbackScoreSummary tag.
PositiveFeedbackCount	Total count of positive feedback entries. Returned within the FeedbackScoreSummary tag.
PositiveFeedbackCountINT1	Count of positive feedback entries for interval 1. Returned within the FeedbackScoreSummary tag.
PositiveFeedbackCountINT2	Count of positive feedback entries for interval 2. Returned within the FeedbackScoreSummary tag.
PositiveFeedbackCountINT3	Count of positive feedback entries for interval 3. Returned within the FeedbackScoreSummary tag.
TotalFeedbackCountINT1	Total feedback score for interval 1. Returned within the FeedbackScoreSummary tag.
TotalFeedbackCountINT2	Total feedback score for interval 2. Returned within the FeedbackScoreSummary tag.
TotalFeedbackCountINT3	Total feedback score for interval 3. Returned within the FeedbackScoreSummary tag.
UniqueNegativeFeedback Count	Total count of negative feedback entries from unique (distinct) users. Returned within the FeedbackScoreSummary tag.
UniquePositiveFeedback Count	Total count of positive feedback entries from unique (distinct) users. Returned within the FeedbackScoreSummary tag.
Score	Total feedback score for target user.

The GetSellerEvents Interface

The GetSellerEvents interface returns the price changes, item revisions, description revisions, and any other changes that a specific seller has made during the last 48 hours. When calling GetSellerEvents, you specify the starting time and ending for the inquiry. You can filter the results using one of three ways:

- By when items auctions ended using EndTimeFrom and EndTimeTo

- By when items were modified using ModTimeFrom and ModTimeTo

- By when items went up for auction using StartTimeFrom and StartTimeTo

These filters are exclusive.

In addition to these arguments, the NewItemFilter tag indicates whether you want to return items that include new listings (by default, the API's notion of "modified" is literally that of a changed listing; new listings are not considered modified). If you specify false (0), the results include newly listed items.

The returned items are contained in individual nodes of XML (encapsulated by the I tag) indicating the reason for their inclusion in the response. Table 9-10 summarizes the tags returned by GetSellerEvents. Note that GetSellerEvents can only return a maximum of 3,000 items if you set DetailLevel tag to 0, and 2,000 items if you set DetailLevel to 1. If the returned value Count attribute is greater than or equal to one of these maximums, eBay can provide more information if you repeat the request with a smaller time window.

Table 9-10. Tags Returned by GetSellerEvents

Tag	Purpose
Count	Number of item changes that fit the criteria that you specified in your GetSellerEvents request.
I	Container node for item information.
BC	Number of bids that the item has received. Returns zero for fixed-price items. Returned within the I tag.
BIN	Buy It Now price for the item. Only returned for items with a Buy It Now price. Returned within the I tag.
CP	Current price for the item. Returned within the I tag.
ET	Time that the listing is scheduled to end. Returned within the I tag.

Table 9-10. Tags Returned by GetSellerEvents (continued)

Tag	Purpose
HB	User ID for the current high bidder for an item that has received bids. Returned only when a high bidder for the item exists. Not returned for fixed-price items. For eBay stores, Fixed-Price, and Dutch auction listings, have your application call GetSellerTransactions or GetHighBidders for additional item information. Returned within the I tag.
HBE	E-mail address for the current high bidder. Returned only if the item has received bids. Not returned for fixed-price items. Returned within the I tag.
HBF	Overall feedback score for the current high bidder. Returned only if the item has received bids. Returned within the I tag.
Id	Item ID.
Q	For non-Chinese auction items, the quantity of items initially offered for sale. For stores fixed-price (US only) or Buy It Now Only items, the remaining quantity (I.Q) equals the original quantity minus the quantity sold (I.QS). Not returned for Chinese format listings.
QS	Number of items sold.
SI	eBay site on which the specified item is listed.
Ti	Item title, returned as character data.
Ty	Listing type for the item. Possible values are 0: Unknown auction type 1: Chinese auction 2: Dutch auction 5: Live Auctions–type auction 6: Ad-Type auction 7: eBay stores inventory (stores fixed-price) listing (US only) 8: Personal offer 9: Basic fixed-price item
TimeTo	If you specify a value in the EndTimeTo, ModTimeTo, or StartTimeTo filter, TimeTo returns that value. If you don't specify a value for one of these entities, TimeTo returns the current time in GMT.

WARNING *You can't call* GetSellerEvents *more than once every 30 minutes. If you do, your application may not pass eBay certification.*

The GetSellerTransactions Interface

The GetSellerTransactions interface returns a list of the fixed-price and auction transactions for the seller you specify. (An auction is treated as a transaction only if it has ended, has had at least one bid, and the buyer has begun the checkout process for the auction by choosing a payment process, requested the details of the transaction, or paid the seller; or the seller has specified the details of the transaction.) Like GetAccount and other API calls that can return a large number of items, this method provides a paged response; use PageNumber and TransactionsPerPage to indicate the page number and how many items per page should be returned. Table 9-11 shows the argument tags you may pass to the GetSellerTransactions interface.

> **TIP** *To get the transactions for a specific item, use* GetItemTransactions *instead.*

The returned XML contains a series of Transaction nodes, each containing the specific details of a single transaction. Table 9-12 summarizes the response tags you can expect.

Table 9-11. Tags Passed to GetSellerTransactions

Tag	Purpose
LastModifiedFrom	Use the LastModifiedFrom and LastModifiedTo filter to return transactions that were last modified between the specified date and time. Use GMT time in the format YYYY-MM-DD HH:MM:SS. You can use this filter for fixed-price items that haven't gone through checkout. The date range can't be greater than 30 days.
LastModifiedTo	Use the LastModifiedFrom and LastModifiedTo filter to return transactions that were last modified between the specified date and time. Use GMT time in the format YYYY-MM-DD HH:MM:SS. You can use this filter for fixed-price items that haven't gone through checkout. The date range can't be greater than 30 days.
TransactionsPerPage	Number of transactions to return in a single call. Default is 100, maximum is 200.
PageNumber	Specifies which virtual page of data to return in the current call. Default is 1.

Table 9-12. Tags Returned by GetSellerTransactions

Tag	Purpose
HasMoreTransactions	Indicator of whether there are more transactions to be retrieved beyond those returned in the last function call.
PageNumber	Number for the virtual page of data returned by the last function call.
ReturnedTransaction CountActual	Number of Transaction nodes actually returned by the last function call.
User	Data about the buyer or seller. User node fields are described in the section "The GetUser API," later in this chapter.
Transactions	Data on multiple transactions and one or more Transaction nodes.
Count	Total number of transactions that meet the input argument criteria and could be returned through one or more calls to GetSellerTransactions. Contained within the Transactions tag.
TotalNumberOfPages	Total number of pages that can be returned.
Transaction	Container node for each transaction. Contained within the Transactions tag.
AllowEditPayment	If 1, indicates if seller allowed buyers to edit payment information at the time that the transaction occurred. Returns 0 otherwise. Contained within the Transaction tag.
AmountPaid	Amount the buyer paid for the item or agreed to pay, depending on how far into the checkout process the item is.
ApplicationData	Custom, application-specific data associated with the item. The data in this field is stored with the item in the items table at eBay, but isn't used in any way by eBay. Use ApplicationData to store such special information as a part or SKU number. Returned as character data with a maximum of 32 characters in length.
Buyer	Container node for data about each transaction's buyer. Except for shipping address fields (explained later in this table). Its User node fields are described in the section "The GetUser API," later in this chapter. Contained within the Transaction tag.
CountryCode	Two-letter abbreviation for the buyer's country. Contained within the User tag of a Transaction tag.

Table 9-12. Tags Returned by GetSellerTransactions (continued)

Tag	Purpose
ShippingAddress	Container node for the buyer's shipping address. Contained within the User tag of a Transaction tag.
City	City portion of buyer's shipping address. Contained within the ShippingAddress tag of a User tag of a Transaction tag.
Country	Country portion of buyer's shipping address. Contained within the ShippingAddress tag of a User tag of a Transaction tag.
Name	Name portion of buyer's shipping address. Contained within the ShippingAddress tag of a User tag of a Transaction tag.
Phone	Phone number portion of buyer's shipping address. Contained within the ShippingAddress tag of a User tag of a Transaction tag.
StateOrProvince	State (or region) portion of buyer's shipping address. Contained within the ShippingAddress tag of a User tag of a Transaction tag.
Street1	First line of street address portion of buyer's shipping address. Contained within the ShippingAddress tag of a User tag of a Transaction tag.
Street2	Second line of street address portion of buyer's shipping address. Contained within the ShippingAddress tag of a User tag of a Transaction tag.
Zip	Zip or postal code portion of buyer's shipping address. Contained within the ShippingAddress tag of a User tag of a Transaction tag.
BuyerProtection	Indicates the status of the item's eligibility for the Buyer Protection Program. Contained within the Transaction tag. Possible values are 0: Item is ineligible (e.g., category not applicable) 1: Item is eligible per standard criteria 2: Item marked ineligible per special criteria (e.g., seller's account closed) 3: Item marked eligible per other criteria Applicable for items listed to the US site and for the Parts & Accessories category (6028) or Everything Else category (10368) (or their subcategories) on the eBay Motors site.
BuyItNowPrice	Amount a buyer would need to bid to take advantage of the Buy It Now feature. Not applicable to fixed-price items or ad format listings. For fixed-price items, see StartPrice instead. Contained within the Transaction tag.

Table 9-12. Tags Returned by GetSellerTransactions (continued)

Tag	Purpose
Category	Container for data on the primary category of listing. Contained within the Transaction tag.
CategoryId	ID for the category in which the item is listed. Contained within the Category tag of a Transaction tag.
Category2	Container for data on the secondary category of listing. Contained within the Transaction tag.
Category2Id	ID for the optional second category (if specified) in which the item is listed. Contained within the Category2 tag of a Transaction tag.
CharityListing	If true (1), indicates that the seller has chosen to use eBay Giving Works to donate a percentage of the item purchase price to a selected nonprofit organization. Contained within the Transaction tag.
Checkout	Container node for post-sale data for the transaction. Contained within the Transaction tag.
Details	Container node for payment details data for the transaction. Contained within the Transaction tag's Checkout tag.
AdditionalShipping Costs	Any additional shipping costs beyond those indicated in ShippingHandlingCosts. Contained within the Transaction tag's Details tag, found within the Checkout tag.
AdjustmentAmount	Adjustment amount entered by the buyer. A positive amount indicates the amount is an extra charge being paid to the seller by the buyer. A negative value indicates this amount is a credit given to the buyer by the seller. Contained within the Transaction tag's Details tag, found within the Checkout tag.
CheckoutDetails Specified	Indicator of whether seller has specified payment details. Contained within the Transaction tag's Details tag, found within the Checkout tag.
Checkout Instructions	Seller's return policy and instructions. Contained within the Transaction tag's Details tag, found within the Checkout tag.
Converted AdjustmentAmount	Value returned in the AdjustmentAmount field, converted to the currency indicated by SiteCurrency. Contained within the Transaction tag's Details tag, found within the Checkout tag.
ConvertedAmountPaid	Value returned in the AmountPaid field, converted to the currency indicated by SiteCurrency. Contained within the Transaction tag's Details tag, found within the Checkout tag.

Table 9-12. Tags Returned by GetSellerTransactions (continued)

Tag	Purpose
Converted TransactionPrice	Value returned in the TransactionPrice field, converted to the currency indicated by SiteCurrency. Contained within the Transaction tag's Details tag, found within the Checkout tag.
InsuranceFee	Amount of insurance. Contained within the Transaction tag's Details tag, found within the Checkout tag.
InsuranceOption	Indicator of whether insurance fee is required. Contained within the Transaction tag's Details tag, found within the Checkout tag. Possible values are 0: Insurance not offered 1: Insurance optional 2: Insurance required 3: Insurance included in shipping and handling costs
InsuranceTotal	Total cost of insurance for the transaction. Contained within the Transaction tag's Details tag, found within the Checkout tag.
InsuranceWanted	Indicator of whether buyer selected to have insurance. Contained within the Transaction tag's Details tag, found within the Checkout tag.
PaymentEdit	Indicator of whether the buyer edited the payment amount. Contained within the Transaction tag's Details tag, found within the Checkout tag.
SalesTaxAmount	Amount of the sales tax to be collected for the transaction. Contained within the Transaction tag's Details tag, found within the Checkout tag (US only).
SalesTaxPercent	Sales tax for the transaction, expressed as a percentage. Contained within the Transaction tag's Details tag, found within the Checkout tag (US only).
SalesTaxState	State of collection for the sales tax for the transaction. Contained within the Transaction tag's Details tag, found within the Checkout tag (US only).
ShippingHandling Costs	Amount charged for shipping and handling. Contained within the Transaction tag's Details tag, found within the Checkout tag.
ShippingInTax	Indicator of whether shipping is included in the tax. Contained within the Transaction tag's Details tag, found within the Checkout tag (US only).

Table 9-12. Tags Returned by GetSellerTransactions (continued)

Tag	Purpose
Status	Container node for checkout status data for the transaction. Contained within the Transaction tag's Checkout tag.
eBayPaymentStatus	Indicator of the success or failure of an eBay Online Payment for the transaction. If the payment failed, the value returned indicates the reason for the failure. Contained within the Transaction tag's Checkout tag, inside the Status tag. Possible values are 0: No payment failure 3: Buyer's eCheck bounced 4: Buyer's credit card failed 5: Buyer failed payment as reported by seller 7: Payment from buyer to seller is in PayPal process, but hasn't yet been completed
IncompleteState	Current state of the checkout process for the transaction. Contained within the Transaction tag's Checkout tag. Possible values are 0: Checkout complete. 1: Checkout incomplete. No details specified. 2: Buyer requests total. 3: Seller responded to buyer's request.
LastTimeModified	Last date and time checkout status or incomplete state was updated (in GMT). Contained within the Transaction tag's Checkout tag.
PaymentMethodUsed	Payment method used by the buyer. Contained within the Transaction tag's Checkout tag. Possible values are 0: No payment method specified 3: Money order/cashier's check 4: Personal check 5: COD 6: Visa or MasterCard 7: Other (or see item description) 12: PayPal
StatusIs	Indicates whether checkout process is complete. Contained within the Transaction tag's Checkout tag. Possible values are 1: Incomplete 2: Complete
CheckoutEnabled	Indicator of whether the seller had Checkout enabled at the time that the transaction completed. Returns 0 otherwise. Contained within the Transaction tag.

Table 9-12. Tags Returned by GetSellerTransactions (continued)

Tag	Purpose
CreatedTime	For fixed-price, stores inventory, and Buy It Now items, indicates when the purchase occurred. Contained within the Transaction tag.
Currency	Numeric ID for the currency used for the transaction. Contained within the Transaction tag.
CurrentPrice	For auction-format listings, highest bid (closing price) for the item. This field doesn't reflect the closing price of the item if it's a fixed-price item and the price has been revised. Contained within the Transaction tag.
DepositType	Deposit type for eBay Motors items. If item isn't a Motors item, then returns None. Contained within the Transaction tag. Possible values are 0: None 1: Other method 2: Fast deposit
EndTime	Time stamp for the end of the listing. Contained within the Transaction tag.
ItemId	Unique item ID for the auction associated with the transaction. Contained within the Transaction tag.
PaymentTerms	Container node for data pertaining to each transaction's payment terms. Not applicable for real estate listings. Contained within the Transaction tag.
Amex	American Express is accepted by seller as payment method in the transaction. For Motors, this payment method is available for the deposit. Contained within the Transaction tag's PaymentTerms tag.
CCAccepted	Credit card is accepted by seller as payment method in the transaction. Contained within the Transaction tag's PaymentTerms tag.
COD	Cash on delivery (COD) is accepted by seller as payment method in the transaction. For Motors, this payment method is available for the deposit. Contained within the Transaction tag's PaymentTerms tag.
Discover	Discover Card is accepted by seller as payment method in the transaction. Contained within the Transaction tag's PaymentTerms tag.

Table 9-12. Tags Returned by GetSellerTransactions (continued)

Tag	Purpose
MOCashiers	Money order (or cashier check) is accepted by seller as payment method in the transaction. For Motors, this payment method is available for the deposit. Contained within the `Transaction` tag's `PaymentTerms` tag.
MoneyXferAccepted	Money transfer is accepted by seller as payment method in the transaction. Contained within the `Transaction` tag's `PaymentTerms` tag.
MoneyXferAcceptedin Checkout	Direct transfer of money is an acceptable payment method in `Checkout`. Contained within the `Transaction` tag's `PaymentTerms` tag.
Other	Some custom method is accepted by seller as payment method in the transaction. For Motors, this payment method is available for the deposit. Contained within the `Transaction` tag's `PaymentTerms` tag.
OtherPaymentsOnline	Non-eBay online payment is an acceptable payment method. Not applicable for real estate listings. Contained within the `Transaction` tag's `PaymentTerms` tag.
PayPalAccepted	If true (1), indicates that the seller accepts PayPal as a form of payment for this item. Not applicable for real estate listings. Contained within the `Transaction` tag's `PaymentTerms` tag.
PersonalCheck	Personal check is accepted by seller as payment method in the transaction. For Motors, this payment method is available for the deposit. Contained within the `Transaction` tag's `PaymentTerms` tag.
SeeDescription	Payment method accepted by seller is cited in the item's description. For Motors, this payment method is available for the deposit. Contained within the `Transaction` tag's `PaymentTerms` tag.
VisaMaster	Visa or MasterCard are accepted by seller as payment method in the transaction. For Motors, this payment method is available for the deposit. Contained within the `Transaction` tag's `PaymentTerms` tag.
Price	Current price of the item. This may be different for stores inventory items because the price of the item can be revised even after a transaction occurs. For Motors items, this is the current price of the vehicle. Contained within the `Transaction` tag.

Table 9-12. Tags Returned by GetSellerTransactions (continued)

Tag	Purpose
Quantity	Total number of items originally available in the listing. Use Quantity minus QuantitySold to calculate the remaining quantity available. Contained within the Transaction tag.
QuantityPurchased	Number of individual items the buyer purchased in the transaction. Contained within the Transaction tag.
QuantitySold	Total number of items in the listing that have sold so far. Use Quantity minus QuantitySold to calculate the remaining quantity available. Contained within the Transaction tag.
RelistID	New item ID for a relisted item. Contained within the Transaction tag.
ShippingOption	Basic shipping options. May contain either SiteOnly, WorldWide, or SiteAndRegions. A value of SiteAndRegions indicates the seller will ship within the country associated with the item's site plus any region represented with a true value in the tags within ShippingRegions: NorthAmerica, Europe, Oceania, Asia, SouthAmerica, Africa, LatinAmerica, MiddleEast, and Caribbean. Contained within the Transaction tag.
ShippingRegions	Container node for regions that seller will ship to. Contained within the Transaction tag.
ShippingTerms	Container node for shipping term information. Contained within the Transaction tag.
SellerPays	Seller pays all shipping. Contained within the Transaction tag's ShippingTerms tag.
SiteCurrency	Numeric code corresponding to the currency of the site specified in SiteId. Contained within the Transaction tag.
SiteId	ID for the eBay site on which the item was listed. Contained within the Transaction tag.
StartPrice	Starting price for the item. For fixed-price items, if the item price (MinimumBid) was revised, this field returns the new price. Contained within the Transaction tag.
StartTime	Time stamp for the start of the listing. Contained within the Transaction tag
Title	Name of the item as listed in its auction. Contained within the Transaction tag.

Table 9-12. Tags Returned by GetSellerTransactions (continued)

Tag	Purpose
TransactionId	Identifier for each transaction returned. Returns 0 when the auction is a Chinese auction. Use ItemId with TransactionId to uniquely identify a transaction. Contained within the Transaction tag.
TransactionPrice	Price of the item, before shipping and sales tax. For Motors, this isn't the price of the vehicle (which is returned in Price), but the Deposit amount. Contained within the Transaction tag.
Type	Type of auction associated with the transaction. Contained within the Transaction tag. Possible values are 0: Unknown auction type 1: Chinese auction 2: Dutch auction 5: Live Auctions–type auction 7: Fixed-Price auction 8: Personal offer
TransactionsPerPage	Number of Transaction nodes per function call.

WARNING *Although this (and other) eBay APIs can return PayPal-relevant data even when you use the Sandbox, the PayPal information is not part of the Sandbox! Put simply, the eBay Sandbox doesn't extend to PayPal transactions.*

The GetUser Interface

The GetUser interface lets your application access the information about another eBay user. The interface takes at least a single parameter, UserId, which must contain the eBay user ID of the user whose information you want to obtain. Table 9-13 shows the returned parameters when invoking GetUser. (Note that the setting you specify for your request's DetailLevel has a huge impact on the data you receive from eBay; for details, see the text that follows this table and Table 9-14.)

Table 9-13. Tags Returned by GetUser

Tag	Purpose
AboutMe	Indicates whether the user has an About Me page.
AllowPaymentEdit	If 1, indicates whether a seller is allowing buyers to edit the total cost of an item.
CheckoutEnabled	Returns 1 if the user is a seller and has enabled Checkout. Returns 0 if the user isn't a seller or hasn't enabled Checkout.
CIPBankAccountStored	If 1, specifies that a user has stored bank account information with eBay in order to use the CIP in checkout function. Applicable to German site only.
eBayGoodStanding	If 1, indicates that the user is in good standing with eBay.
Email	Specifies the e-mail address for the user. As an antispam measure, e-mail addresses are only returned when the UserId in the request matches the RequestUserId. When an e-mail address can't be returned, the string "Invalid Request" is returned in the Email node instead.
Feedback	Indicates node to contain the user's feedback information.
Score	Specifies aggregate feedback score for the specified user, contained within the Feedback tag. Score is only returned if the user specified in UserId hasn't chosen to make his or her feedback private. If private is selected for the user, then Score is only returned if the RequestUserId input argument matches the UserId input argument.
IDVerified	Indicates whether the user has been verified.
IsLAAuthorized	If 1, indicates that a user is authorized to list Live Auction items.
MerchandisingPref	Indicates whether the user has elected to participate as a seller in the Merchandising Manager feature of eBay. Will be one of these values: 0: User as seller opted out of merchandising 1: User as seller opted in to merchandising, including display on the View Item page
NewUser	Identifies a new user. If 1, indicates that the user has been a registered eBay user for 30 days or less. Always 0 after the user has been registered for more than 30 days.
Private	Indicates whether the user selected to have feedback information private.

Table 9-13. Tags Returned by GetUser (continued)

Tag	Purpose
RegDate	Indicates the date the specified user originally registered with eBay.
RegistrationAddress	Contains user registration address data. As an antispam measure, e-mail addresses are only returned when the UserId in the request matches the RequestUserId. Contains tags for the address's City, Country, Name, Phone, StateOrProvince, Street, and Zip.
SchedulingInformation	Specifies the container for scheduling limits for the user. Will contain the tags MaxScheduledTime, MaxScheduledItems, and MinScheduleTime.
SellerLevel	Indicates the user's eBay PowerSeller tier. Possible values are 11: Bronze 22: Silver 33: Gold 66: Platinum 77: Titanium Other values are valid, but indicate that the user is a not a PowerSeller.
SellerPaymentAddress	Contains seller payment address data. As an antispam measure, e-mail addresses are only returned when the UserId in the request matches the RequestUserId. Contains tags for the address's City, Country, InternationalName, Name, Phone, StateAndCity, StateOrProvince, InternationalStreet, Street1, Street2, and Zip.
SiteId	Defines eBay site the user is registered with.
Star	Provides a visual indicator of user's feedback score.
Status	Indicates the user's registration/user status.
StoreLocation	Specifies URL pointing to the seller's eBay stores page.
StoreOwner	Indicates whether the user is an eBay stores storefront owner.
UserId	Defines a unique identifier for the user.
UserIdChanged	Identifies a user whose ID has changed. If 1, indicates that the user's ID has changed within the last 30 days.
UserIdLastChanged	Specifies time stamp the user's data was last changed.

Table 9-13. Tags Returned by GetUser (continued)

Tag	Purpose
VATBusinessAvailable	Indicates that the seller is living in a country for which business features are available (currently Germany, Austria, or Switzerland).
VATStatus	If present, indicates whether or not the user is subject to VAT. Users who have registered with eBay as VAT exempt are not subject to VAT. Not returned for users whose country of residence is outside the EU. Possible values for the user's status are 2: Residence in an EU country but user registered as VAT exempt 3: Residence in an EU country and user not registered as VAT exempt

Because of the potentially large number of returned tags, the GetUser interface uses the DetailLevel parameter to determine which fields to return in its response. Table 9-14 shows the relationship between DetailLevel values and tags returned by the eBay service.

Table 9-14. Tags Returned by GetUser Depending on the DetailLevel

Tag	DetailLevel 0	DetailLevel 2	DetailLevel 4	DetailLevel 8
AboutMe	✔	✔	✔	✔
Checkout Enabled	✔	✔	✔	✔
eBayGood Standing	✔	✔	✔	✔
Email	✔	✔	✔	✔
Feedback 1	✔	✔	✔	✔
Feedback 2	✔	✔	✔	✔
IdVerified	✔	✔	✔	✔
IsLAAuthorized	✔	✔	✔	✔
NewUser	✔	✔	✔	✔
Private	✔	✔	✔	✔
RegDate	✔	✔	✔	✔

Table 9-14. Tags Returned by GetUser Depending on the DetailLevel (continued)

Tag	`DetailLevel 0`	`DetailLevel 2`	`DetailLevel 4`	`DetailLevel 8`
Registration Address				✔
Scheduling Information		✔		
SellerLevel	✔	✔	✔	✔
SellerPayment Address			✔	

The `GetWatchList` Interface

The `GetWatchList` interface returns a list of items being watched by the specified user. It takes a single argument, the `WatchSort` argument, which indicates how the results should be sorted as follows:

- A value of 1 indicates that the results should be sorted by item ID.

- A value of 3 indicates that the results should be sorted by the amount of time remaining in the auction. This is the default.

- A value of 4 indicates that the results should be sorted by current price.

- A value of 5 indicates that the results should be sorted alphabetically by item title.

- A value of 15 indicates that the results should be sorted by the bid count.

The returned XML contains a set of `Item` tags, each with information about a specific item on the user's watch list. The list of `Item` tags is contained within an `Items` tag, which is also accompanied by a `Count` tag that indicates how many items were returned. Table 9-15 summarizes the tags you'll find within each `Item` tag.

Table 9-15. Tags Returned by GetWatchList Within the Item Tag

Tag	Purpose
BidCount	Number of bids placed up to this point.
BuyItNowPrice	Minimum acceptable bid for a Buy It Now auction for the item. Only returned for auctions with Buy It Now option.
CurrentPrice	For auction-format listings, current minimum asking price or the current highest bid for the item if bids have been placed. Shows minimum bid if no bids have been placed against the item.
GalleryURL	Not currently used.
Id	Unique identifier for each item.
SiteId	eBay site on which the item is listed.
TimeLeft	Time remaining in the item's auction, in days, hours, and minutes.
Title	Textual title of the item, as is displayed in browse lists and search results on the eBay site.
Type	Auction type for the item(s) specified in the Id input argument. Will be one of these values: 0: Unknown auction type 1: Chinese auction 2: Dutch auction 5: Live Auctions–type auction 6: Ad-Type auction 7: Stores inventory (stores fixed-price) item (US only) 8: Personal offer 9: Basic fixed-price item (Buy It Now only)

The LeaveFeedback Interface

The LeaveFeedback interface lets your application leave feedback for a user as a result of buying or selling an item. To leave feedback, simply fill in the tags described in Table 9-16. The return XML will have a single tag, the Status tag, which will contain the value Success on success, or Failed on failure.

Table 9-16. Tags Passed to LeaveFeedback

Tag	Purpose
ItemId	Unique identifier of an item for which an auction has just been completed.
TransactionId	Unique identifier for a purchase from an eBay stores inventory (stores fixed-price) listing. Only required for feedback resulting from these type of listings.
TargetUser	Unique identifier (eBay user ID) for the user about whom feedback is being submitted.
CommentType	Type of feedback being left. Valid values for CommentType are positive, negative, or neutral.
Comment	Textual feedback and explanation or justification of good, bad, or neutral feedback. Maximum length is 80 characters for all sites except Taiwan, where the length is 125.

The SetSellerPaymentAddress Interface

The SetSellerPaymentAddress interface overwrites a user's shipment and payment address with new data. To update a user's payment address, specify the new address in the XML, and test the returned value's Status tag for the value Success. When specifying new values, all fields are overwritten—you must specify a value for each tag, because omitting a tag will clear that tag's value in eBay's database. Table 9-17 shows the tags you pass to SetSellerPaymentAddress.

Table 9-17. Tags Passed to SetSellerPaymentAddress

Tag	Purpose
Name	Name for seller's shipping address. Maximum is 64 characters.
Street1	First line of street address for seller's shipping address. Maximum is 64 characters.
Street2	Second line of street address for seller's shipping address. Maximum is 64 characters.
City	City for seller's shipping address. Maximum is 64 characters.
StateOrProvince	State or province for seller's shipping address. Pass as CDATA. Maximum is 64 characters.

Table 9-17. Tags Passed to SetSellerPaymentAddress (continued)

Tag	Purpose
Country	Country for seller's shipping address.
Zip	Zip or postal code for seller's shipping address. Maximum is 12 characters.
Phone	Phone number for seller's shipping address. Maximum is 32 characters.

The ValidateTestUserRegistration Interface

The ValidateTestUserRegistration interface lets you validate a test user in the eBay Sandbox. To use ValidateTestUserRegistration, simply pass the user name and password in the RequestUserId and RequestPassword tags, and check the results for the ValidateTestUserRegistrationStatus tag, which will contain the result of the request.

Understanding eBay API Calls for Items

This section describes interfaces that pertain to eBay items, including the interfaces to add and search for items, as well as relist items and determine who has bid on a specific item.

Listing Items and Revising Listings with the AddItem, VerifyItem, and ReviseItem Interfaces

The AddItem interface lets your application put up an item for auction. Using AddItem is simple: Just fill in the XML tags that describe the item to add (shown in Table 9-18), and make the AddItem request. However, some caveats are in order:

- At least one payment method (MOCashiers, PersonalCheck, VisaMaster, AmEx, Discover, PaymentOther, COD, etc.) must be set to 1 to indicate a valid payment method.

- Payment methods are not appropriate for real estate listings.

- Payment methods indicate the means of payment of a deposit, not the entire sale price, of eBay Motor listings.

- The Quantity field can't be greater than 1 for eBay Motor or real estate auctions.

- Finally, when specifying regions where the seller will ship an item, the various ShipTo... tags are only applicable when a value of SitePlusRegions is passed in the ShippingOption argument.

Table 9-18. Tags Passed to AddItem

Tag	Purpose
AdditionalShipping Costs	Any additional shipping costs for the item. Default is 0.00.
AmEx	American Express is an acceptable payment method.
ApplicationData	Tag used to pass custom, application-specific data to be associated with the new item. The data in this argument is stored with the item in the items table at eBay, but isn't used in any way by eBay. This argument can be used to pass information as a part or SKU number. Maximum size is 32 characters.
ApplyShippingDiscount	Indicator of whether a shipping discount is applied for the item when its transaction is combined into a buyer-created combined payment order.
AutoPay	Indicator of whether the seller requires immediate payment. Default is 0 (false).
BoldTitle	Indicator of whether the title for the item's listing will be in boldface type.
BusinessSeller	If 1 (true), the seller is a business user and intends to use listing features that are offered to business users only. This declaration is up to the seller and isn't validated by eBay. Applicable for business sellers residing in Germany, Austria, or Switzerland, and listing in a B2B VAT-enabled category on the eBay Germany (DE), Austria (AT), or Switzerland (CH) sites only. Required and must be set to 1 (true) if RestrictedToBusiness is set to 1 (true). No effect if RestrictedToBusiness is set to (0) false.
BuyItNowPrice	Buy It Now price for the item.
CashOnPickupAccepted	Payment on delivery is an acceptable payment term.

Table 9-18. Tags Passed to AddItem (continued)

Tag	Purpose
Category	Category ID of the category in which the item is listed on eBay. Maximum length is 10.
Category2	Optional second category in which the item is listed on eBay.
CategoryMapping Allowed	If 1, eBay will look up new categories for obsolete categories on your behalf and substitute them in the listing. If 0, if you submit an invalid category ID, the request fails with an error.
CCAccepted	Credit card an acceptable payment term (but not for all sites).
CheckoutInstructions	Seller's instructions to the buyer and return policy. Default is null. Maximum length is 500.
COD	Cash on Delivery is an acceptable payment method.
Counter	Optional hit counter for the item's listing page.
Country	Country for location. Use the two-letter abbreviation.
Currency	Currency for the eBay site on which the item is being listed.
Description	Brief description of the item.
Discover	Discover Card is an acceptable payment method.
Duration	Number of days the auction will be active. Only certain values are allowed, and the choice of values depends on the listing type.
Escrow	Online escrow paid for by buyer. If used, can't be used with EscrowBySeller.
EscrowBySeller	Online escrow paid for by seller. If used, can't be used with Escrow.
Featured	Item appears at the top of item listings for a category.
Gallery	Indicator of whether to include this item in the gallery.
GalleryFeatured	Indicator of whether this item is featured in the gallery.
GalleryURL	URL for a picture for the gallery.
GiftExpressShipping	If 1, the seller is offering to ship the item via an express shipping method as described in the item description.
GiftIcon	Code for a small, attention-getting image denoting seasonal sales times. If specified, the gift icon displays in the listing's title.
GiftShipToRecipient	If 1, the seller is offering to ship to the gift recipient, not the buyer, when payment clears.

Table 9-18. Tags Passed to AddItem (continued)

Tag	Purpose
GiftWrap	If 1, the seller is offering to wrap the item (and optionally include a card) as described in the item description.
Highlight	If 1, item's listing appears highlighted.
InsuranceFee	Amount of insurance, if InsuranceOption is optional or required. Value specified should be the total cost of insuring the item.
InsuranceOption	Indicator of whether insurance fee is required. Don't specify a value in this field unless CheckoutDetailsSpecified is 1. Default is 0. Valid values are 0: Insurance not offered 1: Insurance optional 2: Insurance required 3: Insurance included in shipping and handling costs
IsAdFormat	If true, a real estate item is listed as an ad.
LayoutId	ID for the template to use when displaying the new item's description.
Location	Geographical location of the item. Maximum length is 45.
MinimumBid	For auction listings, MinimumBid is the minimum acceptable bid for the item. For fixed-price listings, MinimumBid is the fixed price at which the seller is selling the item.
MOCashiers	Money orders and cashier's checks are acceptable payment methods.
MoneyXferAccepted	Direct transfer of money is an acceptable payment method.
MoneyXferAcceptedin Checkout	Direct transfer of money is an acceptable payment method in Checkout. Must be set if MoneyXferAccepted is 1.
PackagingHandling Costs	Optional fees a seller might assess for the shipping of the item.
PaymentOther	Another payment modes (not defined by eBay) is an acceptable payment method.
PaymentOtherOnline	Non-eBay online payment is an acceptable payment method.
PaymentSee Description	Acceptable payment method is in description.
PayPalAccepted	If true, indicates that the seller accepts PayPal as a form of payment. Payment methods are not applicable for real estate listings.

Table 9-18. Tags Passed to AddItem (continued)

Tag	Purpose
PayPalEmailAddress	Seller's e-mail address on file with PayPal that is associated with the item.
PersonalCheck	Personal check is an acceptable payment method.
PhotoCount	Number of photos used for PhotoHosting slide show.
PhotoDisplayType	Type of display for photos used for PhotoHosting slide show. 0: No special Picture Services features 1: Slideshow of multiple pictures 2: Large format picture 3: Picture Pack
PictureURL	URL for one or more pictures for the item's listing. Maximum length is 1,024.
Private	Private auction. Not applicable to fixed-price items.
Quantity	Number of items being sold in the listing. Must be greater than 0.
Region	Numeric code for a region, used to list an item regionally.
ReservePrice	Minimum price that the seller is willing to sell the item.
RestrictedToBusiness	If 1, the seller elects to offer the item exclusively to business users. If 0, the seller elects to offer the item to all users. Applicable for business sellers residing in Germany, Austria, or Switzerland and listing in a B2B VAT-enabled category on the eBay Germany (DE), Austria (AT), or Switzerland (CH) sites only.
SalesTaxPercent	Sales tax for the item. If you specify a SalesTaxPercent, you must also specify a SalesTaxState. Don't specify a value in this field unless CheckoutDetailsSpecified is 1.
SalesTaxState	State that is associated with the SalesTaxPercent. Pass a two-letter abbreviation for the state.
ScheduleTime	Tag that allows a user to schedule a listing to start at the specified time in the future. Specifies the time at which the item is scheduled to be listed on eBay.
SellerPays	Seller pays all shipping.
ShipFromZipCode	Zip code from which the seller is shipping the item. Only specify this tag if ShippingType is 2.
ShippingHandlingCosts	Primary shipping and handling costs for the item. Don't specify a value in this field unless CheckoutDetailsSpecified is 1.

Table 9-18. Tags Passed to AddItem (continued)

Tag	Purpose
ShippingInTax	Indicator of whether shipping costs are included in the tax amount. Don't specify a value in this field unless CheckoutDetailsSpecified is 1.
ShippingIrregular	An item that can't go through the stamping machine at the shipping service office when 1 and requires special or fragile handling. Only specify this tag if ShippingType is 2.
ShippingOption	Specifies where the seller is willing to ship the item. Valid values are SiteOnly (the default) WorldWide SitePlusRegions WillNotShip
ShippingPackage	Size of the package to be shipped. Valid values are 0: None 1: Letter 2: Large envelope 3: USPS flat-rate envelope 4: Package/thick envelope 5: USPS large package/oversize 1 6: Very large package/oversize 2 7: UPS letter
ShippingService	Shipping carrier for the item. Valid values are 3: UPS Ground 4: UPS 3rd Day 5: UPS 2nd Day 6: UPS Next Day 7: USPS Priority 8: USPS Parcel 9: USPS Media 10: USPS First Class 11: USPS Express Mail
ShippingType	Indicator of whether shipping costs are flat rates or calculated rates. Default value is 1. Valid values are 1: Flat shipping rate 2: Calculated shipping rate
ShipToAfrica	Seller will ship to Africa.
ShipToAsia	Seller will ship to Asia.
ShipToCaribbean	Seller will ship to Caribbean.

Table 9-18. Tags Passed to AddItem (continued)

Tag	Purpose
ShipToEurope	Seller will ship to Europe.
ShipToLatinAmerica	Seller will ship to Latin America.
ShipToMiddleEast	Seller will ship to Middle East.
ShipToNorthAmerica	Seller will ship to North America.
ShipToOceania	Seller will ship to Oceania (Pacific region other than Asia).
ShipToSouthAmerica	Seller will ship to South America.
SubtitleText	Subtitle to use in addition to the title. Provides more keywords when buyers search in titles and descriptions.
SuperFeatured	Item is shown on the eBay home page and appears at the top of the category listings.
ThemeId	ID for the template to use when displaying the new item's description.
Title	Title of the item being placed up for auction.
Type	Auction type. Possible values are 0: Unknown auction type 1: Chinese auction 2: Dutch auction 6: Ad-Type auction 7: eBay stores inventory (stores fixed-price) listings (US only) 9: Fixed-price item (BIN only)
UUID	Universally unique constraint tag. Use UUID as a precaution if you are listing many items at once.
VATPercent	VAT rate for the item, if the item price includes the VAT rate. Specify VATPercent if you want include the net price in addition to the gross price in the listing (i.e., on the View Item page).
Version	Used to specify which set of shipping/handling and tax tags to use.
VisaMaster	Visa and MasterCard are acceptable payment methods.
WeightMajor	Number of units for shipping weight unit of measure.

Table 9-18. Tags Passed to AddItem (continued)

Tag	Purpose
WeightMinor	Fractional number of units for shipping weight unit of measure.
WeightUnit	Unit of measure for shipping weight. Default value is 1. Valid values are 1: WeightMajor specifies pounds, WeightMinor specifies ounces 2: WeightMajor specifies kilograms, WeightMinor specifies decimal number of fractions of a kilogram

> **NOTE** *The semantics of the* AddItem *call are slightly different depending on whether you're listing a conventional item, an item in an eBay store, an eBay real estate listing, or an eBay Motors listing. Be sure to check the latest version of the eBay documentation for details.*

Although you may be tempted to code your application using only the AddItem call, it's best if you use VerifyAddItem first to determine if a request to add an item is correct. It takes the same arguments as AddItem and validates all of the arguments as if to add the item, *without actually adding the item.* The key difference in result parameters is that the result Id field will always contain 0, because the item isn't added to eBay, and isn't assigned a unique ID. You can also use VerifyAddItem to have eBay calculate the insertion fees for an item without actually putting the item up for auction.

> **WARNING** *When adding multiple items, always use* AddItem, *and don't use* VerifyAddItem *for each item in the batch to add (it's intended to provide user validation and an estimation of fees for the user).* VerifyAddItem *is designed for interactive use by your application's users; calling it instead of* AddItem *or calling it on items that have already been added may result in your application failing certification.*

When adding an item, the resulting XML contains a description of the insertion fees for the item added along with the item ID of the newly created item. Table 9-19 summarizes the tags in the response XML.

Table 9-19. Tags Returned by AddItem

Tag	Purpose
Category	Category ID of primary category for listing.
Category2	Category ID of secondary category for item listing.
DuplicateItemId	Tag returned with error 488 when a duplicate UUID is specified. Unique identifier for the existing auction item.
EndTime	Date and time the item's listing ends, in GMT.
Fees	Container node for fee information. EU residents who sell items on EU sites may be subject to VAT.
LengthFee	Fee for 10-day auctions. Contained within the Fees tag.
BoldFee	Fee to boldface the title for the item's listing. Contained within the Fees tag.
BuyItNowFee	Fee to add the Buy It Now option to the item.
CategoryFeaturedFee	Fee to have the item featured in its category. Contained within the Fees tag.
CurrencyId	Billing currency of the seller. Contained within the Fees tag.
FeaturedFee	Fee to have the item appear at the top of item listings. Contained within the Fees tag.
FeaturedGalleryFee	Fee to have the item featured in its gallery. Contained within the Fees tag.
FixedPriceDurationFee	Fee for listing a fixed-price item for a certain duration. Contained within the Fees tag.
GalleryFee	Fee to have the item included in the gallery. Contained within the Fees tag.
GiftIconFee	Fee for displaying a gift icon next to the listing. Contained within the Fees tag.
HighLightFee	Fee to have the item's listing appear highlighted. Contained within the Fees tag.
InsertionFee	Basic fee for listing the item. EU residents who sell items on EU sites may be subject to VAT. Contained within the Fees tag.
ListingDesignerFee	Fee charged for the optional use of a Listing Designer layout or theme template. Contained within the Fees tag.
ListingFee	Total fee for listing the item. Includes basic fee (InsertionFee) plus any specialty listing features. EU residents who sell items on EU sites may be subject to VAT. Contained within the Fees tag.

Table 9-19. Tags Returned by AddItem (continued)

Tag	Purpose
PhotoDisplayFee	Fee for use of Photo Hosting feature, a slideshow of multiple images. Contained within the Fees tag.
PhotoFee	Fee for associating 1–6 photos with an item's listing. Contained within the Fees tag.
ReserveFee	Fee for specifying a reserve price for the item's auction. Contained within the Fees tag.
SchedulingFee	Fee for scheduling the item to be listed at a later date. Contained within the Fees tag.
SubtitleFee	Fee to add a subtitle to the item. Contained within the Fees tag.
Id	Unique identifier for the new auction item.
ListedBy RequestAppId	Tag returned with error 488 when a duplicate UUID is specified. A value of 1 in ListedByRequestAppId indicates the item represented by the value in DuplicateItemId was listed by the calling application. A value of 0 in ListedByRequestAppId indicates the item represented by the value in DuplicateItemId was *not* listed by the calling application.
StartTime	Date and time the item's listing starts, in GMT.

WARNING If AddItem *doesn't return a result, attempt to add the same item again with the same* UUID *as the original item. If the first* AddItem *succeeded, the second will fail because you can't add a duplicate item with the same* UUID. *Also, you shouldn't perform end-to-end testing in the Sandbox with PayPal payments, because these payments aren't part of the eBay Sandbox, and actual funds may be transferred between the test buyer and seller!*

Once you have added an item to eBay, you can change many of its fields using the ReviseItem interface. By passing an item ID in its ItemId parameter and item attributes describing the revision from Table 9-18, you can change the various fields of an item. In response, eBay sends a document that contains the item ID of the revised item and the fees associated with that item as described in Table 9-19. Of course, you can't revise just any field of an item once it's been listed on eBay; there are some restrictions you should be aware of. For an auction less than 12 hours old with no bids, you can edit any field that doesn't change the format of the auction. On the other hand, once the auction is more than 12 hours old or a user has bid on the item, you can't change any field that changes the core description. You can, however, change the second category, add optional features of the listing such as a bold title, add new shipping details and payment details, and add counters to your listing.

Adding Items to a Second Chance Auction Using the AddSecondChanceItem and VerifyAddSecondChanceItem Interfaces

You can call AddSecondChanceItem to create a Second Chance auction for an item that didn't complete a sale after its previous action. The arguments to AddSecondChanceAuction and its verify-only counterpart VerifyAddSecondChanceItem are similar to AddItem and VerifyAddItem. Table 9-20 shows the argument tags you may pass to these interfaces. These interfaces return the fees applicable for the auction along with the item ID for the newly created item, described in Table 9-19.

Table 9-20. Tags Passed to AddSecondChanceItem and VerifyAddSecondChanceItem

Tag	Purpose
BuyItNowPrice	Price the offer recipient would need to pay to purchase the item through the second chance offer.
CopyEmailToSeller	Indicator of whether seller receives copy of notification e-mail sent to the recipient bidder. If 1, then seller receives a copy of the notification e-mail. Default is 0.
Duration	Number of days the second chance offer is good for. May be 1, 3, 5, or 7.
OriginalItemId	Valid item ID for an item that qualifies for a second chance offer.
RecipientBidderUserId	Valid eBay user ID for the user to whom the seller is extending the second chance offer.

WARNING *As with* AddItem *and* VerifyAddItem, VerifyAddSecondChanceItem *is designed for interactive use with your application's users. Don't verify additions of multiple items using* VerifyAddSecondChanceItem, *but instead use* AddSecondChanceItem *directly and handle any errors that may occur.*

The AddToItemDescription Interface

The AddToItemDescription interface lets you add additional information to an item's description. It takes two arguments: the ItemId of the item to update, and a Description tag that contains the text to append to the item's description. The response contains a Status tag that specifies the value Success on success, or Failure on failure of the request, and a Message tag contained within an eBay node that provides an optional message.

> **WARNING** *Only use* AddToItemDescription *when a seller needs to change item information after listing the item. Your application shouldn't use* AddToItemDescription *as part of the standard listing process.*

The EndItem Interface

The EndItem interface lets your application instantly end any active eBay auction. The item for auction must be listed by the eBay user specified in the RequestUserId argument. When invoking EndItem, you must also pass the ItemId of the item whose auction should end, and a EndCode with one of the following values:

- A value of 1 indicates that the item was lost or broken.

- A value of 2 indicates that the item is no longer available for sale.

- A value of 3 indicates that the minimum or reserved price is inaccurate.

- A value of 4 indicates that the listing (other than the minimum or reserved price) is in error.

The XML eBay returns contains an EndTime indicating when the auction actually ended, along with the ItemId of the item whose auction was terminated.

You can't end just any auction. For your EndItem call to succeed, you must satisfy the following conditions:

- The value specified in the RequestUserId input argument must be a valid eBay user ID.

- The user specified in RequestUserId must not be currently blocked by eBay.

- The user specified in RequestUserId must be the seller of the item specified in the ItemId argument.

- The item specified in ItemId must have been listed on the site specified in the SiteId argument.

- The item specified in ItemId must still be an active auction (can't have already ended as a successful or unsuccessful auction).

- In a call to EndItem, the value passed in the RequestUserId argument (or RequestToken) identifies the seller of the item being ended.

The GetAllBidders Interface

The GetAllBidders interface returns a list of all bidders for the item you specify in the ItemId parameter. This call is most often used in conjunction with second-chance auctions, in which case you should also pass the value 1 in the SecondChanceEnabledOnly parameter. To view all bidders in the indicated auction, also pass 1 in the ViewAllBidders parameter.

The return value will contain a Bids tag, inside of which will be a Bid tag describing each bid. A crucial element of the Bid tag is the User tag, which describes the user who made the specific bid. Table 9-21 shows the tags within the Bid returned by GetAllBidders. In addition, the Count attribute indicates the total number of Bid nodes in the Bids node, whereas the HighBidderUserId tag contains the user ID of the highest bidder and the HighestBid indicates the amount that that bidder has bid.

Table 9-21. Tags Within the Bid Tag Returned by GetAllBidders

Tag	Purpose
Cause	Type of bid. Will be one of these values:
	0: Unknown
	1: Bid
	2: Not used
	3: Retraction
	4: Auto-retraction
	5: Cancelled
	6: Auto-cancel
	7: Absentee
	8: Buy It Now
	9: Purchase
ConvertedPrice	Converted value of the CurrentPrice in the currency indicated by SiteCurrency.
Currency	Numeric ID for the currency for the auction.
CurrencyId	Currency symbol for the auction.

Table 9-21. Tags Within the Bid Tag Returned by GetAllBidders (continued)

Tag	Purpose
MaxBid	Amount each bidder has extended as a bid. May not be the same amount as the user actually pays when the auction is finalized, per the way Dutch auctions work.
Quantity	Number of items for which each bidder extended a bid. Always returns a value of 1.
SecondChanceEnabled	User's preference to accept second chance offers.
SiteCurrency	Numeric code corresponding to the currency of the site that is requesting the item.
TimeBid	Date and time each bid was placed.
User	Parent node for each high bidder. See Table 9-13 for the tags in this node.

The GetBidderList Interface

The GetBidderList interface returns a list of all items on which the indicated user has bid. Pass the user's eBay ID in the UserId attribute. Use the Active argument to restrict the list of returned items to only active auctions, or use the EndTimeFrom and EndTimeTo argument to restrict the results to a particular interval in time.

The return value consists of a Count tag, which indicates the number of Item nodes returned. Each Item node contains the tags described in the section "The GetItem Interface" later in this chapter. The returned data also depends on the DetailLevel you specify, just as the GetItem call does.

> **WARNING** *Item details don't change very often. If you are going to retrieve information for a bidder more than once, don't retrieve the item details in subsequent calls. If the bidder has bid on items whose details weren't retrieved in the initial call, your application should use* GetItem *to retrieve item details. Failure to do this may result in your application not receiving eBay certification.*

The GetCategoryListings Interface

The GetCategoryListings interface returns a list of all items for auction within a specific category on the eBay site you specify with the SiteId argument. This interface is a paged interface; in addition to passing the CategoryId of interest, you must also pass the ItemsPerPage and PageNumber attributes to specify how many items should be returned on a page, and the page to return. You can filter the results using the ItemTypeFilter tag, which can contain 1 to return all items, 2 to return auction items, or 3 to return fixed-price items. You can also filter items by SiteId with SiteIdFilterType, restricting results to those items listed in the currency implied by that site, located in the country implied by that site, available from the country implied by that site, or regardless of currency and location, by passing integer 1, 2, 3, or 4, respectively; you can also limit the search to a specific region using the RegionId argument. Finally, you can specify whether to return all items or only those listed in the last 24 hours using the OrderBy attribute; if you specify 1, only new items in the last 24 hours are returned.

The XML eBay returns contains Category and CategoryTitle tags that indicate the ID and name of the category you requested. The Count tag indicates the number of items returned, whereas the GrandTotal tag indicates the total number of items matching the search criteria you specified in your request. The PageNumber attribute indicates the page number of the returned data, whereas the TotalNumberOfPages lets you determine the total number of pages available. The items themselves are returned as individual Item entities within an Items container node; each Item node contains the tags described in the section "The GetItem Interface" later in this chapter.

> **WARNING** *Don't call* GetCategoryListings *more than once per category per 30 minutes. If you do, your application may not receive eBay certification.*

The GetHighBidders Interface

The GetHighBidders interface returns a list of all high bidders for a Dutch auction. It returns one Bid node for each high bid in the auction. To determine the high bidders for an item, pass the item's ID in the ItemId attribute. Table 9-22 summarizes the returned tags in the result's Bid nodes. The result will also contain a Count node, indicating the number of returned Bid nodes.

Table 9-22. Tags Within the Bid Tag Returned by GetHighBidders

Tag	Purpose
Cause	Type of bid. Will be one of these values: 0: Unknown 1: Bid 2: Not used 3: Retraction 4: Auto-retraction 5: Cancelled 6: Auto-cancel 7: Absentee 8: Buy It Now 9: Purchase
ConvertedPrice	Converted value of the CurrentPrice in the currency indicated by SiteCurrency.
Currency	Numeric ID for the currency for the auction.
CurrencyId	Currency symbol for the auction.
MaxBid	Amount each bidder has extended as a bid. May not be the same amount as the user actually pays when the auction is finalized, per the way Dutch auctions work.
Quantity	Number of items for which each bidder extended a bid. Always returns a value of 1.
SecondChanceEnabled	Indicates the user's preference to accept second chance offers.
SiteCurrency	Numeric code corresponding to the currency of the site that is requesting the item.
TimeBid	Date and time each bid was placed.
User	Parent node for each high bidder. See Table 9-13 for the tags in this node.

> **WARNING** *When retrieving high bidders, the application should only retrieve new data. Older data records should be cached. Failure to do this may result in your application not receiving eBay certification.*

The GetItem Interface

The GetItem interface returns a description of the item you specify by its item ID. To use GetItem, pass the item ID in the Id attribute. You can also specify an optional

`DescFormat` attribute, which when set to 1 (the default) returns the description with the various templates supported by eBay applied.

This call is highly dependent on the detail level you specify via the `DetailLevel` tag; for specific details, consult the eBay API documentation.

The returned XML contains the tags shown in Table 9-23.

Table 9-23. Tags Returned by GetItem

Tag	Purpose
`ApplicationData`	Tag returns custom, application-specific data associated with the item. The data in this field is stored with the item in the items table at eBay, but isn't used in any way by eBay. Use `ApplicationData` to store such special information as a part or SKU number. Maximum is 32 characters in length.
`AutoPay`	If 1, the seller requested immediate payment for the item.
`BidCount`	Number of bids placed so far against the item. Returned as null for international fixed-price items.
`BidIncrement`	Smallest amount a bid must be above the current high bid.
`BuyerProtection`	Indicator of the status of the item's eligibility for the Buyer Protection Program. Contained within the `Transaction` tag. Possible values are 0: Item is ineligible (e.g., category not applicable) 1: Item is eligible per standard criteria 2: Item marked ineligible per special criteria (e.g., seller's account closed) 3: Item marked eligible per other criteria Applicable for items listed to the US site and for the Parts & Accessories category (6028) or Everything Else category (10368) (or their subcategories) on the eBay Motors site.
`BuyItNowPrice`	Amount a buyer would need to bid to take advantage of the Buy It Now feature. Not applicable to fixed-price or ad-type items (`ItemProperties.Type` returns a 6, 7, or 9). For fixed-price items, see `StartPrice` instead. See `http://pages.ebay.com/services/buyandsell/buyitnow.html` to learn more about Buy It Now.
`BuyItNowPrice`	Amount a buyer would need to bid to take advantage of the Buy It Now feature. Not applicable to fixed-price items or ad format listings. For fixed-price items, see `StartPrice` instead. Contained within the `Transaction` tag.
`Category`	Container for data on the primary category of listing. Contained within the `Transaction` tag.

Table 9-23. Tags Returned by GetItem (continued)

Tag	Purpose
CategoryId	ID for the category in which the item is listed. Contained within the Category tag of a Transaction tag.
Category2	Container for data on the secondary category of listing. Contained within the Transaction tag.
Category2Id	ID for the optional second category (if specified) in which the item is listed. Contained within the Category2 tag of a Transaction tag.
CharityListing	If true (1), the seller has chosen to use eBay Giving Works to donate a percentage of the item purchase price to a selected nonprofit organization. Contained within the Transaction tag.
CharityListingInfo	Container node with information about the Giving Works item and beneficiary.
CharityName	Name of the benefiting nonprofit organization the seller selected. Contained within the CharityListingInfo node.
CharityNumber	Number assigned to the nonprofit organization by the provider of the Giving Assistant for eBay Giving Works. Maximum length is 10 digits. Contained within the CharityListingInfo node.
DonationPercent	Percentage of the purchase price that the seller chose to donate to the selected nonprofit organization. Possible values: 1 to 100. Contained within the CharityListingInfo node.
Checkout	Container node with post-sale information.
Details	Container node with payment details information. Returned within the Checkout node.
Additional ShippingCosts	Any additional shipping costs for the item beyond those indicated in ShippingHandlingCosts. Returned within the Details node.
AllowPaymentEdit	If 1, at the time that the item was listed the seller's user preferences allowed buyers to edit payments. Returned within the Details node.
CheckoutInstructions	Seller's instructions to the buyer and return policy. Returned within the Details node.
InsuranceFee	Amount of insurance. Returned within the Details node.

Table 9-23. Tags Returned by GetItem (continued)

Tag	Purpose
InsuranceOption	Indicator of whether insurance fee is required. Returned within the Details node. Possible values are 0: Insurance not offered (default) 1: Insurance optional 2: Insurance required 3: Insurance included in shipping and handling costs
Packaging HandlingCosts	Any additional packaging and handling fees assessed by the item's seller. Returned within the Details node.
SalesTaxPercent	Sales tax for the item, expressed as a percentage. Returned within the Details node.
SalesTaxState	Indicator of whether state sales tax is charged. Returned within the Details node.
ShippingHandlingCosts	Primary shipping and handling costs for the item. Returned within the Details node.
ShippingInTax	Specifies whether shipping costs are included in the tax amount. Returned within the Details node.
ShipFromZipCode	Zip code from which the seller is shipping the item. Returned within the Details node.
ShippingIrregular	When 1, the item can't go through the stamping machine at the shipping service office and requires special or fragile handling.
ShippingPackage	Size of the package to be shipped. Returned within the Details node. Possible values are 0: None 1: Letter 2: Large envelope 3: USPS flat-rate envelope 4: Package/thick envelope 5: USPS large package/oversize 1 6: Very large package/oversize 2 7: UPS letter

Table 9-23. Tags Returned by GetItem (continued)

Tag	Purpose
ShippingService	Shipping carrier for the item. Returned within the Details node. Possible values are 3: UPS Ground 4: UPS 3rd Day 5: UPS 2nd Day 6: UPS Next Day 7: USPS Priority 8: USPS Parcel 9: USPS Media 10: USPS First Class 11: USPS Express Mail
WeightMajor	Number of units for shipping weight unit of measure. Returned within the Details node.
WeightMinor	Fractional number of units for shipping weight unit of measure. Returned within the Details node.
WeightUnit	Unit of measure for shipping weight. Default value is 1. Returned within the Details node. Valid values are 1: WeightMajor specifies pounds, WeightMinor specifies ounces 2: WeightMajor specifies kilograms, WeightMinor specifies fractions of a kilogram
ConvertedBuy ItNowPrice	Converted value of the BuyItNowPrice in the currency indicated by SiteCurrency.
ConvertedPrice	Converted value of the CurrentPrice field in the currency indicated by SiteCurrency.
ConvertedStartPrice	Converted value of the StartPrice field in the currency indicated by SiteCurrency.
Counter	Optional hit counter for the item's listing page. Possible values: 0, 1, 2, or 3 (0, 1, or 2 for non-US items). For more information on counters, see http://pages.ebay.com/help/sellerguide/counters.html.
Country	Country field is a two-letter abbreviation for the country.
Currency	Numeric code for the currency used to list the item.
CurrencyId	Character symbol for the currency used to list the item symbol for the auction.

Table 9-23. Tags Returned by GetItem (continued)

Tag	Purpose
CurrentPrice	For auction-type listings, this tag returns the start price (if no bids have been placed yet) or current high bid (if at least one bid has been placed). For all fixed-price type and ad-type listings, returns the price specified when the item was originally listed or relisted or the new price after the item was revised.
Description	Description of item.
DescriptionLen	Length (in characters) of the text in Description.
EndTime	Time stamp for the end of the listing.
GalleryURL	URL for the gallery for the item.
GiftIcon	If true, a generic gift icon displays in the listing's title.
GiftServices	Values for the various Gift Services offered by sellers. Contains the tags GiftExpressShipping, GiftShipToRecipient, and GiftWrap, each of which may be 1 or 0.
GoodTillCanceled	If 1, the store owner listed the item as good until cancelled. If the item doesn't sell within the specified listing period, the item is automatically relisted at the end of the specified period. Applicable for eBay stores inventory items only.
HighBidder	Contains one User node representing the current high bidder. See Table 9-13 for the entries in this node.
Id	Unique identifier for the item.
ItemProperties	Container node for item property information.
Adult	Indicator of whether item is adult oriented. Users can't retrieve information for items listed in Mature categories unless they have accepted the Mature Category agreement on the eBay site. Contained within the ItemProperties tag.
BindingAuction	For real estate auctions, indicates whether buyers and sellers are expected to follow through on the transaction. Contained within the ItemProperties tag.
BuyItNowAdded	If 1, a Buy It Now price was added for the item. Only returned for Motors items. Contained within the ItemProperties tag.
BuyItNowLowered	If 1, indicates that the Buy It Now price was lowered for the item. Only returned for Motors items. Contained within the ItemProperties tag.

Table 9-23. Tags Returned by GetItem (continued)

Tag	Purpose
BoldTitle	Indicator of whether the bolding option was used. Contained within the ItemProperties tag.
CheckoutEnabled	Indicator of whether Checkout is enabled for this item. Contained within the ItemProperties tag.
Featured	Indicator of whether the item is a featured item. Contained within the ItemProperties tag.
Gallery	Indicator of whether to include this item in the gallery. Contained within the ItemProperties tag.
GalleryFeatured	Indicator of whether this item is featured in the gallery. Contained within the ItemProperties tag.
Highlight	If true, item's listing is highlighted. Contained within the ItemProperties tag.
Private	Private auction. Limits participation in auction. Contained within the ItemProperties tag.
Reserve	If true, indicates that the item has a reserve price. Contained within the ItemProperties tag.
ReserveLowered	If true, indicates that the reserve price was lowered for the item. Only returned for Motors items. Contained within the ItemProperties tag.
ReserveMet	Returns 1 if the reserve price was met or no reserve price was specified. Contained within the ItemProperties tag.
ReserveRemoved	If 1, indicates that the reserve price was removed from the item. Only returned for eBay Motors items. Contained within the ItemProperties tag.
RestrictedToBusiness	If 1, the seller elects to offer the item exclusively to business users. Applicable for business sellers residing in Germany, Austria, or Switzerland and listing in a B2B VAT-enabled category on the eBay Germany (DE), Austria (AT), or Switzerland (CH) sites only. Contained within the ItemProperties tag.
VATPercent	VAT rate that the business seller entered for the item, if any. The StartPrice is assumed to include the VAT rate. Applicable when the seller is a business seller residing in Germany, Austria, or Switzerland and the item is listed in a B2B VAT-enabled category on the eBay Germany (DE), Austria (AT), or Switzerland (CH) sites only. Contained within the ItemProperties tag.

Table 9-23. Tags Returned by GetItem (continued)

Tag	Purpose
SuperFeatured	Indicator of whether item is a super featured item. Contained within the ItemProperties tag.
Type	Auction format. Possible values are 0: Unknown auction type 1: Chinese auction 2: Dutch auction 5: Live Auctions–type auction 6: Ad-Type auction 7: eBay stores inventory (stores fixed-price) listing (US only) 8: Personal offer 9: Basic fixed-price item
ItemRevised	Indicator of whether the item was revised since the auction started.
LeadCount	Tag that is applicable to ad-format items only. Indicates how many leads to potential buyers are associated with this item. For item types other than ad-format items, returns a value of 0.
ListingDesigner	Container tag in which are returned data elements with Listing Designer information. Contains the LayoutId and ThemeId tags.
Location	Where the item is at time of auction.
MinimumToBid	Smallest amount the next bid on the item may be. Only applicable to auction-type listings; returns zero for all fixed-price and ad-type listings.
OriginalItemId	Item ID for the original item a seller offers through a second chance offer listing.
PaymentTerms	Container node for payment information. Not applicable for real estate listings. Contains the AmEx, CashOnPickupAccepted, CCAccepted, COD, Discover, Escrow, EscrowBySeller, MOCashiers, MoneyXferAccepted, MoneyXferAcceptedinCheckout, Other, OtherPaymentsOnline, PayPalAccepted, PayPalEmailAddress, PersonalCheck, SeeDescription, and VisaMaster tags, each of which may be 1 or 0. See Tables 9-13 and 9-18 for use.
PhotoCount	Number of photos used for Photo Hosting slide show.
PhotoDisplayType	Type of display for photos used for Photo Hosting slide show. 0: No special Picture Services features 1: Slideshow of multiple pictures 2: Large format picture 3: Picture Pack

Table 9-23. Tags Returned by GetItem (continued)

Tag	Purpose
PictureURL	URL for one or more pictures for the item's listing. Maximum length is 1,024.
Private	Private auction. Not applicable to fixed-price items.
Quantity	Number of items being sold in the listing. Must be greater than 0.
Region	Numeric code for a region, used to list an item regionally.
QuantitySold	Number of items purchased so far. (Subtract from the value returned in the Quantity field to calculate the number of items remaining.)
Region	Region where the item is listed.
RelistID	Tag returns the new item ID for a relisted item.
ReservePrice	Reserve price for a reserve auction.
SecondChance Eligible	If 1, item is eligible to be offered as a second chance offer listing.
Seller	Container node for information about the seller. Contains User-pertinent tags described in Table 9-13.
ShippingOption	Where the seller is willing to ship the item. Valid values are SiteOnly (the default) WorldWide SitePlusRegions WillNotShip
ShippingRegions	Where the seller is willing to ship the item if ShippingOption is SitePlusRegions. Tags within this tag will have a value of 1 if the seller will ship to the specified location.
Africa	Seller will ship to Africa. Contained within the ShippingRegions tag.
Asia	Seller will ship to Asia. Contained within the ShippingRegions tag.
Caribbean	Seller will ship to Caribbean. Contained within the ShippingRegions tag.
Europe	Seller will ship to Europe. Contained within the ShippingRegions tag.
LatinAmerica	Seller will ship to Latin America. Contained within the ShippingRegions tag.

Table 9-23. Tags Returned by GetItem (continued)

Tag	Purpose
MiddleEast	Seller will ship to Middle East. Contained within the ShippingRegions tag.
NorthAmerica	Seller will ship to North America. Contained within the ShippingRegions tag.
Oceania	Seller will ship to Oceania (Pacific region other than Asia). Contained within the ShippingRegions tag.
SouthAmerica	Seller will ship to South America. Contained within the ShippingRegions tag.
ShippingTerms	Container node for shipping term information, containing the SellerPays tag, which when 1, indicates that the seller will pay all shipping.
SiteCurrency	Numeric code corresponding to the currency of the site that is requesting the item.
SiteId	eBay site on which the requested item is listed.
StartPrice	Tag returns the price the seller specified when originally listing or relisting the item.
StartTime	Time stamp for the start of the listing.
StorefrontInfo	Tag contains the eBay stores-specific item attributes DepartmentNumber and StoreLocation.
StorefrontItem	If 1, the item is an eBay stores item.
SubtitleText	Subtitle used in addition to the title.
TimeLeft	Container node for the amount of time left in an active auction.
Days	Time left for active auction period, days portion. Contained within the TimeLeft tag.
Hours	Time left for active auction period, hours portion. Contained within the TimeLeft tag.
Minutes	Time left for active auction period, minutes portion. Contained within the TimeLeft tag.
Seconds	Time left for active auction period, seconds portion. Contained within the TimeLeft tag.
Title	Name of the item as it appears for auctions. Returned as CDATA.

Table 9-23. Tags Returned by GetItem (continued)

Tag	Purpose
TitleBarImage	Indicator of whether an image for the item appears in the title bar of the item's listing page (View Item page) on the eBay site.
UUID	Universally unique constraint tag. The UUID is unique to a category. The UUID can only contain digits from 0 to 9 and letters from A to F. The UUID must be 32 characters long.
Zip	Zip code for the seller.

The GetItemShipping Interface

You use the GetItemShipping interface to determine the shipping costs for an item. When using GetItemShipping, pass the arguments in Table 9-24.

Table 9-24. Tags Passed to GetItemShipping

Tag	Purpose
ItemId	Item for which shipping should be calculated.
QuantitySold	Number of objects sold in the auction to a single buyer that would be shipped together. Default is 1.
ShipToZipCode	Zip code to which the seller is shipping the item.

The GetItemShipping interface returns a summary of shipping costs with the tags you see in Table 9-25.

Table 9-25. Tags Returned by GetItemShipping

Tag	Purpose
InsuranceFee	Insurance fees associated with shipping the item(s). Calculated from the value in the PriceSold argument. If no PriceSold is specified, InsuranceFee returns zero.
PackagingHandlingCosts	Seller packaging or handling fees.
ShipFromZipCode	Zip code from which the seller is shipping the item.
ShippingFee	Shipping costs for the item. (Doesn't include any seller packaging or handling fees.)

Table 9-25. Tags Returned by GetItemShipping (continued)

Tag	Purpose
ShippingIrregular	When 1, item can't go through the stamping machine at a post office.
ShippingPackage	The size of the package to be shipped. Possible values are 0: None 1: Letter 2: Large envelope 3: USPS flat-rate envelope 4: Package/thick envelope 5: USPS large package/oversize 1 6: Very large package/oversize 2 7: UPS letter
ShippingRate ErrorMessage	Tag contain any error message associated with the attempt to calculate shipping rates. If there was no error, returns No Error.
ShippingService	Shipping carrier for the item. Valid values are 3: UPS Ground 4: UPS 3rd Day 5: UPS 2nd Day 6: UPS Next Day 7: USPS Priority 8: USPS Parcel 9: USPS Media 10: USPS First Class 11: USPS Express Mail
ShippingType	Indicator of whether shipping costs are flat rates or calculated rates. Possible values are 1: Flat shipping rate 2: Calculated shipping rate
WeightMajor	Weight of the item(s): Number of units for shipping weight unit of measure specified by WeightUnit.
WeightMinor	Weight of the item(s): Fractional number of units for shipping weight unit of measure, either pounds or fractions of a kilogram, depending on WeightUnit.

Table 9-25. Tags Returned by GetItemShipping (continued)

Tag	Purpose
WeightUnit	Unit of measure for shipping weight. Default value is 1. Valid values are 1: WeightMajor specifies pounds, WeightMinor specifies ounces 2: WeightMajor specifies kilograms, WeightMinor specifies fractions of a kilogram

The GetItemTransactions Interface

The GetItemTransactions interface returns information about an item that has been purchased. A transaction isn't an auction; rather, it's a summary of the money that changes hands once an auction is complete. The interface is paged; in addition to specifying the item ID or the time interval for which transactions are of interest, you must also specify the page number and number of transactions per page that should be returned. Table 9-26 summarizes the arguments to GetItemTransactions.

Table 9-26. Arguments to the GetItemTransactions API

Tag	Purpose
ItemId	Unique ID of item that you are retrieving transactions for.
LastModifiedFrom	Use the LastModifiedFrom and LastModifiedTo filters to return transactions that were last modified between the specified date and time. The date range can't be greater than 30 days.
LastModifiedTo	Use the LastModifiedFrom and LastModifiedTo filters to return transactions that were last modified between the specified date and time. The date range can't be greater than 30 days.
TransactionsPerPage	Maximum number of transactions to return per call to GetItemTransactions. Default is 100, maximum is 200. Pagination for GetItemTransactions is the same as for GetSellerTransactions.

Table 9-26. Arguments to the GetItemTransactions API (continued)

Tag	Purpose
PageNumber	Number of the virtual page to return in using the current call to GetItemTransactions. Pagination for GetItemTransactions is the same as for GetSellerTransactions.
TransactionId	Unique ID for a transaction. Use to return data for a single transaction. If you specify the TransactionId argument to retrieve only a single transaction, then you don't need to use pagination.

The return tags in the XML generated by eBay are the same as the tags returned by the GetSellerTransactions interface. See Table 9-12 for a summary of these tags.

The GetSearchResults Interface

GetSearchResults provides a paged interface to search for items matching arbitrary criteria on eBay. The interface provides a Boolean AND search mechanism across the arguments you specify in your query, letting you refine your query by keywords in item descriptions, category, low and high prices, region, and sellers. Table 9-27 describes the arguments you may pass to GetSearchResults.

Table 9-27. Tags Passed to GetSearchResults

Tag	Purpose
Active	If 1, limits the result set to active listings. If 0, limits the result set to listings that have ended.
Category	Numeric ID of the category to be searched. Defaults to all categories if 0 is specified or the tag isn't present.
CharityListing	If 1, limits the results to Giving Works listings and no other listings. If 0, has no effect on the search results.
Currency	Numeric ID for a currency type.
ExcludeSellers	Tag excludes the specified sellers from the search. Use either a seller's user ID or e-mail address. Separate multiple sellers with a comma. A maximum of 100 sellers can be listed.
HighestPrice	Highest price in the Current Price field that any item returned by the search results should have.

Table 9-27. Tags Passed to GetSearchResults (continued)

Tag	Purpose
IncludeSellers	Tag restricts search to the sellers specified. Use either a seller's user ID or e-mail address. Separate multiple sellers with a comma. A maximum of 100 sellers can be listed. Can't be used with ExcludeSellers and PayPal arguments. StoreSearch overrides IncludeSellers.
ItemTypeFilter	Tag filters items returned by the type of listing. Valid values are 1: Auction items only 2: Fixed-price items (both fixed-price and Buy It Now) 3: All items
LowestPrice	Lowest price in the Current Price field that any item returned by the Search results should have.
MaxResults	Maximum number of items matching search criteria to return. Maximum value is 100; default value is 100. Use Skip to specify the number of items to skip when building the result set. Use MaxResults and Skip together to paginate your results set.
Modifier	Tag used with ModifierCode argument. Restricts items returned based on country availability.
ModifierCode	Country code to specify which country you want to limit the results to.
Order	Specifies the sort order of the returned list of items.
PayPal	When 1 (true), items returned are restricted to only those for which PayPal is accepted as a buyer payment option. Default is 0 (false).
Query	Search string, which consists of one or more keywords to search for in the listing title and/or description. Embed the search string in a CDATA construct.
Region	Numeric ID for a region. Limits the search to items listed in a specified region.
SearchInDescription	If true (1), item titles, subtitles, and descriptions are searched for the string specified in Query. Defaults to false (0) to search the title only.
SearchType	Tag restricts items returned to, selectively, only gallery items or gallery and nongallery items. Valid values are 0: Search for gallery and nongallery items 1: Search for gallery items only and display a preview (thumbnail) image of gallery picture 2: Same as 0

Table 9-27. Tags Passed to GetSearchResults (continued)

Tag	Purpose
SiteIdFilterType	Tag that allows a user to filter the category listings by SiteID. Limits items returned to 1: Items listed in the currency implied by SiteID 2: Items located in the country implied by SiteID 3: Items available to the country implied by SiteID 4: Items listed on the site implied by SiteID, regardless of listing currency 5: (Belgium site only) Items located in Belgium or listed on one of the two Belgian sites
Skip	Number of items to skip over (counting from the first) in paginating results.
StoreID	Tag restricts the search to the specified store. Used only in the test environment.
StoreName	Tag restricts the search to the specified Store. Used only in the production environment. You must specify a value in StoreName in the production environment if StoreSearch = 0, 1, or 2. Pass the value using the CDATA modifier. The StoreName argument is case sensitive.
StoreSearch	Tag restricts the search to items that are listed in eBay stores: 0: Within a single store for all items (use with StoreName) 1: Within a single store for auction items (use with StoreName) 2: Within a single store for Buy It Now items (use with StoreName) 3: Across all stores for Buy It Now items

The XML eBay returns contains an Items node, which contains an Item node for each returned item. (The tags in the Item node are described previously in this chapter in Table 9-23.) In addition, the returned XML contains the HasMoreItems tag, which indicates if more items are available, and the Count and GrandTotal entities, which return the number of items in the response and the total number of items matching the request, respectively.

> **WARNING** *When collecting new listings that match the search criteria, the application should limit request frequency to once every 30 minutes. By specifying a value of* MetaNewSort *for the* Order *argument, the listings are sorted by listing date in descending order of time, and the application should make only as many requests as needed to return newly listed items. A newly listed item, in this case, is an item that was listed after the time of the previous call. Also, don't use* GetSearchResults *to track current bid prices. Most users are interested in only tracking a small subset of the items that are returned by a search query. Instead, use* GetItem *to track price changes for the items that a user selects to track. Failure to follow these guidelines may result in your application not receiving eBay certification.*

The GetSellerList Interface

The GetSellerList interface returns a list of the items listed by a specific eBay user. Like other interfaces that can return a large number of items, GetSellerList paginates its results; be prepared to determine the total number of items and request the data in pages from eBay. Using the interface, you can filter by the start time or end time of auctions. The arguments to the call are similar to those for GetSellerEvents:

- Specify the UserId field to indicate for which user to list items.

- Specify PageNumber to indicate what page of the results should be returned, and ItemsPerPage to indicate how many items should be returned on a page.

- Select whether to search based on auction start or end time by setting the StartTimeFrom and StartTimeTo arguments to the desired auction start time to search, or the EndTimeFrom and EndTimeTo arguments to the desired auction end time.

The return values are the same as for GetSearchResults; see Table 9-23 for a summary of the tags returned by eBay in the Item nodes of the result. Note that in some cases, you may not be able to get all of the data you need; should this happen, consider lowering the detail level of your request to return fewer item fields.

> **WARNING** *Only use the* GetSellerList *call if you can't use the* GetSellerEvents *call. An example of an exception to this would be when you import a seller's items to your local application for the first time. Failure to do this may result in your application not receiving eBay certification.*

The RelistItem Interface

RelistItem lets you relist an item that didn't sell at a previous auction. To relist an item, you must pass its original item ID in the ItemId argument, and any other arguments for listing the item as you would when you call AddItem. (Refer to Table 9-18 for a summary of the arguments you can pass to AddItem.)

Relisting an item returns the newly created item's ID and the fees applicable for listing the item. The returned XML follows the same scheme as for AddItem; see Table 9-19 for a summary of returned tags.

> **WARNING** *The same guidelines for* AddItem *also hold true for* RelistItem; *don't call* VerifyAddItem *to relist items in bulk, and use the* UUID *field to determine if* RelistItem *succeeds if you receive no response.*

The ReviseCheckoutStatus Interface

The ReviseCheckoutStatus interface lets you change the status of an item after its buyer has finished the checkout process. Your application may invoke this interface to note that the buyer didn't remit payment correctly. The arguments you pass must include the item's ID and the transaction ID for the item. Table 9-28 shows the other arguments you may pass to ReviseCheckoutStatus.

Table 9-28. Tags Passed to ReviseCheckoutStatus

Tag	Purpose
ItemId	Unique ID for the item associated with the checkout.
TransactionId	Unique ID for the transaction associated with the checkout. For Chinese auctions, the value passed in the TransactionId argument must be 0, or the call will fail with an error. For all other auction types, the TransactionId argument accepts the actual, nonzero transaction ID.
OrderId	Unique ID for a multi-item order. If specified, ItemId and TransactionId are ignored in the same call. Changes to the checkout status are applied to the specified order as a whole.
AmountPaid	Amount the buyer paid for the item specified in ItemId.
StatusIs	Indicator of whether the checkout process has been completed. Valid values are 1: Incomplete 2: Complete

Table 9-28. Tags Passed to ReviseCheckoutStatus (continued)

Tag	Purpose
PaymentMethodUsed	Payment method used by the buyer. Default is 0. Valid values are
	0: No payment method specified
	3: Money order/cashier's check
	4: Personal check
	5: COD
	6: Visa or MasterCard
	7: Other (or see item description)
	9: Cash on pickup
SendEmailToBuyer	Indicator of whether seller is sending an e-mail containing a personalized message about the transaction to the buyer. If SendEmailToBuyer is 1, the seller must specify a message to the buyer in the MessageToBuyer tag.
MessageToBuyer	Message seller is sending to the buyer.

The XML eBay returns includes a Status tag, which contains either Success or Failure to indicate whether the request succeeded or failed.

Using the eBay API Within a Web Site

This chapter's example demonstrates how to use the eBay API within a simple Web site that lets you search eBay for items at auction by keywords in the item title and description. Although simplistic (there's little business reason why such a simple site would likely garner enough users to be profitable from a business perspective), it demonstrates several key points about the eBay API and Web integration of the API with your site, including

- Displaying and caching the URL for the eBay Marketplace Logo that your application must show

- Paging an interface such as GetSearchResults

- Managing error handling within your Web-based application

The interface is very simple. In the entry page, you simply enter your eBay account name and password, along with the keywords for the item search to perform. Then you click the button labeled Submit Query, and the server performs as many GetSearchResults requests as are required to obtain the full list of items for auction matching your search, and presents the results.

The sample code is written in Perl using the Perl module CGI.pm, which provides a flexible interface to the Common Gateway Interface (CGI) used between Web servers and the scripts they execute. The underlying implementation has a few additional requirements that keep the code simple too.

- When debugging the scripts, you can use the Data::Dumper Perl module to dump the contents of arrays and hashes using print.

- The underlying code that executes eBay API calls uses the LWP::UserAgent, HTTP::Headers, and HTTP::Request modules to perform the Web requests of eBay, just as the example in the last chapter does.

- The relatively complex XML returned by eBay when invoking GetSearchResults requires some heavy lifting; I chose to use XML::Smart to parse the resulting XML because it has nice facilities for obtaining multiple nodes with the same name (see the section "Obtaining a List of Items Matching the Search Criteria" later in the chapter for details.)

The resulting code is very portable; I've successfully run it on both Microsoft Windows platforms and UNIX with no difficulty. If you need to obtain one of the modules I name here, the easiest way to do so is with ppm, the Perl Package Manager, or by visiting http://www.cpan.org, the Comprehensive Perl Archive Network site.

> **TIP** *In a production environment, it makes more sense to use the Apache mod_perl module to execute code like this, because with mod_perl, you don't have the overhead of bringing up the Perl interpreter for every request. However, the relative complexity of having you install mod_perl if you don't already have it just to run one sample application makes little sense. Instead, for simplicity, these scripts use the CGI interface and will work with any Web server that supports CGI, such as the Apache Web Server or Microsoft Internet Information Services.*

Obtaining the Search Parameters

The first page of the Web site is a simple HTML form, which you see in Listing 9-1.

Listing 9-1. The Search Parameter Form

```
1: <html>
2: <head>
3: <title>eBay Search</title>
```

```
 4: </head>
 5: <body>
 6: <h1><img src="logo.pl">eBay Search</h1>
 7: <p>
 8: This page uses the eBay API with Perl to search
 9: the eBay service for items currently up for auction
10: with key words you specify in the item's title
11: or description.
12: </p>
13: <p>
14: <form method="POST" action="getsearchresult.pl">
15: <table>
16:   <tr>
17:     <td>
18:       Your eBay User Id:
19:     </td>
20:     <td>
21:       <input type="TEXT" name="userid">
22:     </td>
23:   </tr>
24:   <tr>
25:   <td>
26:       Your eBay Password:
27:   </td>
28:   <td>
29:     <input type="PASSWORD" name="password">
30:   </td>
31:   </tr>
32:   <tr>
33:     <td>
34:       Find items with the following words in their
35:       title or description.
36:     </td>
37:     <td>
38:       <textarea name="querydata">shoes</textarea>
39:     </td>
40:   </tr>
41: </table>
42:
43: <input type="submit">
44: </form>
45: </p>
46:
47: <hr/>
```

```
48: <p>
49: This web page is part of the book
50: <i>Developing Applications with eBay</i>
51: written by Ray Rischpater and available
52: from <a href="http://www.apress.com">Apress, L.P.</a>
53: </p>
54: </body>
55: </html>
```

The HTML for this form is very simple, consisting of a header (line 6), a form you fill out (lines 13–45), and an obligatory credit message on lines 48–55.

The form on lines 13–45 are at the heart of the application. This form has three fields and a Submit button. The fields for eBay authentication (your eBay account name and password, on lines 21 and 29, respectively) are simple input elements, the first a text input, and the second a password input (to obscure the password that you enter). The third element, a textarea, accepts the space-delimited keywords for your search. Named userid, password, and querydata respectively, the Web browser gathers the values you enter and submits them via a HTTP POST request when you press the Submit Query button (defined on line 43).

The image at the top of the query page deserves special note: It's the eBay logo provided by the eBay API GetLogoUrl. This URL is captured using a simple script, updatelogo.pl, which I show you later in this chapter in the section "Looking Behind the Scenes: Periodic Maintenance Tasks." For now, it's enough to know that this script creates the file logo.pl, which contains the lines you see in Listing 9-2.

Listing 9-2. The logo.pl Script

```
1: use CGI;
2: $query = new CGI;
3: print $query->redirect("https://scgi.sandbox.ebay.com/saw/pics/
   api/ebay_market_108x44.gif"); #wrapped from previous line
```

This script simply sends a redirection Location HTTP header when it's executed, telling the Web browser to load the content from the indicated URL instead of from logo.pl directly.

Obtaining a List of Items Matching the Search Criteria

Obtaining the items that match your search request is the responsibility of the getsearchresults.pl script, aided by the module CallEBayAPI.pm, which I wrote for this example and which you can modify and use in your own Perl applications. Listing 9-3 shows getsearchresults.pl.

Listing 9-3. Getting Search Results with getsearchresults.pl

```
 1: use CallEBayAPI;
 2: use Data::Dumper;
 3: use CGI qw(:standard);
 4: use strict;
 5:
 6:
 7: # Get the arguments for the search.
 8: my $query = new CGI;
 9: my $userid = param( "userid" );
10: my $password = param( "password" );
11: my $querydata = param( "querydata" );
12:
13:
14: #my $userid = "sandy2718";
15: #my $password ="ebaytest";
16: #my $querydata = "phone";
17:
18:
19: # Create the eBay interface.
20: my $eBayInterface = CallEBayAPI->new;
21:
22: # Output the header first
23: print header();
24: print start_html("eBay Search Results");
25: print h1( "<img src=\"logo.pl\">eBay Search Results");
26:
27: # Now perform the request.
28: my $skip = 0;
29: my $done = 0;
30: my $request;
31: my $response;
32:
33:
34: while( !$done )
35: {
36:     $request = $eBayInterface->newRequest( {
37:                         Verb => 'GetSearchResults',
38:                         DetailLevel => '0',
39:                         RequestUserId => $userid,
```

```
40:                        RequestPassword => $password,
41:                        Active => '1',
42:                        SearchInDescription => '1',
43:                        ItemTypeFilter => '3',
44:                        Order => 'MetaEndSort',
45:                        Query => $querydata,
46:                        MaxResults => '3',
47:                        SiteIdFilterType => '2',
48:                        Skip => $skip } );
49:
50:    $response = $eBayInterface->request( $request );
51:
52:    if ( $response->{eBay}->{Errors}->{Error}->{LongMessage} )
53:    {
54:      if ( $skip > 0 )
55:      {
56:        # End the table first.
57:        print "</table>\n";
58:      }
59:      my $error = $response->{eBay}->{Errors}->{Error};
60:      print p("An error occurred. The eBay service returned: " .
61:              i( blockquote( $error->{LongMessage} ) ) );
62:      last;
63:    }
64:
65:    # If we are just starting, print the total number of items.
66:    if ( $skip == 0 &&
67:         $response->{eBay}->{Search}->{GrandTotal} == 0   )
68:    {
69:      print p( "No items matched your query." );
70:    }
71:    if ( $skip == 0 &&
72:         $response->{eBay}->{Search}->{GrandTotal} != 0   )
73:    {
74:      print p( "There were " .
75:               "$response->{eBay}->{Search}->{GrandTotal} " .
76:               "items matching your query."), "\n";
77:      print "<table>\n";
78:      print "<tr>";
79:      print td( "Item #" );
80:      print td( "Title" );
81:      print td( "Number of Bids" );
82:      print td( "Current Price" );
```

```
 83:      print td( "Start Time" );
 84:      print td( "End Time" );
 85:      print "</tr>\n";
 86:    }
 87:
 88:
 89:    # Print the table row for each item returned.
 90:    my @items = @{$response->{eBay}->{Search}->{Items}->{Item}};
 91:    foreach my $item (@items)
 92:    {
 93:      if ( $item->{Id} )
 94:      {
 95:        print "<tr>";
 96:        print td( "<a href=\"$item->{Link}\" target=\"_new\">" .
 97:                      $item->{Id} . "</a>" );
 98:        print td( $item->{Title} );
 99:        print td( $item->{BidCount} );
100:        print td( "\$" . $item->{CurrentPrice} );
101:        print td( $item->{StartTime} );
102:        print td( $item->{EndTime} );
103:        print "</tr>\n";
104:        $i++;
105:      }
106:    }
107:    $skip += $response->{eBay}->{Search}->{Count};
108:    # and if we're done, exit the loop
109:    $done = !$response->{eBay}->{Search}->{HasMoreItems};
110:    if ( $done )
111:    {
112:      print "</table>";
113:    }
114: }
115:
116:
117: # Output a note about the app.
118: print hr();
119: print p( "This web page is part of the book ",
120:          i("Developing Applications with eBay"),
121:          "written by Ray Rischpater and available ",
122:          "from ",
123:          "<a href=\"http://www.apress.com\">Apress, L.P.</a>" );
124: # Close the HTML tags and end the document.
125: print end_html();
```

After importing the CallEBayAPI.pm, Data::Dumper, and CGI.pm modules on lines 1–3, the script next gets the values of the form elements userid, password, and querydata using the CGI.pm module's param function, which collects their values from the data you sent when you submitted the form. (Lines 14–16, if uncommented, provide defaults you can use for stand-alone testing.)

Line 20 creates an instance of the CallEBayAPI.pm module, which encapsulates making eBay API calls and managing application keys.

Lines 23–25 send the first bits of HTML to the device: the initial title, page heading, and eBay logo. As you can see, the code makes extensive use of the CGI.pm module's support for generating well-formed HTML.

The while loop on lines 24–114 perform the bulk of the work in this script. This loop is responsible for querying eBay for search results as many times as necessary, satisfying the paged interface provided by GetSearchResults, and formatting the results as items in an HTML table. In addition, the loop also has provisions for printing error messages in the event that no items are found, or in case the eBay queries fail. This loop executes as long as no error occurs and the current search can return more eBay items. Let's take the loop a segment at a time.

Line 36 creates a new request object using the eBay interface returned by the new method of the CallEBayAPI.pm module. This request is actually just the XML document describing the request, created using the hash you pass to newRequest. The fields defined on lines 37–49 are those required for the GetSearchResults function, as described here:

- The Verb field indicates the name of the eBay API call to execute, GetSearchResults.

- The DetailLevel field indicates the detail level for this request, which is 0. The GetSearchResults call only takes a detail level of 0.

- The RequestUserId field indicates the eBay user account to use with the request.

- The RequestPassword field indicates the password for the named eBay account.

- The Active field indicates that the eBay service should only return items currently at auction.

- The SearchInDescription field indicates that the eBay service should search both item titles and item descriptions.

- The ItemTypeFilter field indicates that the eBay service should return all items including both those at auction and with fixed prices.

- The Order field indicates that the eBay service should sort the results by the auction end time.

- The Query field contains the text you entered in the search form.

- The MaxResults field indicates how many results should be returned per request page. For this example, I set this value artificially low to ensure that the script's management of eBay's result pages works correctly; a more realistic value might be 50 or even 100 (the default).

- The SiteIdFilterType field indicates that results should be returned only for the SiteId indicated in the request (the United States).

- The Skip field indicates how many results should be skipped when generating the result document; this lets the script obtain successive pages of the result set.

Line 50 makes the API call, sending the XML the script just created to eBay and collecting the response and parsing its XML into a hash.

Lines 52–63 handle any errors returned by the eBay service or the CallEBayAPI.pm module by first ending the table if it's already opened (lines 54–58), printing the error string in a paragraph (lines 59–61), and then exiting the while loop with Perl's last statement on line 62. (The last statement is analogous to C#'s break statement.) The $skip counter does double duty here: If it's 0, this is the first time through the loop, and it shows that you haven't started the HTML table yet. Later in the loop the code increments the counter by the number of items returned, and it gets passed back to the eBay service to indicate the number of items that should be skipped in subsequent requests.

Lines 65–86 print the table head if it's the first pass through the loop: first printing the number of items found (lines 66–76), a table head (line 77), and then a first row labeling each column of the table (lines 78–85).

Lines 90–106 iterate across each of the returned items, printing a single item's information on each row of the table. Line 90 itself shows a slick feature: XML::Smart: nodes in the parsed XML tree are available as both hashes and arrays; evaluating the node $response->{eBay}->{Search}->{Items}->{Item} (which corresponds to the <Item> tags contained within the <Items> node of the <Search> node of the <eBay> result) in array context returns an array of all <Item> tags as Perl hashes. With this array, fetching each item is as easy as using foreach and building the HTML by hand, enclosing the whole thing in a table row <tr> tag (line 95, line 103), and generating table columns for the item ID (which links to the eBay page describing the item on lines 96–97), item title (line 98), bid count (line 99), current price (line 100), auction start time (line 101), and the auction end time (line 102).

Line 107 increments the variable `$skip` by the number of items just processed, so that when making another request, the script doesn't fetch the same items. Line 109 determines whether or not to continue making requests of eBay by using the return parameter `HasMoreItems` of the `GetSearchResults` API, which is 1 when more items are available, and 0 when no more items can be returned.

After the loop finishes, lines 118–123 print the closing message on the page, attributing the content to the book you're reading. Finally, line 125 closes the HTML with the help of the CGI.pm module.

The implementation you see in Listing 9-3 is all well and good, but relies on the CallEBayAPI.pm module to do its dirty work. Listing 9-4 shows you the CallEBayAPI.pm module.

Listing 9-4. The CallEBayAPI.pm Module

```
 1: package CallEBayAPI;
 2:
 3: # Dependencies
 4: use LWP::UserAgent;
 5: use HTTP::Request;
 6: use HTTP::Headers;
 7: use XML::Smart;
 8: use Data::Dumper;
 9:
10: use strict;
11:
12: # Constants
13: use constant True => 1;
14: use constant False => 0;
15: use constant COMPATIBILITY_LEVEL => 335
16: use constant EBAY_API_URL =>
17:    'https://api.sandbox.ebay.com/ws/api.dll';
18: use constant DEBUG => 0;
19: use constant SITE_ID => '0';
20:
21: # Module variables
22: my $_xmlRequest = '<?xml version="1.0"?><request>' .
23:    '<ErrorLevel>1</ErrorLevel><SiteId>0</SiteId>';
24: my $_xmlError =    '<?xml version="1.0""?>' .
25:    '<eBay><Errors><Error><Code>0</Code>' .
26:    '<ErrorClass>NetworkError</ErrorClass>' .
27:    '<SeverityCode>1</SeverityCode>' .
28:    '<Severity>SeriousError</Severity>' .
29:    '<ShortMessage>' .
```

```
30:      'Could not connect to eBay.' .
31:      '</ShortMessage><LongMessage>' .
32:      'Could not connect to eBay. ' .
33:      'There was a problem with the client or the ' .
34:      'network.' .
35:      '</LongMessage></Error></Errors></eBay>';
36:
37: sub new
38: {
39:    my ($class) = @_;
40:
41:    my $self = bless
42:    {
43:     useragent => LWP::UserAgent->new,
44:    }, $class;
45:
46:    $self->getKeys;
47:
48:    return $self;
49: }
50:
51: sub newRequest
52: {
53:    my $self = shift;
54:    my $ref = shift;
55:    my $result = $_xmlRequest;
56:
57:    foreach my $key (keys(%$ref))
58:    {
59:      $result .= "" . $ref->{$key} . "</$key>";
60:    }
61:    $result .= "</request>";
62:
63:    return $result;
64: }
65:
66: sub request
67: {
68:    my $self = shift;
69:    my $requestXML = shift;
70:    my $header = HTTP::Headers->new;
71:    my $requestHash = XML::Smart->new( $requestXML );
72:
73:    print "CallEBayAPI request\n" if DEBUG;
```

```
74:    print $requestXML, "\n"   if DEBUG;
75:
76:    $header->push_header( 'X-EBAY-API-COMPATIBILITY-LEVEL' =>
77:                          COMPATIBILITY_LEVEL );
78:    $header->push_header( 'X-EBAY-API-SESSION-CERTIFICATE' =>
79:      "$self->{devkey};$self->{appkey};$self->{crtkey}");
80:    $header->push_header( 'X-EBAY-API-DEV-NAME' =>
81:                          $self->{devkey} );
82:    $header->push_header( 'X-EBAY-API-APP-NAME' =>
83:                          $self->{appkey} );
84:    $header->push_header( 'X-EBAY-API-CERT-NAME' =>
85:                          $self->{crtkey} );
86:    $header->push_header( 'X-EBAY-API-CALL-NAME' =>
87:                          "$requestHash->{request}{Verb}" );
88:    $header->push_header( 'X-EBAY-API-SITEID' =>
89:                          SITE_ID );
90:    $header->push_header( 'X-EBAY-API-DETAIL-LEVEL' =>
91:      "$requestHash->{request}{DetailLevel}" );
92:    $header->push_header( 'Content-Type' =>
93:                          'text/xml' );
94:    $header->push_header( 'Content-Length' =>
95:                          length( $requestXML ) );
96:
97:    # Make the request.
98:    my $request = HTTP::Request->new( "POST",
99:                                      EBAY_API_URL,
100:                                     $header,
101:                                     $requestXML );
102:   my $response = $self->{useragent}->request( $request );
103:
104:   print "NETWORK ERROR\n" if DEBUG && $response->is_error;
105:   return ( XML::Smart->new( $_xmlError ) )
106:     if $response->is_error;
107:
108:   print $response->content() if DEBUG;
109:   return XML::Smart->new( $response->content() );
110: }
111:
112:
113: sub testWithGetLogoUrl
114: {
115:   my $self = shift;
116:   my $user = shift;
117:   my $password = shift;
```

```
118:
119:    return $self->getLogoUrl( $user, $password );
120: }
121:
122: sub getLogoUrl
123: {
124:    my $self = shift;
125:    my $user = shift;
126:    my $password = shift;
127:    my $eBayRequest = $self->newRequest(
128:                        {
129:                          Verb => 'GetLogoUrl',
130:                          Size => 'Small',
131:                          RequestUserId => $user,
132:                          RequestPassword => $password } );
133:    # Issue the request.
134:    my $eBayResponse = $self->request( $eBayRequest );
135:
136:    my $url = $eBayResponse->{eBay}{Logo}{URL};
137:
138:    return $url;
139: }
140:
141: sub getKeys
142: {
143:    my $self = shift;
144:    my $ttyInput;
145:    my $input;
146:    my $devid;
147:    my $appid;
148:    my $crtid;
149:
150:    # Try to open the file.
151:    open( IDS, "c:\\Documents and Settings\\All Users\\ebayrc" )
152:    or die "No keys available.";
153:
154:    # Read them from the file.
155:    # The file should have the keys in the order
156:    # developer ID
157:    # application ID
158:    # certificate ID.
159:    my $line = 0;
160:    while ( <IDS> )
161:    {
```

```
162:    chomp( $_ );
163:    $devid = $_ if $line == 0;
164:    $appid = $_ if $line == 1;
165:    $crtid = $_ if $line == 2;
166:    $line++;
167:  }
168:
169:  # Return a list with the keys.
170:  $self->{devkey} = $devid;
171:  $self->{appkey} = $appid;
172:  $self->{crtkey} = $crtid;
173:
174:  return ( $devid, $appid, $crtid );
175: }
176:
177: 1;
```

As you see when skimming this listing, it's really just a glorified abstraction of the ValidateTestUser example you encountered in the previous chapter. Lines 4–8 outline the dependencies this module has on other Perl modules: LWP::UserAgent, HTTP::Request, and HTTP::Headers for making queries of the eBay service, XML::Smart for XML parsing, and Data::Dumper for debugging. Lines 13–19 define a number of constants used by the module, or that you can use in your application. Lines 22–35 define XML templates for the beginning of a valid request and a canned error message in the event of a network failure; these are broken into multiple lines in the listing here to fit the printed page.

The module's constructor, new, spans lines 37–49, and does two things. First, on lines 41–44, it creates a new Perl object by blessing the hash containing a new LWP::UserAgent module instance. Next, on line 46, it loads your eBay keys from disk using its getKeys function, which is defined later in the module. Finally, it returns the new class instance on line 48.

The newRequest method on lines 51–61 is a rather simpleminded hash-to-XML converter; I chose to show you one I wrote from scratch after experimenting with the output from XML::Simple and XML::Smart, preferring the hand-rolled XML over what these modules automatically generate. The code's simple: On line 55 the result is seeded first with the XML preamble

```
1: <?xml version="1.0"?><request>
```

and then the loop on lines 57–60 builds up the XML tag by tag from the incoming hash, terminating the XML on line 61 with a closing </request> tag. The resulting XML is returned on line 63 to the caller as a new request item.

Actually making the request is the purview of the request method, on lines 66–110: This was copied nearly verbatim from the ValidateUser example in the last chapter, so I'll only point out the differences. Most important, this code must determine both the X-EBAY-API-CALL-NAME and the X-EBAY-API-DETAIL-LEVEL headers from the request; the code does this by parsing the XML in the request and using the resulting hash to obtain the necessary values. Lines 98–102 make the request, first by creating a new POST request and then actually issuing the request. In the event of a network error between this host and eBay, lines 105–106 return a hash based on the error XML defined on lines 24–35, making it easy for clients to handle both network errors and errors from the eBay service.

The testWithGetLogoURL method on lines 113–120 is a rather simpleminded unit test that you use in a separate Perl script to make sure that the basic flow of the CallEBayAPI.pm module is working correctly. It uses the getLogoUrl method on lines 122–139, which makes one eBay API call *all* applications have to make, returning the eBay logo URL.

The GetKeys method on lines 141–175 loads the keys from a default configuration file; this code is lifted directly from the eBaySampleApplication Perl module I discuss in the Appendix.

Looking Behind the Scenes: Periodic Maintenance Tasks

Besides the usual requirements of running a Web server—network maintenance, periodic backups, and such—running a site that uses the eBay service has additional demands. All sites should cache the logo URL or the eBay Marketplace as provided by the eBay API, and more complex applications will need to cache and regularly update data such as category data.

The example in this chapter needs the small eBay logo to display on both the search and results pages. To get this logo, the script updatelogo.pl, shown in Listing 9-5, must be called periodically (once per day is ideal) to update the file logo.pl, which you saw in the section "Obtaining the Search Parameters" previously in this chapter.

Listing 9-5. The updatelogo.pl Script

```
 1: use CallEBayAPI;
 2: use strict;
 3:
 4: my $filename = "logo.pl";
 5:
 6: my $eBayInterface = CallEBayAPI->new;
 7: # login, password variables in the following call
 8: my $url = $eBayInterface->getLogoUrl( $user, $pass );
 9: exit if !$url;
10: open FILE, ">$filename";
11: print FILE "use CGI;\n";
12: print FILE "\$query = new CGI;\n";
13: print FILE "print \$query->redirect(\"$url\");\n";
14: close FILE;
```

The script simply creates a new CallEBayAPI.pm module instance (line 6) and uses it to fetch the logo URL using a developer's account and password (here represented using the $user and $pass variables). Once it's obtained the URL, it writes the result to the file logo.pl on lines 10–14 if the returned value $url contained any data.

This script is sufficient for use with a cron job, or you can invoke it from getsearchresults.pl by first checking the last modified time of the file logo.pl when getsearchresult.pl first starts.

> **TIP** *A production application would probably be better off obtaining the image at the GetLogoUrl location and caching the image, rather than just redirecting the client's Web browser to the URL returned by GetLogoUrl.*

Key Points

In this chapter, you learned the following key points:

- Writing a Web application that uses the eBay API is essentially the same as writing any other Web application.

- You must cache category data when using the GetCategories function because of the large amount of data it can return. (If you don't, your application won't pass certification.)

- You must cache and show the eBay logo somewhere within your application's user interface, such as its About box. This holds true for both Web and stand-alone applications.

- You can't call GetSellerEvents, and most of the other calls that get information, more than once every half hour.

- Use VerifyAddItem to verify the attributes of an item without actually adding the item before using AddItem.

- The AddItem call may not return a result. If it doesn't, attempt to add the same item with the same UUID. If that fails, the original AddItem call succeeded.

- Don't do end-to-end testing with PayPal in the eBay Sandbox! These payments aren't part of the actual eBay Sandbox, and will cost you real money. (If you do need to test the PayPal relationship, make sure the buyer and seller are both PayPal accounts of yours!)

- Only use `AddItemToDescription` when a seller needs to change information after listing an item. This call shouldn't be part of the standard use case for adding items.

- Item details don't change very often. Cache the results of `GetItem`, or at least don't fetch all of the item details by supplying an appropriate `DetailLevel`.

- Don't call `GetCategoryListings` more than once every half hour. Instead, cache the results for later inquiries.

- When calling `GetHighBidders`, cache the previous results and use it only to retrieve new data.

- When using `GetSearchResults` to fetch listings, limit request frequency to once every half hour for the same inquiry. Moreover, don't use it just to get an item's price; instead, use `GetItem` on the item in question.

- Only call `GetSellerList` if you can't use `GetSellerEvents` instead, such as when you're importing a list of seller's items into your application for the first time.

Examining the Container for the Sample Applications

THROUGHOUT THIS BOOK, I've shown you sample applications based on a *container application* that encapsulates the details of application startup, initializing eBay interfaces, and collecting configuration information such as your eBay access keys, user account, and password.

This code isn't difficult to understand, but deserves some explanation. However, scattering the explanation across the various chapters isn't fair to you, because in those chapters you're intent on learning an interface such as GetUserCall. Hence this appendix: It shows you the container application the samples use, unfettered by the actual eBay calls you've learned. In this appendix, you'll learn why I chose the user interface behind the container application, what's in it, and what it does. When you're done reading this chapter, you can use the container application in C# and Perl to quickly write small stand-alone applications that let you examine the behavior of specific eBay interfaces or test small parts of a larger application that you want to build.

Understanding the Purpose of the Container Application

When writing the container application I use throughout this book, I had the following goals:

- Provide an easy division in code between the eBay interfaces and logic I want to show you and the housekeeping necessary to support those eBay interfaces.

- Provide a simple and effective container with a minimum of user interface complexity, letting me focus on showing you what you want to see when you buy this book: how to use eBay—not how to use C#, classes in the Microsoft .NET Framework, or Perl/Tk. (There are *lots* of good books on these topics already!)

- Provide an application that lets you enter your eBay access keys and a test user account without needing to hand-edit text files or the registry.

- Provide an isomorphic implementation between C# and Perl wherever possible so that you can see how to interact with eBay in these languages, letting you gain insight as to which language is best for your application.

Thus, the container application concept: a container window responsible for presenting a sample-specific form demonstrating an aspect of eBay, and an associated configuration form that lets you enter your access information. Behind the scenes, to ensure that you could enter your information in one place and make it available to all applications, is a simple flat-text file that stores your eBay access information.

In addition to providing application startup, configuration management, and a container for the sample code, the container application offers two additional services. Each of these map to the appropriate GUI (.NET Framework for C#, Perl/Tk for Perl) calls when set with a new value.

The StatusBarText property reflects the status bar text on the lower-left side of the main window. Updating this text property updates the contents of this text box. In a similar vein, the Busy property, when true (1 in Perl), causes the cursor to change to the wait cursor (the hourglass). When false (0 in Perl), the default, the cursor returns to the default cursor.

Figure A-1 shows a sample application in its simplest form, the container application itself.

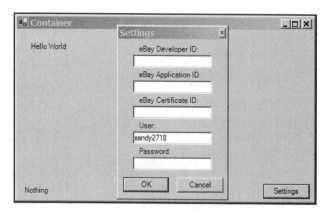

Figure A-1. A sample application using the book's container code

The application makes some notable deviations from how a production eBay application should behave, including the following:

- Production applications should have far more error handling, including try/catch blocks around the allocation of objects and interfaces, error handling for file management, and so on. With few exceptions, the only error handling you see in the sample applications is directly applicable to using an eBay interface.

- Most (but not all) application users have only a single eBay account. Entering account information should be the responsibility of a simple preferences screen seldom accessed by the user.

- eBay keys should be stored as an application resource or in the registry in an encrypted form, not as a plain-text entry in a text file for everyone to see.

- eBay user account passwords shouldn't be stored in a manner in which they can be easily read.

- The eBay Marketplace Logo (available by calling GetLogoUrlCall) should be shown in the application's splash screen. (The container application doesn't even have a splash screen!)

In the context of learning about the interfaces to manipulate eBay users, items, accounts, and such, these are small cosmetic issues. Moreover, how you address them in your application is largely a function of how your application performs. The user interface and data storage requirements for a back-office application that integrates eBay with your inventory system are going to be very different from the requirements for an eBay application to help the owner of the local comic book shop unload her unsold inventory on eBay with little effort.

Examining the Container Application in C#

The container application in C# has two classes: eBaySampleApplication and ConfigDialog, both of which inherit from System.Windows.Forms.Form. The eBaySampleApplication form is the base class of all sample applications and the container per se, holding the form specific to a single sample application. A button on this form, the Settings button, creates and shows an instance of the ConfigDialog class, letting you enter your eBay access information. eBaySampleApplication manages ApiSession, which you use to access eBay, as well as loading keys from the configuration file. In a similar vein, ConfigDialog is responsible for updating the configuration file in the event of changes to your eBay access information.

To use the container application, you must provide a third class that contains a Main entry point and inherits from the eBaySampleApplication class. It must create an eBaySampleApplication subclass instance, configure it by setting the Gui property to a control or container with controls for the main layout, and then relinquish control to the runtime.

Starting the Application

Application bootstrap is the responsibility of the sample application class itself. Listing A-1 shows the simplest of sample applications using the container, a Hello World application.

Listing A-1. The Hello World Sample Application

```
 1: using System;
 2: using System.IO;
 3: using System.Drawing;
 4: using System.Collections;
 5: using System.ComponentModel;
 6: using System.Windows.Forms;
 7: using System.Data;
 8: using eBay.SDK.API;
 9:
10: namespace com.lothlorien.ebaysdkbook
11: {
12:    /// <summary>
13:    /// HelloWorld provides a container application for the sample.
14:    /// </summary>
15:    public class HelloWorld :
16:         com.lothlorien.ebaysdkbook.eBaySampleApplication
17:    {
18:      public HelloWorld()
19:      {
20:         System.Windows.Forms.Label label =
21:           new System.Windows.Forms.Label();
22:         System.Windows.Forms.Control  container =
23:           new System.Windows.Forms.Control();
24:         label.Location = new System.Drawing.Point(10, 10);
25:         label.Name = "Example";
26:         label.Size = new System.Drawing.Size(180, 24);
27:         label.Text = "Hello World";
28:
29:         container.SuspendLayout();
30:         container.Controls.AddRange(
31:           new System.Windows.Forms.Control[] {label} );
32:         container.ResumeLayout(false);
```

```
33:
34:        this.Gui = container;
35:
36:        this.StatusText = "Nothing";
37:    }
38:
39:    [STAThread]
40:    static void Main()
41:    {
42:        Application.Run(new HelloWorld());
43:    }
44:  }
45: }
```

As you can see from Listing A-1, the eBaySampleApplication parent class makes writing a sample application very easy. The constructor need only create whatever components are necessary and start the application (and then, of course, manage the events from those controls). This sample uses a container with a single label-created constructor on lines 20–24 to display the text "Hello World". Once initialized (lines 22–27), the constructor adds the control to the form's layout on lines 29–32, and then points the application at the container using its Gui property. This property, defined in the eBaySampleApplication class, simply adds the container with its elements to the application's form. This property resizes the incoming container to a size that fits within the bounds of the root form and adds it to the control list for the root form.

The remainder of the startup is done within the eBaySampleApplication class. To keep things simple, I mimic the convention set by the Microsoft Windows Designer interface, and use a method named InitializeEBayComponent, called after the InitializeComponent method in the class's constructor. Listing A-2 shows InitializeEBayComponent.

Listing A-2. The InitializeEBayComponent Method

```
 1: private void InitializeEBayComponent( )
 2: {
 3:    // Create the API session.
 4:    apiSession = new ApiSession();
 5:
 6:    apiSession.Url = "https://api.sandbox.ebay.com/ws/api.dll";
 7:    // Set the API session's access credentials.
 8:    // Load our access info.
 9:    LoadKeys();
10: }
```

The InitializeEBayComponent method creates a new APISession object, sets the Url property of the session to the URL for the eBay sandbox, and then loads the keys using the LoadKeys method.

If I were writing *only* an application using the .NET Framework, I might well choose to use a Microsoft-centric mechanism for storing the eBay keys and access information, such as the Windows registry or an XML configuration file. However, to make it easy for you to run the samples, I wanted to share the contents of the configuration file between applications that use the .NET Framework and those written in Perl. Although it's true that with the additional modules provided by ActiveState, ActiveState Perl applications can read registries and parse the XML the .NET Framework uses when creating configuration files, that seemed more complexity in a sample application than necessary. Consequently, I decided that access keys and other configuration information should be kept in a flat text file. Although admittedly primitive by today's standards, it has the benefit of being easy to parse in any language, and equally easy for people like you and me to open with a text editor and examine the contents. (This last feature, however, although an asset in a sample application, is emphatically a detriment when storing something as important as access keys in a commercial application!) Another, equally valid, choice would be to store this information in a simple XML file. Listing A-3 shows the LoadKeys function.

Listing A-3. The LoadKeys Function

```
 1: private void LoadKeys()
 2: {
 3:    FileStream stream;
 4:    StreamReader streamreader;
 5:    String keystring;
 6:    String [] keys;
 7:    Char [] eol = {'\n'};
 8:
 9:    apiSession.Developer = "unknown";
10:    apiSession.Application = "unknown";
11:    apiSession.Certificate = "unknown";
12:    apiSession.RequestUserId = "unknown";
13:    apiSession.RequestPassword = "unknown";
14:
15:    try
16:    {
17:      stream =
18:        new FileStream(
19:          "c:\\Documents and Settings\\All Users\\ebayrc",
20:          System.IO.FileMode.Open );
21:      streamreader = new StreamReader( stream );
22:      keystring = streamreader.ReadToEnd();
```

```
23:     streamreader.Close();
24:     stream.Close();
25:     keys = keystring.Split( eol );
26:     apiSession.Developer = keys[0].Trim();
27:     apiSession.Application = keys[1].Trim();
28:     apiSession.Certificate = keys[2].Trim();
29:     apiSession.RequestUserId = keys[3].Trim();
30:     apiSession.RequestPassword = keys[4].Trim();
31:   }
32:   catch
33:   {
34:     // Abbreviated for brevity.
35:     MessageBox.Show( this,
36:             "Please set your...",
37:             "Error" );
38:   }
39: }
```

LoadKeys is one of those longish, boring functions that doesn't do anything exciting. It begins by trying to open the file named ebayrc, and if it succeeds, splits the contents of the file into strings, one string for each line of the file (lines 21–25). Next, lines 26–30 trim the white space from each line and assign successive lines to the apiSession object's properties, such as the Developer, Application, and Certificate properties (lines 26–28) that contain your eBay application keys, or the RequestUserId and RequestPassword properties (lines 29–30). In the event of an error, the try/catch block prints an error message (truncated in the sample code for brevity).

Once the application has finished starting up, the APISession object is available via the property APISession.

Configuring the Application

All of the application configuration is done within the ConfigDialog class. An object of this type is created and used as a model dialog box when you press the Settings button, as you can see from Listing A-4.

Listing A-4. Invoking a ConfigDialog

```
1: private void setting_Click(object sender, System.EventArgs e)
2: {
3:   if ( configDialog == null )
4:     configDialog = new ConfigDialog();
5:   configDialog.ShowDialog( this );
6:   // Blocking; this happens when the dialog box closes.
```

```
7:    LoadKeys();
8: }
```

I chose to use a modal dialog box (line 5), because it makes little sense (and could potentially wreak havoc on the application) to let the user change configurations while an eBay transaction is in process, which would happen if the dialog box was a regular window and you changed the configuration while accessing eBay.

The configuration dialog box itself is a typical Windows form; the only thing of note is that when closing, if you choose to accept the changes you made, it writes the new settings to the configuration file so that the application can reload the keys (line 7 of Listing A-4). Listing A-5 shows how these keys get written to the configuration file when the configuration dialog box closes.

Listing A-5. Saving Configuration Information in ConfigDialog

```
 1: private void ok_Click(object sender, System.EventArgs e)
 2: {
 3:    this.DialogResult = DialogResult.OK;
 4:    // Save settings.
 5:    try
 6:    {
 7:      FileStream stream = File.OpenWrite(
 8:            "c:\\Documents and Settings\\All Users\\ebayrc" );
 9:      StreamWriter streamWriter = new StreamWriter( stream );
10:      streamWriter.Write( devid.Text );
11:      streamWriter.Write( "\n" );
12:      streamWriter.Write( appid.Text );
13:      streamWriter.Write( "\n" );
14:      streamWriter.Write( crtid.Text );
15:      streamWriter.Write( "\n" );
16:      streamWriter.Write( user.Text );
17:      streamWriter.Write( "\n" );
18:      streamWriter.Write( password.Text );
19:      streamWriter.Write( "\n" );
20:      streamWriter.Flush();
21:      streamWriter.Close();
22:      stream.Close();
23:    }
24:    catch
25:    {
26:      MessageBox.Show( this, "Could not save settings.", "Error" );
27:    }
28: }
```

This is the reverse of LoadKeys; the code opens the file for writing on lines 7–9, and then writes each of the entered keys on lines 9–20 before flushing and closing the file on lines 20–22. In the event of a file system error, line 26 informs you that the changes weren't saved.

Examining the Container Application in Perl

Although the container application in Perl has the same user interface and configuration file implementation, it differs significantly from the C# version. On the surface, an obvious difference is that it uses the Perl/Tk library. Because of this and the nature of Perl, I constructed the Container application as a Perl module, which exports a Gui property and a Main function that starts the sample application. Thus, unlike the C# version, sample applications don't subclass the eBaySampleApplication module, but instead include it and use its functionality.

> **NOTE** *Of course, it's actually fairly easy to create Perl classes that can inherit from other classes. However, given the nature of the example applications, this implementation is even easier than using a parent class–child class relationship.*

Starting the Application

Application startup using the eBaySampleApplication module is simple, in some ways even simpler than the C# version. Just include the module, create the Tk components for your interface, and then call the module's Main function. Listing A-6 demonstrates this.

Listing A-6. Starting an eBay Application Written with the eBaySampleApplication Module

```
1: require eBaySampleApplication;
2: my $application = eBaySampleApplication->new;
3: my $ui = $application->{MAINWINDOW}->Label(
4:    -text => 'Hello World' );
5: $application->Gui( $ui );
6:
7: $application->Main;
```

The crucial line is the second, invoking the new method of eBaySampleApplication. You can see it in Listing A-7.

Listing A-7. The new Function of eBaySampleApplication.pm

```
1: sub new
2: {
3:    my $class = shift;
4:
5:    return if $app;
6:
7:    $app = bless {}, $class;
8:
9:    $app->{MAINWINDOW} = MainWindow->new;
10:   $app->{APISESSION} = Win32::OLE->new(
11:            "eBay.SDK.API.ApiSession" );
12:   $app->{APISESSION}->{Url} =
13:   "https://api.sandbox.ebay.com/ws/api.dll";
14:
15:   # Load your settings and keys.
16:   $app->_loadKeys;
17:
18:   return $app;
19: }
```

Unsurprisingly, this looks an awful lot like the constructor for the eBaySampleApplication class in C#. The code begins by creating an empty object on line 7, and then fills out three key slots in its hash:

- The Tk MainWindow (line 9) to contain the application's interface

- The ApiSession to use when connecting with eBay (lines 10–11)

- The URL to use when contacting the eBay sandbox

Next, the routine loads the keys (line 16) it will use to access eBay using _loadKeys. This function uses a bit of Perl to do what Perl does best: parse strings. Listing A-8 shows _loadKeys.

Listing A-8. Loading eBay Keys in Perl

```
1: sub _loadKeys
2: {
3:     # Try to open the file.
4:     $devid = "developerid";
5:     $appid = "applicationid";
6:     $crtid = "certificateid";
7:     $user = "user";
```

```
 8:      $password = "password";
 9:
10:      if ( !open( IDS,
11:            "c:\\Documents and Settings\\All Users\\ebayrc" ) )
12:      {
13:        # Read them from the file.
14:        $line = 0;
15:        while ( <IDS> )
16:        {
17:          chomp( $_ );
18:          $app->{APISESSION}->{Developer} = $_
19:            if $line == 0;
20:          $app->{APISESSION}->{Application} =
21:            if $line == 1;
22:          $app->{APISESSION}->{Certificate} = $_
23:            if $line == 2;
24:          $app->{APISESSION}->{RequestUserId} = $_
25:            if $line == 3;
26:          $app->{APISESSION}->{RequestPassword} = $_
27:            if $line == 4;
28:          $line++;
29:      }
30:      close IDS;
31:      }
32: }
```

Without the benefit of exception handling, this code is a little less clear than its analog in C#, but it does basically the same thing. First, it sets default values in the event of an error (lines 4–8), and then attempts to open the configuration file (lines 10–11). If this succeeds, the routine reads one line at a time (line 15), trims the trailing end-of-line characters (line 17), and then assigns the resulting string to a named slot in the object.

Configuring the Application

The configuration dialog box appears when you press the Configuration button; its declaration includes a command attribute that contains a reference to configDialog_ShowDialog, shown here in Listing A-9.

Listing A-9. Showing the Configuration Dialog Box

```
1: sub _configDialog_ShowDialog
2: {
3:   my $configDialog = $app->{MAINWINDOW}->DialogBox(
```

```
4:      -title => "Settings",
5:      -buttons => [ "OK", "Cancel" ] );
6:
7:   $configDialog->add( 'Label',
8:     ( -text => "eBay Developer ID:" ) )->pack();
9:   $configDialog->add( 'Entry', (
10:     -textvariable =>\$app->{APISESSION}->{Developer} ) )->pack();
11:   $configDialog->add( 'Label', (
12:     -text => "eBay Application ID:" ) )->pack();
13:   $configDialog->add( 'Entry', (
14:     -textvariable => \$app->{APISESSION}->{Application} ) )->pack();
15:   $configDialog->add( 'Label', (
16:      -text => "eBay Certificate ID:" ) )->pack();
17:   $configDialog->add( 'Entry', (
18:      -textvariable => \$app->{APISESSION}->{Certificate} ) )->pack();
19:   $configDialog->add( 'Label', ( -text => "User:" ) )->pack();
20:   $configDialog->add( 'Entry', (
21:     -textvariable => \$app->{APISESSION}->{RequestUserId} ) )->pack();
22:   $configDialog->add( 'Label', (
23:   -text => "Password:" ) )->pack();
24:   $configDialog->add( 'Entry', (
25:     -textvariable =>\$app->{APISESSION}->{RequestPassword} ) )->pack();
26:
27:   my $result = $configDialog->Show();
28:   if ( $result == "OK" )
29:   {
30:     $app->_saveKeys;
31:   }
32: }
```

This routine simply contains a lot of unglamorous Perl/Tk code to construct a new configuration dialog box and show it each time one is required. Lines 3–5 create the base dialog box. The add invocations, on lines 7–26, add each of the interface elements (labels or their corresponding input lines) to the dialog box. Line 27 shows the dialog box, whereas lines 28–30 save the results of an update once you press the confirmation button.

The _saveKeys method is the inverse of _loadKeys (shown here in Listing A-10).

Listing A-10. Saving Application Configuration

```
1: sub _saveKeys
2: {
3:   if ( !open( IDS,
4:     ">c:\\Documents and Settings\\All Users\\ebayrc" ) )
5:   {
```

```
 6:      print IDS $app->{APISESSION}->{Developer}, "\n";
 7:      print IDS $app->{APISESSION}->{Application}, "\n";
 8:      print IDS $app->{APISESSION}->{Certificate}, "\n";
 9:      print IDS $app->{APISESSION}->{RequestUserId}, "\n";
10:      print IDS $app->{APISESSION}->{RequestPassword}, "\n";
11:      close IDS;
12:   }
13:   else
14:   {
15:      $app->{MAINWINDOW}->messageBox( -title => "Error",
16:         -message => "Could not save settings."
17:         -icon => "error" );
18:   }
19: }
```

This routine is simple, too. It begins by opening the configuration file for writing (lines 3–4), and if it succeeds, writes each of the configuration items to the file (lines 6–11). If the open fails, lines 15–17 show an error message.

Index

Symbols

$resultText object, 101
$theAccount variable, 101
$theUser object, 93
$ttyInput variable, 36
$variable variable, 35
_loadKeys function, 288–89
_saveKeys method, 290–91

A

AboutMe property, 74, 86
AboutMe tag, 222, 224
Access database, using Integration
    Library with, 125–27
AccessRule class, 40
Account class, 79–80
account management, 72
Account object, 96, 97
Account OLE class, 101
Account tag, 206
AccountActivity class, 42, 80–81
AccountActivity collection, 97
AccountActivity objects, 42, 81
AccountActivityCollection class, 42,
    80–81
AccountCollection class, 79–80
AccountForm class, 113, 113–14
AccountId tag, 204
AccountInvoiceView, 81–83, 87
AccountInvoiceView class, 42, 43, 79, 81
AccountOnHold value, 78
AccountPageType tag, 203, 206
AccountPaymentEnum, 42
AccountPaymentMethodImpl class, 42,
    82, 83–84
AccountPeriodView class, 42, 43, 79,
    81–83
AccountPeriodView object, 82, 84
accounts
    defined, 17
    vs. user accounts, 44
    vs. users, 71–72
AccountState tag, 204
AccountStatus
    implementing in C#, 94–97
    implementing in Perl, 97–101
AccountViewEnum, 87
Active field, 268
Active tag, 256

ActivePerl, 21, 22
Activities property, 79, 80
Activity property, 80
ActivityCollection, 101
Add method, 48
additem function, 158
AddItem interface, 228–38
AddItemCall, 51, 103, 112, 117
AdditionalAccount class, 43, 84
AdditionalAccount object, 82, 84
AdditionalAccount tag, 206
AdditionalAccountCollection, 43, 84
AdditionalAccounts property, 82
AdditionalAccountsCount tag, 205
AdditionalBalance tag, 206
AdditionalCurrency tag, 206
AdditionalId tag, 206
AdditionalShippingCosts tag, 215, 229,
    245
AddRange method, 48
Address class, 40
AddRootNodes method, 64, 65
AddToItemDescription interface, 239
AddToItemDescriptionCall, 51, 103
AdjustmentAmount tag, 215
Ad-Type auction, 15
Adult property, 108
Adult tag, 248
Africa property, 109
Africa tag, 251
AirConditioning property, 44
AllowEditPayment tag, 213
AllowPaymentEdit property, 74
AllowPaymentEdit tag, 222, 245
AmEx property, 108
AmEx tag, 218, 229
AmountPaid tag, 213, 260
AmountPastDue property, 82
AmountPastDue tag, 205
API, eBay. *See* eBay API
api object, 31
api variable, 31
APIAccessRules tag, 195
ApiCallSession property, 27, 35, 36, 50,
    90
APIException class, 40
ApiSession object, 31, 32, 54–55, 285
ApiSession property, 85
apiSession variable, 30–31
AppData property, 74, 104, 118, 133
appID variable, 32